THE AIR PILOT'S MANUAL

Volume 3

Air Navigation

Trevor Thom

graphics by
Robert Johnson

Airlife

England

Nothing in this manual supersedes any legislation, rules, regulations or procedures contained in any operational document issued by Her Majesty's Stationery Office, the Civil Aviation Authority, the manufacturers of aircraft, engines and systems, or by the operators of aircraft throughout the world.

Text, Copyright © 1987 Trevor Thom.
Original Illustrations & Diagrams, Copyright © 1987
Trevor Thom & Robert Johnson.

ISBN 1 85310 016 1

First edition published 1987
by Airlife Publishing Ltd.

This second revised edition published 1987.
Reprinted 1988.
Reprinted with amendments 1989.

Printed in England by Livesey Ltd., Shrewsbury.

Airlife Publishing Ltd.

101 Longden Road, Shrewsbury SY3 9EB, Shrewsbury, England.

THE AIR PILOT'S MANUAL Vol. 3

Air Navigation

CONTENTS

PERSONAL PROGRESS TABLE	
Theory	Exercises

FOREWORD .... (vii)

SECTION 1 – BASIC NAVIGATION THEORY.
1. The Pilot/Navigator 2
2. Speed 14
3. Direction 28
4. Wind-Side of the Navigation Computer 45
5. Calculator-Side of the Navigation Computer 79
6. Vertical Navigation 98
7. Time 125
8. The Earth 142
9. Aeronautical Charts 157

SECTION 2 – FLIGHT PLANNING.
10. Introduction to Flight Planning 190
11. Pre-Flight Briefing 195
12. Route Selection and Chart Preparation 204
13. Compiling a Flight Log 210
14. The Flight Plan Form 227

SECTION 3 – EN ROUTE NAVIGATION.
15. En Route Navigation Techniques 232
16. Navigation in Remote Areas 276
17. Entry/Exit Lanes and Low Level Routes 281

APPENDIX 1 —
The Navigation Flight Test 287

APPENDIX 2 — Planning the Climb 291

EXERCISES AND ANSWERS —
Located in Volume 2.

INDEX 299

EDITORIAL TEAM

Trevor Thom.

A current Airbus A320 Captain, Trevor has been active in the *International Federation of Airline Pilots' Associations (IFALPA),* based in London, and a member of the *IFALPA Aeroplane Design and Operations Group.* During this time he also served as IFALPA representative to the *Society of Automotive Engineers (SAE) – Aerospace,* a body which makes recommendations to the aviation industry, especially the manufacturers. Prior to his airline career Trevor worked as a lecturer in Mathematics and Physics, and also as an Aviation Ground Instructor and a Flying Instructor. He is a double degree graduate from the University of Melbourne and holds a Diploma of Education.

Jim Hitchcock.

Supervisor of Pilot Technical Training, Oxford Air Training School, Jim joined the RAF as an apprentice in 1945. Later commissioned as a Navigator, he served in Coastal and Flying Training Commands, and on Photo Reconnaissance. On leaving the RAF he joined CSE in 1967. Jim has organised navigation events for the HCGB, including the 1973 World Championships. He also holds a C Mech E.

Edward Pape.

Director of the Manchester School of Flying and a former Chief Flying Instructor of the Lancashire Aero Club, Ed has over 3000 instructional flying hours and is dedicated to Private Pilot training.

John Fenton.

A Flying Instructor since 1970, John is joint proprietor and assistant CFI of Yorkshire Flying Services at Leeds/Bradford. He is a PPL Examiner and recently received the Bronze Medal from the Royal Aero Club for his achievements and contributions to air rallying. John has made considerable contributions to the field of flying instruction in this country and pioneered the use of audio tapes for training.

Ronald Smith.

A senior Aviation Ground Instructor, Ron's twenty years in aviation include considerable time as a flying instructor, specialised flying in remote areas, fish-spotting, and a period operating his own Air Taxi Service. He is an active member of *California Wheelchair Aviators* and holds a Commercial Pilot's Licence.

Robert Johnson.

An experienced aviator, Bob drew most of the diagrams, designed the cover, and prepared the final edit and layout of the manuals for printing. His aviation experience includes flying a *Cessna Citation* executive jet, a *DC-3* and light aircraft as Chief Pilot for an international University based in Switzerland, and seven years as a First Officer on *Fokker Friendship, Lockheed Electra* and *McDonnell Douglas DC-9* airliners. Prior to this he was an Air Taxi Pilot and also gained technical experience as a Draughtsman on Airborne Mineral Survey work in Australia.

ACKNOWLEDGEMENTS

We greatly appreciate the input that has been made by the following:

The Civil Aviation Authority, Peter Godwin, Brian Harbit (Manchester School of Flying), Bill Ryall and Martin Watts; ICAO, Cessna, Piper and Gulfstream American for technical material, and of course Airtour Flight Equipment Ltd and Robert Pooley Ltd.

'Good, clear Knowledge
minimises
Flight Training Hours'

FOREWORD

This volume of the Air Pilot's Manual – AIR NAVIGATION – presents this important area of training for the Private Pilot's Licence in the logical sequence of Theory, Preparation, and Performance.

THE COCKPIT IS A DIFFICULT ENVIRONMENT IN WHICH TO LEARN.

As with the other Volumes of the Air Pilot's Manual, in AIR NAVIGATION we have avoided the presentation of 'Facts Only', so that a thorough understanding of the principles can enable you to derive maximum benefit from your actual Navigation Exercises.

This approach will not only enable you to become a very competent Pilot/Navigator but will also help to minimise your flight training hours. (It does, however, mean that our book is a little longer than it could be if the aim was only to cram facts in without a reasonable understanding.)

'Understanding makes for Remembering.'

Also, in determining the order of how the knowledge is presented, care has been taken to keep things as logical and practical as possible for you, the student. Consequently, in the first section – Basic Navigation Theory – the simpler, more practical topics of *Speed*, *Direction* and *Using the Navigation Computer* come first to give you the feel of practical operations, before the more involved items of *Vertical Navigation, The Earth, and Aeronautical Charts* are encountered.

OPERATIONAL DECISIONS.

Navigation of an aeroplane consists mainly of making commonsense operational decisions. These decisions are based on knowledge and experience. Very few are difficult to make – most being logical and simple – but occasionally there are difficult decisions (both on the ground and in flight) to be made. These are the ones that we must prepare for.

We have adopted a professional approach right from the start, whether your ultimate aim is to be a Private Pilot or to go on and make Aviation your career.

Operational Decisions will often have to be taken well away from your home base, and to a large extent you will be on your own. They fall into two categories:
- those made **On-The-Ground** during your pre-flight planning; and
- **In-Flight** operational decisions.

Many decisions are so simple and second nature that you don't even realise that you are making them. Others require a calm, cool, but quick assessment, followed by a decision and some action. Proceeding into an area of poor visibility could fall into this category.

The aeroplane will not stand still while you make-up your mind what to do in difficult in-flight situations. You cannot just pull over to the side of the road and study your maps. **Good pre-flight planning,** with many operational decisions taken on the ground – and alternative courses of action considered in the event of in-flight problems occurring – takes a lot of pressure off the Pilot/Navigator.

THE NAVIGATION COMPUTER.

As a Pilot/Navigator you will become adept at **estimating angles, distances, time intervals, fuel consumption, etc.** The *art of estimating* is an important skill to develop. It is also important that you can calculate these various quantities **easily and accurately**. To achieve this you will use a Navigation Computer. It is a simple device (it looks complicated but isn't) that allows us to carry out almost every navigational calculation with speed and accuracy.

The type of computer most commonly used in the UK is the **CRP-1**, manufactured by Airtour Flight Equipment, and this type is featured right throughout the Air Pilot's Manual. One advantage of the CRP-1 is its ability to handle metric conversions without having to put marks and arrows on it yourself.

Electronic navigation computers are available but we suggest you steer away from them, at least initially, because they do not encourage the Pilot/Navigator to visualise each situation – an important ability to develop. Once you are adept at the various computing problems involved in Air Navigation you might elect to 'go electronic'.

The basic concept of the Slide Navigation Computer dates back to early navigation days, and with the incorporation of modern production techniques which allow precision marking of graduations and scales on the latest materials, Navigation Computers such as the excellent CRP-1 are an essential item of equipment for a modern Pilot/Navgator.

The Slide Navigation Computer has two sides:

- a **Wind-Side**, which enables solution of *triangle of velocities* problems for flight-planning and en route navigation; and

- a **Calculator-Side** (the main component of which is a circular slide-rule on the outer scales), used to perform the simple arithmetical calculations involved in flight operations, e.g. distance, speed and time; conversion of units; fuel quantities and consumption; True Air Speed, etc.

Two chapters in the first section are devoted to using the Navigation Computer, one for each side, and, although it may appear a little complicated at first, we have gone to great lengths to set out the text clearly, logically and simply – with ample illustrations to assist you.

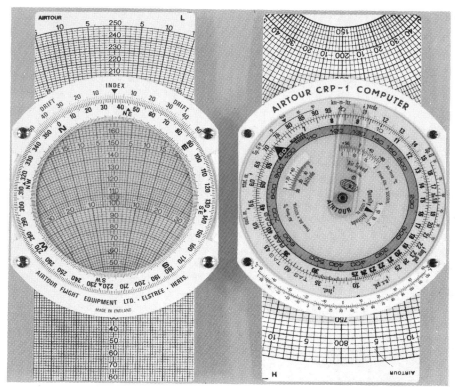

Figs.1a & b. The Two Sides to the CRP-1 Navigation Computer.

THE THEORY EXAMINATION.

Navigation is one of the theory examinations for the UK PPL, for which you will sit at your Flying School. Prior to this you should be achieving considerable success in completing the Exercises which form part of this course. They are mentioned at the relevant places in each chapter, and in this volume some chapters have Exercises interspersed throughout the text to give you practice on a particular aspect of the Chapter before moving on to the next consideration.

The Exercises themselves are located at the back of Volume 2 – in Part (D). They form a very important part of the Course and we recommend you work through them carefully.

This Manual is more than just a text to allow you to pass the examination (even though this is indeed one of its aims) – it is designed to remain as a reference text on your shelves for as long as you fly. In places we have gone a little beyond what is required of you in the Air Navigation examination. For example there is an Appendix to Chapter 13 which shows you how to plan a climb – something which, although not required of you in the PPL examination, will enable you to plan longer, higher altitude flights in the future.

THE NAVIGATION FLIGHT TEST (NFT).

This is the province of your flying instructor.

The test is carried out towards the end of your flying training for the PPL(A). It is designed to assess your ability as a 'Pilot/Navigator', prior to carrying out your (solo) 'qualifying cross-country' flight. Details of the test have been included as an Appendix.

This manual, and your navigation cross-country training, will prepare you fully for this Navigation Flight Test.

OPERATIONAL INFORMATION.

For safe flight operations it is essential that all Pilots refer to current operational information. This basically involves using latest issues of aeronautical charts, and amended flight information publications, Circulars and NOTAMs.

In the UK the primary source of operational information is the *UK Aeronautical Information Publication (AIP)*, a large, frequently amended set of manuals produced to an international standard by the Civil Aviation Authority. Your flying training organisation and ATS units should have amended copies of the UK AIP for reference.

As the AIP is a formidable and bulky set of documents for a Private Pilot (because the major portion covers airline-type instrument flight procedures) there are also available conveniently-sized publications known as Pooley's *Pilots Information Guide (P.I.G.)* and the *United Kingdom and Ireland Flight Guide*. These are revised regularly. The P.I.G. is a compilation of aeronautical information for Private non instrument-rated Pilots, produced with the assistance of the Civil Aviation Authority.

It is worth mentioning that this type of conveniently-sized publication for visual flight operations is often produced by the aviation authorities in many countries (e.g. the Visual Flight Guide in Australia), however in the UK this service has been provided for many years by Pooley's at the behest of the Civil Aviation Authority.

You will find references to Pooley's publications, where applicable, throughout The Air Pilot's Manual, (in addition to the UK AIP). However, if in any doubt, refer to an amended copy of the UK AIP and current air legislation documents; and **always** check latest AICs and NOTAMs prior to flight.

Now we suggest you commence the first chapter, entitled THE PILOT/NAVIGATOR, which is an introductory overview of the Basic Principles of Air Navigation; and good luck with completing your PPL(A).

1

BASIC NAVIGATION THEORY

1. The Pilot/Navigator 2
2. Speed 14
3. Direction 28
4. Wind-Side of the Navigation Computer .. 45
5. Calculator-Side of the Navigation
        Computer 79
6. Vertical Navigation 98
7. Time 125
8. The Earth 142
9. Aeronautical Charts 157

1

THE PILOT/NAVIGATOR

Air Navigation involves basic principles that apply to all aeroplanes, from the simplest trainer to the most sophisticated passenger jets. These basic principles are discussed in this manual.

Since the Air Pilot's Manual is a training programme for the Private Pilot, we concentrate on:
- accurate navigation of a light aircraft;
- flown by a single Pilot;
- in visual conditions.

Fig. 1-1.

The Private Pilot, when flying cross-country, acts as Pilot, Navigator and Radio Operator. He or she must:
- primarily fly the aeroplane safely and accurately;
- navigate correctly;
- attend to the radio and other aspects of his duty in the cockpit.

In short, he or she must *'Aviate, Navigate and Communicate'*.

To conduct a cross-country flight efficiently, the navigational tasks must be co-ordinated with (and not interfere with) the smooth flying of the aeroplane. It is most important that the Pilot/Navigator clearly understands the basic principles underlying navigation so that correct techniques and practices can be applied quickly and accurately without causing too much distraction or apprehension.

SOUND PREPARATION is the Basis for a Confident Navigation Exercise.

Being properly prepared prior to a cross-country flight is essential if it is to be successful. Always **flight plan carefully** and meticulously. This sets up an accurate base against which you can measure your in-flight navigational performance.

Pre-flight consideration should be given to navigational items such as:
- the serviceability of your watch or aircraft clock – *Time* is vital to accurate navigation;
- the contents of your *'Nav Bag'* – pencils, computer, protractor and scale – or a plotter, suitable maps and charts, and relevant flight information publications;
- the preparation of the appropriate maps and charts;
- the desired route;
- the terrain en route;
- the airspace en route (uncontrolled, controlled, special rules, advisory, etc);
- the suitability of the destination and any alternate aerodromes;
- the **forecast** weather en route and at the destination and alternate aerodromes (plus any actual reports that might be available);
- the calculation of accurate headings and ground speeds;
- consideration of fuel consumption, and accurate fuel planning.

It certainly sounds like a lot, but each item considered individually is very simple to understand. After considering them one by one in separate chapters, we will put them all together and see how they fit into a normal cross-country flight.

IN FLIGHT, FLY ACCURATE HEADINGS.

Once the aeroplane is in flight, flying a reasonably accurate **heading** (which involves reference to both the Direction Indicator and outside cues) is essential if the aeroplane is to track towards the desired destination. Maintaining **cruise air speed,** and comparing your progress and **times of arrival** at various fixes with those estimated at the flight planning stage will normally ensure a pleasant and drama-free journey.

NAVIGATIONAL TASKS ARE ADDITIONAL TO FLYING THE AEROPLANE.

Our objective in this Volume of the Air Pilot's Manual is to show you navigational techniques that will not increase your workload in the cockpit to an unacceptable degree, and which will still allow time to fix your position and navigate the aeroplane safely to your desired destination.

We make the assumption that you already know how to fly the aeroplane; the idea here being to add on to these flying skills the Basic Principles of Air Navigation. Other aspects that have a bearing on the conduct of a cross-country flight are covered in their own sections (for instance, Airspace, Radio Procedures and Meteorology in Vol.2).

THE EARTH.

All navigation is done with reference to the surface of the Earth – starting from the elementary exercise of 'navigating' the aeroplane around the circuit during your initial training (which requires visual reference to ground features such as the runway and points ahead of the aeroplane for tracking) and progressing to the large passenger jets using sophisticated instrument navigation techniques to cover vast distances around the Earth.

Direction on Earth.

Direction is the angular position of one point to another without reference to the distance between them. It is expressed as the angular difference from a specified reference direction. In Air Navigation this reference direction is either:

- North (for *'true'* or *'magnetic'* bearings); or
- the heading (or the nose) of the aircraft (for *'relative bearings'*).

The simplest means of describing direction is to consider a circle laid flat and then divided into 360 units, numbered clockwise from 000 in the reference direction all the way around the circle to 360.

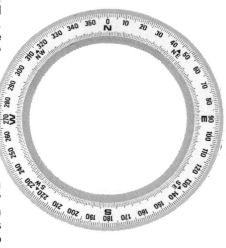

Fig.1-2. To Measure 'Direction', the Full Circle is Divided into 360 Degrees.

It is usual to refer to direction as a three-figure group to prevent any misunderstanding in the transmission of messages. For example, North is referred to as 360, East is referred to as 090, South-West as 225.

Position on Earth.

The main method of specifying the position of a place on the surface of the Earth is the *latitude and longitude* system. This involves covering the surface of a reduced Earth with an evenly spaced *graticule* of lines – North-South lines joining the North and South poles, and East-West lines parallel with the Equator. The North-South lines are known as **meridians of longitude** and the East-West lines are called **parallels of latitude**.

The position of any place on the surface of the Earth can be then be specified with reference to the Equator and a **datum** (or prime) meridian of longitude. The universal base longitude used throughout the world – **Longitude 0°** – is the meridian drawn (North-South) through **Greenwich**, near London, and known as the **prime meridian**.

4

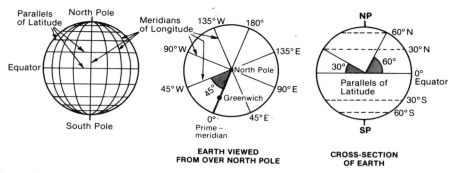

**EARTH VIEWED
FROM OVER NORTH POLE**

**CROSS-SECTION
OF EARTH**

*Fig.1-3. Position on Earth is usually Specified with Reference to
Meridians of Longitude and Parallels of Latitude.*

Distance on Earth.

The separation of two points on Earth is called *distance* and is expressed as
the length of the shortest line joining them.

For most navigational purposes, distance is stated in **nautical
miles** (abbreviation 'nm') – with 1 nm = 1852 metres,
i.e. 1·852 km.

**The nautical mile is related to the size of the Earth in that it is the length
of 1 minute of latitude.** It is slightly longer than the familiar *statute mile*,
1 nm measuring 6076 ft compared to the 5280 ft of the *sm*.

One minute of latitude is measured down the side of a chart, i.e. along a
meridian of longitude, which is a *'Great Circle'*. A *Great Circle* is one whose
centre lies at the centre of the Earth (for example, all meridians of longitude
and also the Equator), and so 1 minute of arc of any Great Circle will be
1 nm. This is explained in more detail later in the Chapter on *The Earth*.

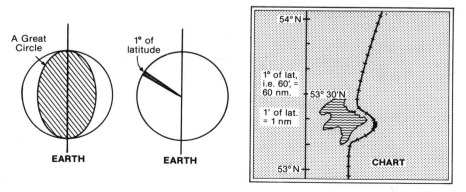

*Fig.1-4. A Great Circle, and 1° of Latitude
on the Earth and on a Chart.*

There are 360 degrees in a circle and each degree has 60 minutes, i.e. a circle has (360 x 60 =) 21,600 minutes – which makes the circumference of the Earth approximately 21,600 nautical miles.

If an aeroplane travels 1 nautical mile through an air mass, we refer to this as 1 **air nautical mile** (anm). As well as the aeroplane moving through the air mass, the air mass will be moving across the ground (in the form of a wind that blows) and will carry the aeroplane along with it. The wind velocity adds an extra effect to the passage of the aeroplane over the ground. If an aeroplane travels 1 nautical mile over the ground or water, we refer to this as 1 **ground nautical mile** (gnm).

NOTE: Whilst navigational distances are referred to in terms of nautical miles, other shorter horizontal distances, such as runway length or horizontal distance from cloud, may be referred to in *metres.*

In Air Navigation we are concerned not only with *'horizontal navigation'* but also with *'vertical navigation'* (covered in Chapter 6). The traditional and standard unit for vertical distance, or *height,* is the *foot* (abbreviated *ft*).

SPEED.

Speed is the rate at which distance is covered, i.e. speed is the *distance per unit time.*

The standard unit for speed is the **knot,** (abbreviated *kt*).
1 knot = 1 nautical mile per hour.

DIRECTION AND SPEED COMBINED.

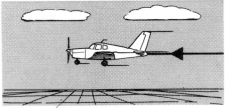

An Aeroplane flies in the medium of air. Its motion relative to the air mass is specified by:
- its Direction (known as **Heading**); and
- its Speed Through the Air Mass (**True Air Speed**).

Fig. 1-5.

Heading (HDG). When flown in balance (as it normally is) the aeroplane will travel **through the air** in the direction in which it is heading. If the aeroplane is headed East (090), then its passage relative to the air mass will be easterly (090) also.

True Air Speed (TAS). This is the actual speed of the aeroplane **relative to the air mass.** *True Air Speed* is normally abbreviated as **TAS,** but occasionally to **V** when used in formulae (such as '½.Rho.V-squared' for *Dynamic Pressure,* or 'Lift = C$_{Lift}$ ½.Rho.V-squared S', an equation you will encounter in the section on Principles of Flight in Vol.4; in which *Rho* represents *Air Density*).

When considered together HDG/TAS constitute what is known as a **Vector** quantity, which requires both **magnitude** (in this case *TAS*) and

direction (here *HDG*) to be completely specified. HDG/TAS is the *Velocity* (direction and speed) of the aeroplane through the air.

The **HDG/TAS** Vector fully describes the Motion of the
Aeroplane Relative to the Air Mass.

HDG/TAS is symbolised by a single-headed arrow –
the direction of the arrow indicating the direction of
movement along the vector line.

Fig.1-6.

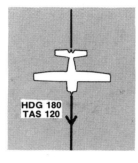

*Fig.1-7. An Aeroplane Heading
South at TAS 120 kt.*

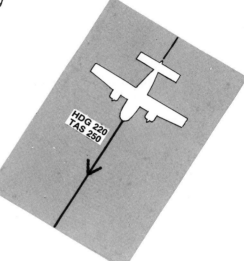

*Fig.1-8. Heading 220 Degrees
at TAS 250 kt.*

*Fig.1-9. An Aeroplane Heading 330°,
TAS 80 kt.*

**An Air Mass Can Move Relative to the Ground –
i.e. a Wind Can Blow.**

The general movement of air relative to the ground is called *Wind Velocity* and is abbreviated as *W/V*. Like HDG/TAS, **W/V** is a vector quantity because both **direction** and **magnitude** are specified. By convention, the wind direction is expressed as the direction **from** which it is blowing. For example, a northerly wind blows *from* the North *towards* the South. **W/V** is symbolised by a triple-headed arrow.

⟶⟫⟫ *Fig.1-10.*

The **W/V** Vector fully describes the horizontal Motion of the Air Mass *Relative* to the Earth's Surface.

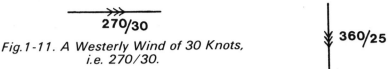

Fig.1-11. A Westerly Wind of 30 Knots, i.e. 270/30.

360/25

Fig.1-12. A Northerly Wind of 25 kt, i.e. 360/25.

030/10

Fig.1-13. A Wind Blowing From 030 Degrees at 10 kt, i.e. 030/10.

Fig.1-14. A Wind Blowing Towards the North at 35 kt, i.e. 180/35.

180/35

With a W/V of 230/20, the air mass will be moving relative to the Earth's surface from a direction of 230 degrees at a rate of 20 nautical miles per hour.

In a 6 minute period, for example, the air mass will have moved 2 nm (6 min = 1/10th hour; 1/10th of 20 nm = 2 nm) from a direction of 230 degrees (and therefore towards 230 – 180 = 050 degrees).

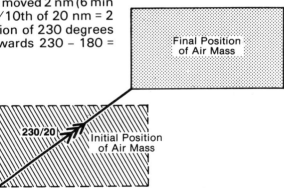

Fig.1-15. A Wind of 230/20.

The motion of the aeroplane relative to the surface of the Earth is made up of two velocities:
- the aeroplane moving relative to the air mass (HDG/TAS); and
- the air mass moving relative to the surface of the Earth.

Adding these two together gives the resultant vector of:
- **the aeroplane moving relative to the surface of the Earth (Track/GS)**.

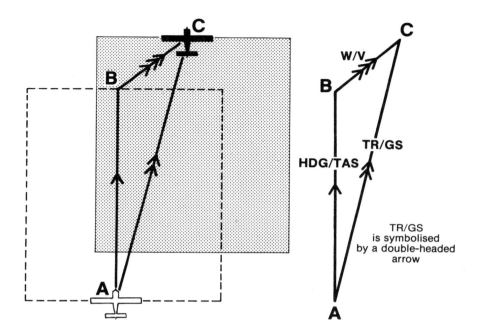

Fig.1-16. HDG/TAS + W/V = TRACK/GS.

An aeroplane flying through an air mass is in a similar situation to you, say, as a swimmer, crossing a fast flowing river. If you dive in at A and head-off through the water in the direction of B, the current will carry you downstream towards C. To an observer (hopefully also able to swim) sitting overhead in the branch of a tree, you will appear to be swimming a little bit sideways as you get swept downstream, even though in fact you are swimming straight through the water.

In the same way, it is quite common to look up and see an aeroplane flying somewhat *'sideways'* in strong wind situations. Of course the aeroplane is not actually flying sideways through the air, rather it is flying straight ahead relative to the air mass (HDG/TAS) and it is the wind velocity (W/V) which, when added to the aeroplane's motion through the air (HDG/TAS), gives it the resultant motion over the ground (TRack/Ground Speed).

To fly from A to C in the above situation, the Pilot must fly on a HDG of *'A:B'* through the air, i.e. maintain the nose of the aeroplane in a direction parallel to *A:B*. The wind will have the effect of *B:C*. The combined effect of these, known as the resultant, will give the aeroplane a track over the ground of *A:C*.

The **TR/GS** Vector fully describes the Motion of the Aeroplane Relative to the Earth's Surface.

THE TRIANGLE OF VELOCITIES.

The two velocities:
1. **HDG/TAS**: the aeroplane moving through the air mass; and
2. **W/V**: the air mass moving over the ground; and, when added together vectorially, give the resultant:
3. **TRack/Ground Speed (TR/GS)** – the aeroplane moving over the ground.

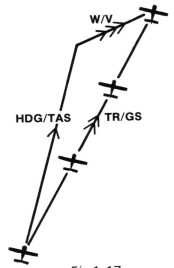

These three vectors form what is known as *'The Triangle of Velocities'*. It is a pictorial representation of the vector addition:

HDG/TAS + W/V = TR/GS

– i.e. the combined effect of HDG/TAS plus W/V will give the resultant TR/GS.

We add the two vectors for HDG/TAS and W/V *'head to tail'*, i.e. starting from A, the head of the HDG/TAS vector at B is the starting point for the tail of the W/V vector which then ends up at C.

Fig.1-17.
The Triangle of Velocities.

The resultant effect of the two combined is the TR/GS vector starting at A and finishing at C. This is the path that the aeroplane would fly over the ground. The angle between the HDG and the Track (TR) is called the **drift** angle.

You may have already seen this *triangle of velocities* illustrated on a navigation computer, as in the next figure.

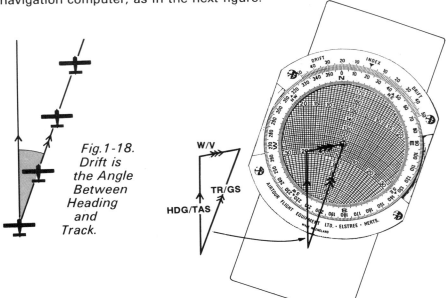

Fig.1-18.
Drift is the Angle Between Heading and Track.

Fig.1-19. The Triangle of Velocities Laid on the 'Wind-Side' of the CRP-1 Navigation Computer.

Do not be frightened by the navigation computer. It is a marvellous device designed to make your navigational tasks easier. A whole chapter is devoted to the 'Wind-Side' of the computer later on to make it all really clear.

At the flight planning stage:
- you will know the **Desired Track** (also known as *Track Required*); and
- will obtain a forecast **Wind Velocity**.

Using the known **True Air Speed**, you will be able to calculate:
- the **Heading** required to *'make good'* the desired track; and also
- the expected **Ground Speed**.

Later on during the flight you may find that, even though you have flown the HDG/TAS accurately, your actual **'Track Made Good' (TMG)** over the ground differs from your desired track; in other words there is a **'Track Error'**. It is most likely due to the actual wind being different from the forecast wind that you used at the flight planning stage. You will then have to make some adjustments to the HDG to carry out your navigational task of rejoining your desired track and continuing on to the destination.

This then is what Air Navigation is basically all about! The essential principles are fairly simple and they have now been covered. All we have to do is expand on them a little in our following chapters and then combine them into practical navigational operations.

SUMMARY OF TERMINOLOGY

HDG/TAS: Heading (HDG) is the actual heading of the aeroplane in degrees steered by the Pilot. It may be related to True North, Magnetic North or Compass North.

True Air Speed (TAS) is the actual speed of the aeroplane through the air. It will differ significantly from the airspeed indicated on the Air Speed Indicator (the Indicated Air Speed) due to the air being less dense the higher the aeroplane flies. The Pilot will need to do a small calculation to convert IAS to TAS when flying at altitude.

The normal unit for airspeed is the *knot*. IAS is useful for aerodynamics, but TAS is necessary for navigation. The normal unit of distance for navigation is the *nautical mile (nm)* and if it is distance relative to the air, we call it an *air nautical mile (anm)*.

TR/GS: Track (TR) is the path of the aeroplane over the surface of the Earth, and is usually expressed in degrees True or Magnetic.

Ground Speed (GS) is the actual speed of the aeroplane over the ground and is measured in knots. A GS of 120 kt means that 120 ground nautical miles would be covered in 1 hour at that GS.

DRIFT: is the difference between the HDG steered by the Pilot and the TRack of the aeroplane over the ground. It is of course the wind that blows the aeroplane from its HDG/TAS through the air onto its TR/GS over the Earth's surface.

Drift is measured from the **HDG** (the nose of the aeroplane) **to the TR**, and is specified in degrees left (port) of HDG or right (starboard) of HDG.

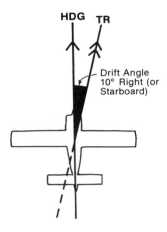

Fig.1-20. Drift is the Angle between Heading and Track.

W/V: **Wind Direction** is expressed in *degrees True or Magnetic* and is the direction **from** which the wind is blowing. **Wind Speed** is in *knots* (kt) – 1 kt being 1 nm per hour.

TRACK ERROR: the actual *Track Made Good (TMG)* over the ground will often differ from the *Desired Track*. The angular difference between the desired track and the TMG is called **Track Error** and is specified in degrees left (port) or right (starboard) of the desired track.

Fig.1-21. Track Error is the Angle Between Desired Track and the Track Made Good (TMG).

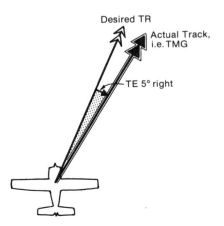

NOTE: *Track Error* is a totally different thing to *Drift*.

LATITUDE: The distance of a place North or South from the Equator, measured in degrees.

LONGITUDE: The distance of a place from the prime meridian (0°), through Greenwich, also measured in degrees.

NAUTICAL MILE: The length of 1 minute of latitude measured along a meridian, i.e. down the side of a chart.

KNOT: Unit of Speed – 1 nautical mile per hour.

GREAT CIRCLE: A circle on the Earth's surface whose centre is the centre of the Earth.

☐ Before continuing on to the next chapter, we recommend that you review what has been covered by completing the exercises for this chapter: **Exercises 1 — The Pilot/Navigator.**

All the Exercises for Air Navigation are located in the last Section of Vol.2, along with the Answers.

2

SPEED

A sound understanding of the factors involved in **Air Speed** is important if you are to become a competent Pilot/Navigator.

The **True Air Speed (TAS)** of an aircraft is its rate of progress or speed through the air mass in which it is flying. Whether this air mass is moving over the ground, or whether it is stationary, is irrelevant to the True Air Speed. TAS is simply the speed of the aircraft *through the air.*

In contrast, a hot-air balloon or a cloud has no horizontal driving force of its own and so just hangs in the air, i.e. the TAS of a balloon or a cloud is **zero** because it is **not moving relative to the air mass.**

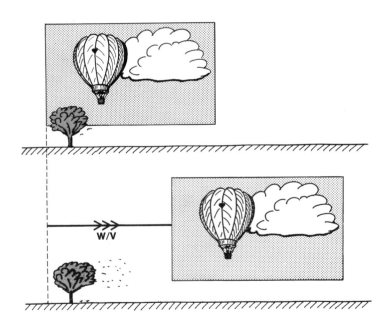

Fig.2-1. An Air Mass Can Be Stationary or Move as Wind.

If the air mass is moving relative to the ground (i.e. the wind velocity is other than zero), then the balloon or cloud will be carried by the air mass across the ground. Being static in the air mass, the balloon or the cloud could theoretically be used as a point against which to measure the True Air Speed (TAS) of an aircraft. In other words, an aircraft will fly past a balloon, or a cloud, at its True Air Speed.

The actual speed of an aircraft relative to the ground is known as the **Ground Speed (GS).** The resultant *Ground Speed* is a combination of:
- the *True Air Speed (TAS –* the movement of the aircraft relative to the air mass); and
- the *Wind Velocity (W/V –* the movement of the air mass relative to the ground).

This is familiar from our discussion on the 'triangle of velocities'.

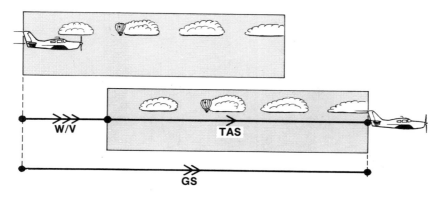

Fig.2-2. The Ground Speed is the Resultant of the True Air Speed (TAS) and the Wind Velocity (W/V).

At this stage we are only interested in *Air Speed –* the speed of the aircraft through the air. (A consideration of *Ground Speed* will follow in a later chapter.)

THE INTERNATIONAL STANDARD ATMOSPHERE.

A *'Standard Atmosphere'* has been defined as a 'measuring stick' against which we can compare the actual atmosphere that exists at a given place on a given day. The *Standard Atmosphere* has a Standard Mean Sea Level (MSL) Pressure of 1013·25* millibars (mb), which decreases by about 1 mb for each 30 ft of altitude gained, and a Standard MSL Temperature of +15°C, which decreases by about 2°C for each 1000 ft of altitude gained. The ISA MSL air density is 1225 gm/cubic metre, and this also decreases as altitude is gained.

NOTE: A new standard **unit of pressure** for aviation, equivalent to millibars, is being adopted in many countries – the *'hectoPascal' (hPa)*. Because 1 mb = 1 hPa, the change has no other significance than the change of name. The UK has decided to remain using *millibars* for the forseeable future, but to remind you of the other unit, (which will be encountered if you fly to the Republic of Ireland or across to the Continent) we will occasionally show pressure as *mb(hPa)*.

*1013 mb is used for practical purposes.

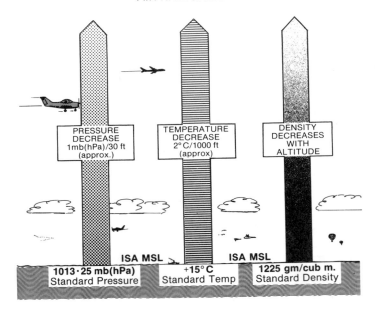

Fig.2-3. The 'hypothetical' International Standard Atmosphere.

THE MEASUREMENT OF SPEED.

To measure the speed of an aircraft is a little more complicated than you might expect. The basic instrument used is the **Air Speed Indicator** (ASI) which is a pressure-operated instrument. The air speed displayed is given the logical name *Indicated Air Speed (IAS)*.

Due to the nature of the atmosphere, in which air pressure and air density decrease with altitude – (and of course our aircraft will be flying at various altitudes) – and due to the design of the ASI system, the *Indicated Air Speed (IAS)* is usually less than the *True Air Speed (TAS)*.

Fig.2-4. The Air Speed Indicator.

The *Indicated Air Speed* as shown on the Air Speed Indicator in the cockpit and the *True Air Speed* of the aeroplane through the air will only be the same value when *International Standard Atmosphere Mean Sea Level conditions* exist. (Such conditions are usually not experienced.)

In conditions other than *ISA MSL*, the Pilot must make some straightforward calculations (either mentally, or by navigation computer) to convert the IAS he or she reads on the Air Speed Indicator to the TAS needed for navigational purposes.

To a beginning Pilot, the fact that the word *airspeed* has a number of meanings in aviation may at first be a little confusing but, as Pilots, we must understand the differences quite clearly.

- **Performance** of the aeroplane is related to **Indicated Air Speed (IAS)**, (i.e. whether the plane will stall or not, its rate of climb performance, lift/drag ratio, etc), and is a function of IAS. Indicated Air Speed is related to Dynamic Pressure.

- **Navigation and Flight Planning** depend upon **True Air Speed (TAS), Wind Velocity (W/V)** and **Ground Speed (GS)**. True Air Speed is the actual speed of the aeroplane through the air.

To understand the difference between the two really basic air speeds, *Indicated Air Speed (IAS)* and *True Air Speed (TAS)*, we will need to consider briefly certain properties of the atmosphere and the principles of fluid flow.

STATIC PRESSURE.

Static Pressure at any point in the atmosphere is exerted equally in all directions. It is a result of the weight of all the molecules composing the air above that point. At this very moment, static pressure of the atmosphere is being exerted at all points on the skin of your hand.

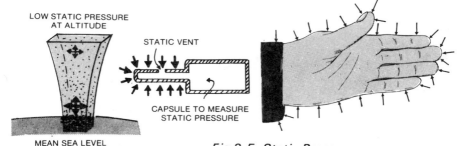

Fig.2-5. Static Pressure.

As its name implies, Static Pressure does not involve any motion of the body relative to the air.

DYNAMIC PRESSURE.

If you hold your hand up in a strong wind or out of the window of a moving car, then an extra wind pressure, or *moving pressure,* is felt due to the air impacting upon your hand.

This extra pressure, over and above the static pressure which is always present, is called **Dynamic Pressure,** or pressure due to relative movement. It is felt by a body which is moving relative to the air, i.e. it could be moving through the air, or the air could be flowing past it.

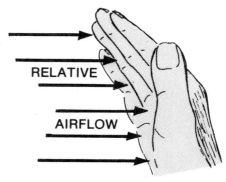

Fig.2-6. Dynamic Pressure.

Just how strong Dynamic Pressure is depends upon a number of things, the two main ones being:

(a) **The Speed of the Body Relative to the Air.** The faster the car drives or the faster the wind blows, then the stronger the extra Dynamic Pressure that you feel on your hand. This is because of the greater number of air molecules that impact upon it per second.

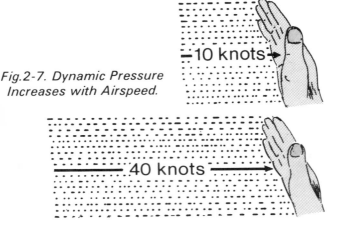

Fig.2-7. Dynamic Pressure Increases with Airspeed.

(b) **The Density of the Air.** In outer space, no matter how fast you travelled, you would not feel any Dynamic Pressure because there are practically no molecules to impact upon you.

By contrast, at sea level, where the atmosphere is densest, then your hand would be struck by very many molecules per second – certainly many more than in the upper regions of the atmosphere. Even though you might be travelling at the same speed, you will feel a much lower Dynamic Pressure in the higher levels of the atmosphere, where the air is less dense, than in the lower levels.

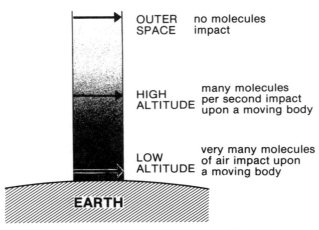

Fig.2-8. Air Density Decreases with Altitude.

So, for an aircraft moving at a constant True Air Speed, less Dynamic Pressure is experienced the higher the altitude. The actual measure of Dynamic Pressure is written:

Dynamic Pressure = ½.**Rho.V-squared**

where:

- **Rho** represents **air density**, which **decreases with altitude**;
- **V** represents the speed of the body relative to the air, i.e. the **True Air Speed**. (It does not matter whether the body is moving through the air, or the air blowing past the body, or a combination of both – as long as they are moving relative to one another there will be an airspeed and a Dynamic Pressure.)

TOTAL PRESSURE.

In the atmosphere some Static Pressure is always exerted, but only if there is motion of the body relative to the air will any Dynamic Pressure (due to relative motion) be felt by the surface exposed to the airflow. Thus:

Total Pressure consists of **Static Pressure** plus **Dynamic Pressure.**

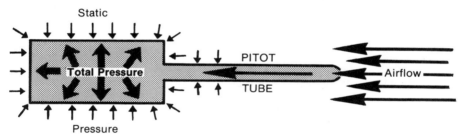

Fig.2-9. Total Pressure is Measured by a Pitot Tube.

Much of this theory about Pressure was developed by the Swiss scientist Daniel Bernoulli, and is expressed in *Bernoulli's Equation,* which, in simplified form, is:

Static Pressure + **Dynamic Pressure** = **Total Pressure**
measured by static   ½.Rho.V-squared   measured by
line (barometer   pitot tube
or altimeter)

An expression for *Dynamic Pressure* can be obtained by subtracting the term *Static Pressure* from both sides of this equation:

Dynamic Pressure = **Total Pressure** – **Static Pressure.**

INDICATED AIR SPEED (IAS).

A measure of Dynamic Pressure can be found by starting with the Total (Pitot) Pressure and from it subtracting the Static Pressure. This is easily done by having a diaphragm with Total Pressure from the pitot tube being fed onto one side, and Static Pressure from the static line being fed onto the other side.

The diaphragm in the ASI system positions itself according to the difference between the Total Pressure and the Static Pressure, i.e. according to the Dynamic Pressure. A pointer connected to the diaphragm through a gearing mechanism then moves around the ASI scale as the diaphragm responds to these pressure variations.

If we assume that the density of air (Rho) remains constant at its Mean Sea Level value (which of course it does not), the scale around which the pointer moves can be graduated in units of speed. This results in an Air Speed Indicator that displays the airspeed accurately only under ISA MSL conditions, i.e. when the air density is 1225 grammes per cubic metre (the same as at +15°C, Pressure Altitude zero).

If the air density (Rho) is precisely 1225 gm/cubic metre, then the Air Speed Indicator will show an Indicated Air Speed that is the same as the True Air Speed of the aeroplane through the air.

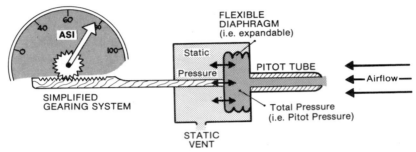

Fig.2-10. The Flexible Diaphragm Drives the Airspeed Pointer to display 'Indicated Air Speed' (IAS).

NOTE: Air Speed Indicators are usually calibrated in **knots** but occasionally indicators graduated in statute miles per hour, the familiar mph, may be encountered.

Indicated Air Speed (IAS) is What We Read on the Air Speed Indicator (ASI).

RECTIFIED AIR SPEED (RAS).

A particular pitot-static system and its cockpit indicator will experience certain small errors, the main two being:

- **Instrument Error** – resulting from poor design and construction of the ASI itself, or from friction within it; and

- **Position Error** – resulting from sensing errors inherent in the positioning on the aircraft of the static vent and the pitot tube. Their position with respect to the airflow is fairly critical and may lead to somewhat incorrect readings when the airflow pattern is disturbed at certain airspeeds, angles of attack, wing flap settings, etc.

The Pilot can correct the reading of Indicated Air Speed shown on the ASI by using a *Calibration Table* (found in the Pilot's Operating Handbook for the aeroplane) to obtain a value known as **Rectified Air Speed (RAS)** or, alternatively, **Calibrated Air Speed (CAS)**.

20

NOTE: *Rectified Air Speed* is the term commonly used for this airspeed in the UK, whereas *Calibrated Air Speed* is used in the United States of America, many European Countries, Australia and New Zealand. Navigation Computers may be labelled with RAS or CAS (or both).

The calculated RAS figure is what the ASI would read if the particular Air Speed Indicator system was perfect. RAS is therefore more accurate than IAS and, if you have taken the trouble to calculate RAS, it should be used in preference to IAS in navigation calculations.

The instrument and position errors of an Air Speed Indicator system are usually no more than a few knots and, for our purposes at Private Pilot level, we can generally assume that Indicated Air Speed (IAS) and Rectified Air Speed (RAS) are equal. Just to remind you of this we will occasionally write *IAS(RAS)*.

☐ Now complete **Exercises 2 — Speed-1**, which review things so far.

TRUE AIR SPEED (TAS).

The aeroplane will rarely be flying in an air mass that has the same density as that under ISA MSL conditions (1225 gm/cubic metre), the basis of the calibration of the Air Speed Indicator. Generally an aeroplane flying at altitude will be experiencing an air density significantly less than this, (because air density *Rho* decreases with altitude). This will also be the case when there is an increase in temperature.

The *Indicated Air Speed* (even if it has been corrected for instrument and position errors to give *Rectified Air Speed*) will need to be further corrected for **density error** if the Pilot is to know the exact speed at which the aeroplane is moving through the air, i.e. the **True Air Speed.**

Whereas the position and instrument error (if any) will be different for each ASI system, the *density error* applies equally to all systems because it is a function of the atmospheric conditions at that time and place.

Air density varies for two main reasons:
(a) **Temperature**: cold air is dense, warm air is less dense, and so on a warm day an aircraft must travel faster through the air for the same number of molecules per second to impact it, and for the same IAS to be indicated.

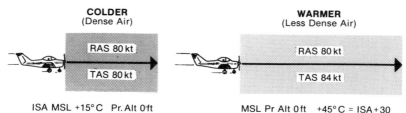

Fig.2-11. Constant IAS(RAS) – TAS Varies with Air Temperature.

TAS varying with temperature (for a constant IAS) is one reason why, on a warm day, an aeroplane requires longer take-off and landing distances. The TAS is higher to give you the same IAS, and the IAS is what you *'fly by'*.

(b) **Pressure**: the greater the Pressure Altitude (i.e. the lower the air pressure), the fewer the molecules per unit volume. For two aircraft with the same True Air Speed (TAS), the higher aircraft will have a lower Indicated Air Speed (IAS) because it will impact fewer molecules of air per second than the lower aircraft.

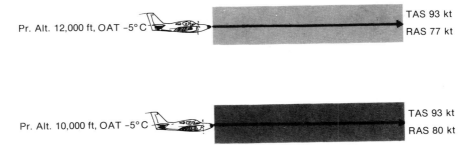

Pr. Alt. 12,000 ft, OAT –5°C TAS 93 kt RAS 77 kt

Pr. Alt. 10,000 ft, OAT –5°C TAS 93 kt RAS 80 kt

Fig.2-12. Same TAS – the Aircraft in Less Dense Air Has a Lower IAS(RAS).

Remember that IAS(RAS) is only equal to TAS under ISA MSL (International Standard Atmosphere – Mean Sea Level) conditions. At higher altitudes the IAS (or RAS) will be less than the TAS because the aircraft will be flying through the thinner air with an airspeed well in excess of that indicated on the ASI.

What Happens When We Climb at a Constant IAS(RAS)?

As an aeroplane gains altitude, the air density (Rho) decreases. If we adopt the usual climb technique of maintaining a **constant** IAS (i.e. a constant Dynamic Pressure '½.Rho.V-squared'), the decrease in Rho is made up by an increase in V (the True Air Speed). Therefore **the higher we climb, when flying at a constant IAS(RAS), the greater the TAS**.

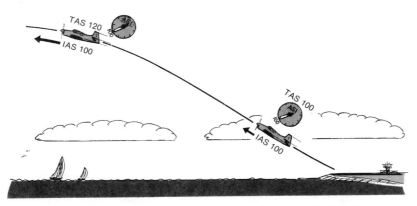

TAS 120
IAS 100

TAS 100
IAS 100

Fig.2-13. The Higher We Climb, the Greater the TAS for a Constant IAS(RAS).

USING THE NAVIGATION COMPUTER TO FIND TAS FROM IAS(RAS).

This calculation has been greatly simplified for us by the invention of the Navigation Computer. The principles illustrated here apply to the *CRP-1* computer, as well as most other types available.

On the Calculator-Side of most Navigation Computers is an *airspeed correction window*, which allows us to:

• match up the *pressure altitude* and the *air temperature* (the main factors determining density – *Rho*); and then:

• from IAS (or RAS/CAS) on the inner scale, read-off TAS on the outer scale.

NOTE: On many computers you will actually have the inner scale labelled *RAS* or *CAS* (or *IAS*) and the outer scale *TAS*. Check if yours is like this.

Ensure that you use the Celsius temperature scale, as all temperatures in UK Meteorology Forecasts (and those for most other countries) are quoted as *degrees Celsius* (formerly *Centigrade*).

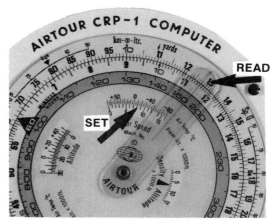

Example 1:

1. Temp –10°C at Pr. Alt. 8000 ft.

2. RAS(CAS) 115 kt gives TAS 127 kt.

Fig.2-14. Finding TAS from IAS(RAS) and Air Temp on the Nav Computer, (Example 1).

As a further example, line up the ISA MSL conditions of +15°C and Pressure Altitude 0. The computer will then show that under these conditions IAS (inner scale) and TAS (outer scale) are the same.

Variation of TAS with Altitude.

Let us assume that the recommended climb speed for our aeroplane is 100 kt IAS. Using your navigation computer see if you can come up with similar answers for the TAS as we have in the table that follows, for a climb at IAS 100 kt from MSL to 20,000 ft. (Assume an International Standard Atmosphere, where temperature decreases by 2°C for each 1000 ft climbed.)

Pressure Altitude	Temp	IAS/RAS	(TAS)
20 000 ft	–25°C	100 kt	(137 kt)
15 000 ft	–15°C	100 kt	(126 kt)
10 000 ft	–5°C	100 kt	(117 kt)
5 000 ft	+5°C	100 kt	(108 kt)
----ISA MSL----	+15°C	100 kt	(100 kt)

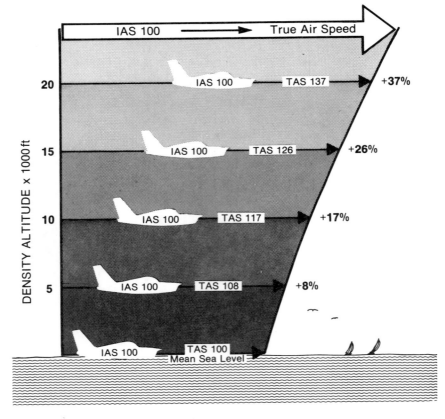

Fig.2-15. IAS 100 kt – TAS Increases with Altitude.

NOTE: at 5000 ft, TAS exceeds IAS by about 8%; and
at 10,000 ft, TAS exceeds IAS by about 17%.

These are handy figures to remember for rough mental calculations and also for when experienced pilots are talking about the speeds at which their aeroplanes *'true-out'*. If you are cruising at 5000 ft with IAS 180 kt showing on the Air Speed Indicator, then your TAS will be approximately 8% greater (8% of 180 = 14), i.e. 194 kt TAS.

☐ Now complete **Exercises 2 — Speed-2.**

The Reverse Situation –
For a Constant TAS, What IAS Is Required?

It is interesting to compare what Indicated Air Speed will be shown in the cockpit if a constant True Air Speed is required at various levels. See if you can obtain the same answers as us for IAS with a constant True Air Speed of 200 kt at various pressure altitudes. Once again, assume a standard atmosphere to be present.

Compare:

Pr. Alt.	Temp	TAS	(IAS/RAS)	
20 000 ft	–25°C	200 kt	(146 kt)	
15 000 ft	–15°C	200 kt	(159 kt)	To fly same TAS, IAS will decrease with
10 000 ft	–5°C	200 kt	(172 kt)	higher altitudes as the air density decreases.
5000 ft	+5°C	200 kt	(185 kt)	
---ISA MSL --	+15°C --	200 kt ---	(200 kt)----	

So, for the same TAS, the greater the Pressure Altitude, the lower the IAS, or, in other words, **the higher an aircraft flies, the more the TAS exceeds the IAS.**

Variation of TAS with Outside Air Temperature (OAT).

Temperature at the one level in the atmosphere will vary from place to place and from time to time. Since temperature affects air density, it will also affect the relationship between IAS and TAS.

(a) The Mean Sea Level situation if temperature varies:

	Temp	IAS/RAS	(TAS)	
	ISA+20 = +35°C	100 kt	(104 kt)	(less dense air)
	ISA+10 = +25°C	100 kt	(102 kt)	
Pressure Altitude 0 ft	ISA = +15°C	100 kt	(100 kt)	
	ISA–10 = +5°C	100 kt	(98 kt)	
	ISA–20 = –5°C	100 kt	(96 kt)	(more dense air)

The Less Dense the Air,
the Greater the TAS, compared to IAS(RAS).

(b) The situation at Pressure Altitude 10,000 ft, if temperature varies:

	Temp	IAS/RAS	(TAS)
	ISA+20 = +15°C	100 kt	(121 kt) (less dense air)
	ISA+10 = +5°C	100 kt	(119 kt)
Pressure Altitude 10,000 ft	ISA = −5°C	100 kt	(117 kt)
	ISA−10 = −15°C	100 kt	(115 kt)
	ISA−20 = −25°C	100 kt	(113 kt) (more dense air)

True Air Speed is Important for Navigation and Flight Planning because TAS is the Actual Speed of the Aeroplane Through the Air Mass.

FURTHER EXAMPLES OF IAS(RAS) to TAS COMPUTER CALCULATIONS.

Example 2: At FL70, OAT −5°C, IAS(RAS) 105 kt. Find the TAS.

Working:

Set the Pressure Altitude 7000 ft against −5°C OAT in the True Air Speed (TAS) window.

Then, against RAS 105 kt on the inner scale, read-off TAS 115 kt on the outermost scale.

TAS is 115 kt (ANS.)

Fig.2-16. Example 2.

In some situations the required pieces of information are not always given directly, but have to be first derived from other information which is provided. We will take an example from a fairly high Flight Level **to illustrate the widening gap between IAS(RAS) and TAS as an aeroplane climbs.**

Example 3: A turboprop plans on flying at FL280 (Flight Level Two Eight Zero), where the temperature is forecast to be ISA+10°C. If its Rectified Air Speed (RAS) will be 150 kt, what TAS can be expected?

Working:
FL280 is Pressure Altitude 28,000 ft.
At FL280, ISA = +15 − (2 x 28)
= +15 − 56 = −41°C
so ISA+10 = −41 + 10 = −31°C

On the computer, set Pr. Alt. 28,000 vs OAT −31 in the Air Speed window, and then, against RAS 150 kt, read-off TAS 240 kt on the outer scale.

Finding the Required IAS(RAS) to Achieve a Particular TAS.

The usual in-flight problem is to determine the TAS from the Indicated Air Speed read-off the ASI. Sometimes, however, you need to be able to work these problems in reverse, say to achieve a certain desired TAS or GS for flight planning purposes, when you will start with these and work back to find the IAS (RAS/CAS) necessary to achieve this.

Example 4: Cruising at FL100 and temperature ISA−10, what is the required RAS (CAS) to give you a True Air Speed of 200 kt?

Working:
Pr.Alt. is 10,000 ft,
where ISA = +15 − (2 x 10)
= +15 − 20
= −5°C
so ISA−10 = −5 − 10
= −15°C

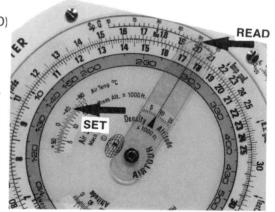

- In the computer *Air Speed* window, set Pr.Alt. 10,000 ft against OAT −15°C.

- Against TAS 200 on the outer scale, read-off RAS 175 kt on the inner.

Fig.2-17. Example 4.

COMMON AIRSPEED TERMINOLOGY:

- **IAS**: Indicated Air Speed;
- **RAS or CAS**: Rectified Air Speed or Calibrated Air Speed (and generally approximately equal to Indicated Air Speed);
- **TAS**: True Air Speed (and, at higher altitudes, usually greater than IAS/RAS/CAS).

☐ Now, finally for this chapter, complete **Exercises 2 − Speed-3**.

3

DIRECTION

Direction is obviously of prime importance to accurate navigation. As all aircraft navigate with reference to the Earth's surface, we begin our study of Direction with a brief consideration of the Earth itself.

There is a geographical axis passing through two physical points on the surface of the Earth about which the Earth rotates. These points are the North and South Geographic Poles. Any 'straight' line drawn around the Earth's surface joining these two points is aligned in a true North-South direction.

By world convention, the basic reference direction is North, with other directions being measured clockwise from this reference in degrees (°). Since there are 360° in a circle, East is described as 090°, South as 180°, West as 270°, and North as 000° or 360°. Any direction (be it the desired track of an aeroplane, the direction from which the wind is blowing, etc.) can be defined in this way.

TRUE DIRECTION.

If Direction is described with reference to **True North** (the direction to the North Geographic Pole), then it is said to be the **True Direction**, and is symbolised by 'T'. East is therefore written as 090°T or 090T. The track between town A and town B illustrated below is 327°T.

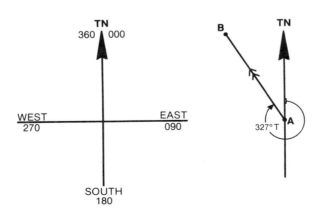

Fig.3-1. True Direction.

A more approximate means of describing direction is using the Cardinal Points, which are the four chief directions of North, South, East and West – further divided by the Quadrantal Points North-East, South-East, South-West and North-West. If necessary, these can be even further divided to give, for instance, NNW ('Nor-Nor-West'). Obviously, the 360° method is superior for aeronautical navigation.

True Direction, however, is a problem for Pilots, because most aeroplanes are not fitted with an instrument that can determine the direction of True North. The Magnetic Compass, the prime source of directional information in the cockpit, aligns itself with **Magnetic North**, rather than with True North.

NOTE: as you will see shortly, this statement is not perfectly correct if there are extraneous magnetic fields, say due to radios or nearby magnetic materials, that are strong enough to affect the magnet within the compass. At this stage, we will assume that the magnet is influenced only by the Earth's magnetic field and none other.

MAGNETIC DIRECTION.

Near to the True North Geographic Pole is an area from which the Earth's magnetic field emanates, known as the North Magnetic Pole to avoid confusion with the geographic pole. Similarly, there is a South Magnetic Pole located near the True South Pole.

A small magnet that is suspended and free to move will seek to align itself with these roughly North-South lines of magnetic force. This is the basis of the Magnetic Compass. If a Compass Card is attached to the magnetic *'needle'*, then the Magnetic Heading of an aeroplane can be read-off against a *'lubber line'*, or *index*, on the compass face.

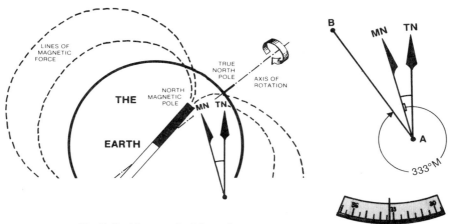

Fig.3-2. Magnetic Direction.

A direction defined by reference to the North-seeking end of a Magnetic Compass is known as a **magnetic direction**. In the case illustrated, the direction between the same two towns, A and B, is now described as 333°**M**.

The actual direction between the two towns of course has not changed, only our description of it has, because of the two different reference directions, TN and MN. 327°T and 333°M in the above case are the same physical direction described differently.

Why Introduce The Complication of Degrees Related to Magnetic North?

Well, it turns out that the simple Magnetic Compass is the most reliable source of directional information. Instruments to display Direction relative to True North are both complicated and expensive, and subject to certain operational limitations not associated with the good old Magnetic Compass. Even in the most sophisticated aircraft flying today, such as the Boeing 767, Airbus A320, and BAe146, a simple Magnetic Compass is installed.

In most light aircraft, the Magnetic Compass is the primary source of directional information, to which other Direction Indicators (often gyroscopic) are aligned.

Fig.3-3.
The Magnetic Compass.

To obtain accurate directional information from the Magnetic Compass, you must understand how it operates, and also its *inaccuracies* whilst the aeroplane is turning or changing speed. This is covered fully in the *Flight Instruments* section of Volume 4 of this series. a summary follows here.

A bar magnet that is freely suspended horizontally will swing so that its axis points roughly North-South. The end of the magnet that points towards the Earth's North Magnetic Pole is called 'the North-seeking POLE' of the magnet.

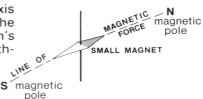

Fig.3-4. Simple Bar Magnet.

THE EARTH'S MAGNETIC FIELD
(also known as TERRESTRIAL MAGNETISM).

The Earth acts like a very large and weak magnet. Its surface is covered by a weak magnetic field – lines of magnetic force that begin deep within the Earth near Hudson Bay in Canada and flow towards a point deep within the Earth near South Victoria Land in Antarctica. Because of their proximity to the North and South Geographic Poles, the magnetic poles are referred to as the *North Magnetic Pole* and the *South Magnetic Pole.*

VARIATION.

The Latitude-Longitude grid shown on charts is based on the geographical poles at either extremity of the axis of rotation, and so the *Meridians of Longitude* run True North and True South, whilst the *Parallels of Latitude* run True East and True West.

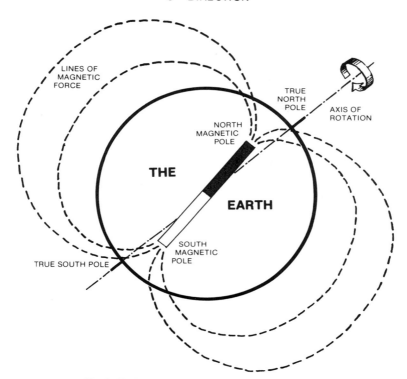

Fig.3-5. The Earth Has a Magnetic Field.

Our small compass magnet, however, does not point exactly at True North and True South. A Magnetic Compass, if it is working perfectly and is influenced only by the Earth's magnetic field, will point at the North **Magnetic** Pole, near Hudson Bay in Canada. At most points on Earth this is a different direction to True North. The angular difference between True North and Magnetic North at any particular point on the Earth is called the **Magnetic Variation** at that point.

If the magnet points slightly East of True North, then the Variation is said to be *East*. If the magnet points to the West of True North, then the Variation is *West* – (West Variation is experienced over the entire UK).

Variation at a point on Earth is measured from True North to Magnetic North. For example, a Magnetic Compass in London will point 5° West of True North, i.e. the Magnetic Variation is 5°W, since Magnetic North lies 5° West of True North. In Liverpool, the Variation is 7°W. In the area between the Towns A and B illustrated previously, the Variation is obviously 6°W (327°T and 333°M being one and the same direction).

VARIATION is the Angular Difference from True North to Magnetic North.

ISOGONALS.

As well as the lines forming the latitude-longitude grid, maps have other lines drawn joining places that have the same magnetic variation, the lines being known as known as **Isogonals.** On the UK 1:500 000 Aeronautical Chart, the Isogonals are shown as dashed lines coloured magenta (purple).

The 6° West Isogonal joins all the places having a Variation of 6° West (e.g. Tees-side, Leeds, Halfpenny Green and Yeovilton). If you are anywhere on this line, then the message that your compass is giving you about Magnetic North can be related to True North; your compass will point at Magnetic North, which will be 6° West of True North.

ISOGONALS are Lines on a Chart joining Places of Equal Magnetic Variation.

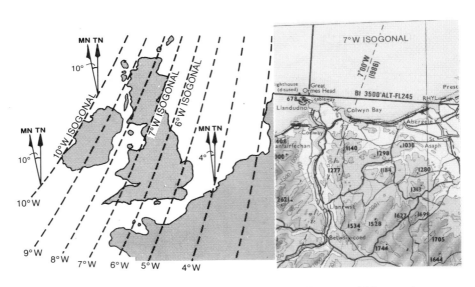

Fig.3-6. Variation is the Angle between True and Magnetic.

If Magnetic North is to the West of True North (i.e. West Variation), then °M will exceed °T. Conversely, if Magnetic North is to the East of True North (i.e. East Variation), then °M will be less than °T. An easy way to remember the relationship between True and Magnetic is:

VARIATION WEST, MAGNETIC BEST,

VARIATION EAST, MAGNETIC LEAST.

Example 1: Whilst flying on the Continent, you are steering your aeroplane on a Heading of 300°M with reference to the Magnetic Compass. From an aeronautical chart you determine that Magnetic Variation in the vicinity is 4°W. What is the aeroplane's Heading in °True?

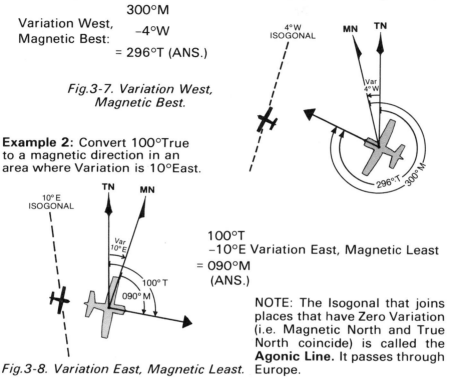

300°M

Variation West,
Magnetic Best: –4°W

= 296°T (ANS.)

Fig.3-7. Variation West,
Magnetic Best.

Example 2: Convert 100°True to a magnetic direction in an area where Variation is 10°East.

100°T
–10°E Variation East, Magnetic Least
= 090°M
   (ANS.)

NOTE: The Isogonal that joins places that have Zero Variation (i.e. Magnetic North and True North coincide) is called the **Agonic Line.** It passes through Europe.

Fig.3-8. Variation East, Magnetic Least.

DEVIATION.

Unfortunately, the magnet in the Magnetic Compass is affected not only by the magnetic field of the Earth, but by any magnetic field that exists in its vicinity, such as the magnetic fields surrounding the metal structure of the aeroplane, rotating parts in the engine, the radios, etc. All can generate their own magnetic fields and affect the Magnetic Compass.

The effect of these additional magnetic fields in a particular aeroplane is to deviate or deflect the compass from indicating Magnetic North precisely. This imprecision is known as **Compass Deviation.**

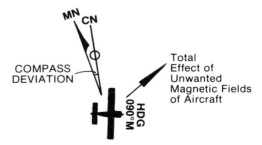

Fig.3-9a. Compass Deviation.

Deviation varies according to the Heading that the aeroplane is on, since these unwanted extra magnetic fields are related to the aeroplane itself. If their resultant is diagonal to the longitudinal axis of the aeroplane (as shown below) then, when the aeroplane is steering 045°, or its reciprocal 225°, it will be aligned with the Earth's magnetic field and so will not cause the compass needle to deviate (i.e. on these headings, Compass Deviation is zero).

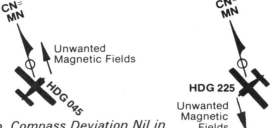

Fig.3-9b. Compass Deviation Nil in this Aeroplane on these Headings.

If, on the other hand, the aeroplane is headed towards the East, the alignment of the unwanted magnetic fields will deviate the Compass as shown, and the compass needle will point towards a *'Compass North'* that is slightly to the East of Magnetic North (by 1° in this case). Even though the Magnetic Heading might be 090°M in actual fact, the Compass will indicate 089°C.

An easy way to remember **the relationship between Magnetic and Compass Directions** is similar to the Variation rhyme:

DEVIATION EAST, COMPASS LEAST;
DEVIATION WEST, COMPASS BEST.

Example 3: A Pilot steers his aeroplane on a Heading of 257° indicated on the Magnetic Compass in the cockpit. If, on that heading, Deviation is 3°W, what is the aeroplane's Magnetic Heading?

257°C
Deviation West, Compass Best: –3
= 254°M
(ANS.)

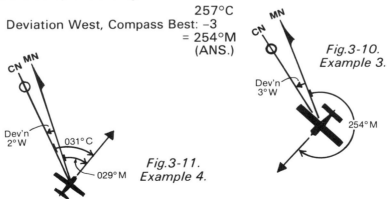

Fig.3-10. Example 3.

Fig.3-11. Example 4.

Example 4: What compass direction must be steered to achieve a Magnetic Heading of 029°M, if the Compass Deviation is 2°West?

Deviation West, Compass Best: 029°M +2 = 031°C (ANS)

THE COMPASS DEVIATION CARD.

Rather than continually having to carry out deviation corrections to the Compass Headings, a simpler approach is for each aircraft to have a small placard known as the **Deviation Card** displayed near the Compass. This Card shows the Pilot what corrections need to be made to the actual magnetic compass reading (described as °C, for compass) in order to obtain the desired magnetic direction in °M. This correction usually involves no more than a few degrees (and in fact, the correction may be so small that the Pilot does not even apply it).

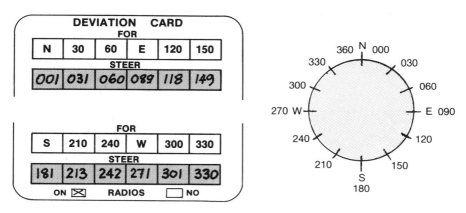

Fig.3-12. *Deviation Card;* *Direction.*

Example 5: To achieve a Magnetic Heading of 270°, steer 271°C **in this aeroplane.**

DEVIATION is the Angular Distance from Magnetic North to Compass North for that Particular Compass and with the Aircraft on that Particular Heading.

PRECAUTIONS WHEN CARRYING MAGNETIC OR METAL GOODS.

The Compass Deviation Card is filled out by an engineer who has actually checked the compass in that particular aeroplane with it headed in different directions. It may be done with electrical services off, or with them on, (which is the normal in-flight situation). Electrical services, such as radios, often generate their own magnetic fields. The Compass Deviation Correction Card allows only for the magnetic influences in the aeroplane that were present when the engineer calibrated the compass in a procedure known as *'Swinging the Compass'.*

Any other magnetic influences introduced into the aeroplane at a time following the *Swinging of the Compass* will not be allowed for, even though they can significantly affect the Compass. Therefore, as Pilot, ensure that no metal or magnetic materials, such as metal pens, clipboards, books with metal binders, key rings, headphones, electronic calculators, transistor radios, or other devices that generate magnetic fields are placed anywhere near the Compass.

Such magnetic or metal materials placed near the Compass may introduce large and **unpredictable** errors. Many pilots have been lost – or should we say more politely *'temporarily uncertain of their position'* – as a result of random deviations in the Compass readings caused by these extraneous magnetic fields.

Common Items in the Cockpit NOT to leave near the Magnetic Compass:
- Headphones;
- Ferrous Metals;
- Transistor Radios, etc;
- Calculators;
- Books with Metal Binders.

CORRECT
Heading 095

INCORRECT
Pilot thinks Heading is still 095
but in reality it is now 130

Fig.3-13. Keep Foreign Objects Away from the Magnetic Compass.

RELATING TRUE, MAGNETIC AND COMPASS HEADINGS.

1. HDG(C) is the actual heading that you observe on the Magnetic Compass in the cockpit and it relates to *Compass North* for that particular compass in that particular aeroplane on that particular heading.

2. Either by referring to the *Deviation Card*, or by applying *'Deviation East, Compass Least; Deviation West, Compass Best'*, allows you to convert HDG(C) to HDG(M), i.e. the aeroplane has not changed its direction in space, but its heading is now related to *Magnetic North* rather than *Compass North* (the peculiarities of that particular compass having been accounted for and corrected). Usually this correction for Deviation is not significant and is often disregarded.

3. Applying **Variation** (found on a topographical chart) to HDG(M) allows you to convert it to HDG(T), which is the heading of the aeroplane related to the *geographic poles*, commonly known as the North and South Poles, or as the *True Poles*. **The correction for Variation can be very significant and should always be applied** (and in the right sense – applying 6°W Variation as if it were 6°E Variation will give you a 12° error). Remember: *'Variation East, Magnetic Least; Variation West, Magnetic Best'*.

The process described above takes you from °Compass to °Magnetic to °True. It is just as easy to carry out the reverse process to go from °T to °M to °C.

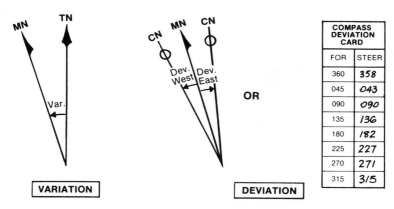

COMPASS DEVIATION CARD	
FOR	STEER
360	*358*
045	*043*
090	*090*
135	*136*
180	*182*
225	*227*
270	*271*
315	*315*

Fig.3-14.

Example 6:

Aircraft Heading	020°T
Variation	7°W
Aircraft Heading	027°M
Deviation	2°E
Aircraft Heading	025°C (ANS)

Example 7:

Aircraft Heading	025°C
Deviation	2°E
Aircraft Heading	027°M
Variation	7°W
Aircraft Heading	020°T (ANS)

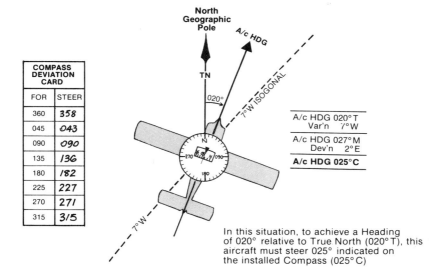

COMPASS DEVIATION CARD	
FOR	STEER
360	*358*
045	*043*
090	*090*
135	*136*
180	*182*
225	*227*
270	*271*
315	*315*

A/c HDG 020°T
Var'n   7°W

A/c HDG 027°M
Dev'n   2°E

A/c HDG 025°C

In this situation, to achieve a Heading of 020° relative to True North (020°T), this aircraft must steer 025° indicated on the installed Compass (025°C)

Fig.3-15. The Relationship of HDG C, M & T – Variation and Deviation.

The maximum accuracy we consider practical in navigation is 1°, hence there is no need for us to consider the further subdivision of 1° into 60 minutes and each of these minutes into 60 seconds. Only apply a Variation or Deviation correction accurate to the nearest degree.

PILOT SERVICEABILITY CHECKS ON THE MAGNETIC COMPASS.

Pre flight, check that the Compass is securely installed and can be easily read. The liquid in which the magnet is suspended should be free of bubbles and should not be discoloured. The glass should not be broken, cracked or discoloured, and it should be secure.

Check the position of the Compass Deviation Card in the cockpit.

Check that the Compass indication is at least approximately correct. Runways are named according to their magnetic direction (for example, a runway pointing 243°M is called *'Runway 24'*), so when pointing in the same direction as this runway, your Compass should indicate this, at least approximately.

When you are taxying out prior to take-off, turn the aircraft left and right and check that the response of the Magnet Compass is correct. Remember that the magnet should remain in the same North-South direction, and the aeroplane turn around it.

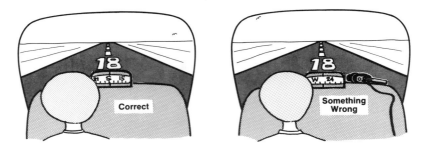

Fig.3-16. Always Cross-Check Compass Direction.

A Magnetic Compass is a Better Indicator of Direction at Middle and Low Latitudes than Near the Poles.

The Earth's magnetic field is fairly weak, and varies in strength and direction over the entire surface of the Earth. The strength of the magnetic field can be resolved into two components:

- a horizontal component parallel to the surface of the Earth, which is used to align the Compass needle with Magnetic North; and

- a vertical component, which causes the magnetic needle to **dip** down.

At the so-called *'Magnetic Equator'* (roughly mid-way between the Magnetic Poles), the lines of magnetic force are parallel with the Earth's surface (i.e. they are horizontal). Consequently, the **horizontal** component of the Earth's magnetic field is at its strongest here and so the magnetic compass is very stable and accurate in these areas.

At the higher latitudes near the Magnetic Poles, where the lines of magnetic force run in through the Earth's surface, the vertical component of the Earth's magnetic field causing dip is stronger, and the horizontal component parallel to the surface of the Earth is weaker. This makes the compass less effective as an indicator of horizontal direction in the polar regions compared to its performance at the lower latitudes.

At latitudes higher than 60 degrees North or South (i.e. closer to the Poles than 60°N or S), the Magnetic Compass is not very reliable at all.

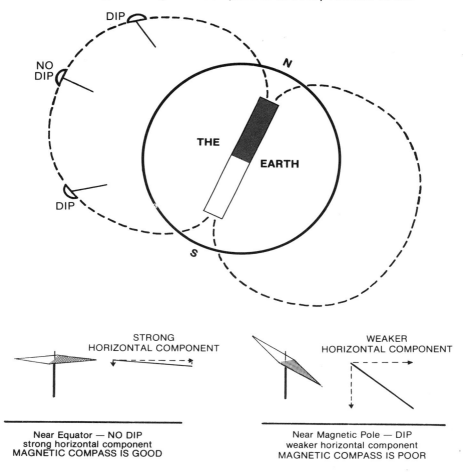

STRONG
HORIZONTAL COMPONENT

WEAKER
HORIZONTAL COMPONENT

Near Equator — NO DIP
strong horizontal component
MAGNETIC COMPASS IS GOOD

Near Magnetic Pole — DIP
weaker horizontal component
MAGNETIC COMPASS IS POOR

Fig.3-17. The Horizontal Component of the Earth's Magnetic Field is Strong Near the Equator and Weak Near the Poles.

As a means of avoiding the compass needle *dipping* down in line with the magnetic force, it is suspended in a manner that displaces its Centre of Gravity (CG) from the pivot point at which it is suspended (and indirectly attached to the aeroplane structure).

The greater the dip, the more the needle dips down towards the nearer Magnetic Pole, and the more its CG is displaced. This causes the Weight force to *balance* the Dip force and at least keep the needle approximately horizontal.

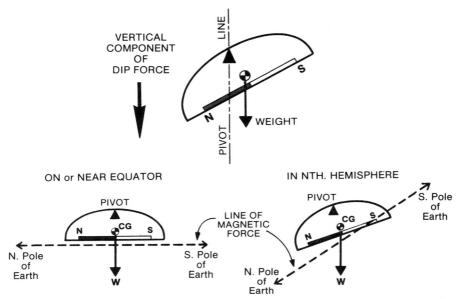

Fig.3-18. To Minimise the Effect of Dip, the Needle's CG is Displaced.

TURNING AND ACCELERATION ERRORS IN THE MAGNETIC COMPASS.

Any acceleration of the aeroplane will be transmitted to the compass needle via its pivot. The needle's CG will tend to continue at its previous velocity and so will be left behind in an acceleration, and will move ahead in a deceleration. **In a turn**, the aeroplane (and the pivot) is accelerating towards the centre of the turn, with the CG trying to *'fly off at a tangent'.*

Indication Errors in the Magnetic Compass and what causes them is a problem dealt with in detail in Volume 4 of the Air Pilot's Manual, Chapter 27. It will suffice us here to summarise the effect of these errors upon the Magnetic Compass indications (which you should know for the examination in this subject):

(1) **Turning Errors** are maximum when turning through Headings of Magnetic North or South (and zero when turning through Headings of East or West).

When heading towards the nearer Magnetic Pole, the Magnetic Compass is *'sluggish'* and will under-indicate the amount of turn (for both left and right turns). You should stop the turn before the Magnetic Compass indicates your desired heading. Once settled into steady straight and level flight, the Compass will settle down and (hopefully) indicate your desired heading. If not, make minor adjustments to your heading.

In the case illustrated below, an aeroplane flying initially on a Heading of 060°M is turning left through North. The CG tends to fly off at a tangent, and so the Compass Card rotates anticlockwise, thereby under-indicating the amount of turn. For example, when the aeroplane is actually turning through 000°M (Magnetic North), the Compass is only indicating 020°M.

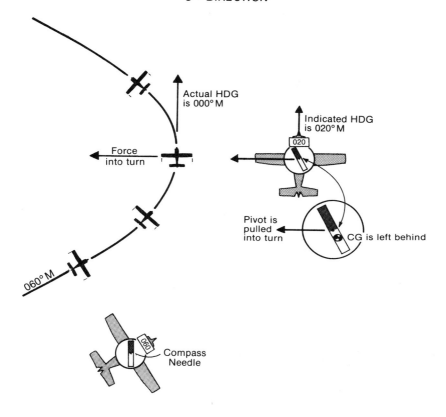

Fig.3-19. The Compass is Sluggish and Lags Behind When Turning Through North (in the Northern Hemisphere).

When heading towards the more distant Magnetic Pole, the Magnetic Compass is *lively* and will over-indicate the amount of turn. You should continue the turn through your desired heading as indicated on the Magnetic Compass during the turn. Once settled into steady straight and level flight, the Compass will settle down and (hopefully) indicate your desired heading. If not, make minor adjustments to your heading.

(2) **Acceleration Errors** are maximum on East and West Magnetic Headings (and zero on North and South Headings).

Acceleration produces a false indication of turning towards the nearer Magnetic Pole (i.e. towards North in the Northern Hemisphere). Increasing speed (accelerating) towards the East will cause the Compass needle and its attached card to rotate clockwise, causing a false indication of say 080° (instead of 090°). Another way of looking at this is that, on accelerating in an Easterly direction, the Centre of Gravity is left behind, causing the Compass Card to rotate to the right. This gives a **false** indication of a turn towards North.

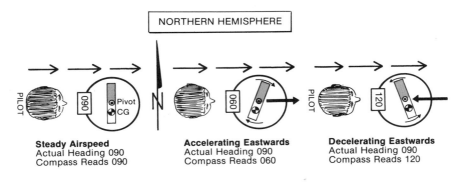

NORTHERN HEMISPHERE

Steady Airspeed
Actual Heading 090
Compass Reads 090

Accelerating Eastwards
Actual Heading 090
Compass Reads 060

Decelerating Eastwards
Actual Heading 090
Compass Reads 120

Fig.3-20. Acceleration East Produces a 'False' Indication of a Turn towards the North.

Considering an acceleration on a westerly heading, again the Centre of Gravity is left behind, the compass card in this case turning anticlockwise and indicating (incorrectly) a turn towards North.

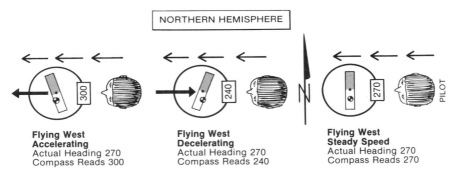

NORTHERN HEMISPHERE

**Flying West
Accelerating**
Actual Heading 270
Compass Reads 300

**Flying West
Decelerating**
Actual Heading 270
Compass Reads 240

**Flying West
Steady Speed**
Actual Heading 270
Compass Reads 270

Fig.3-21. Acceleration West Produces a 'False' Indication of a Turn Towards North.

Conversely, **deceleration on an easterly or westerly heading** produces a false indication of turning towards the further Magnetic Pole (i.e. towards South in the Northern Hemisphere).

If the aeroplane is heading North or South, the pivot supporting the compass needle and the needle's Centre of Gravity are in line, and so the needle will **not** be displaced by accelerations or decelerations in the North-South directions.

On intermediate headings, the acceleration error will increase with the proximity of the aeroplane's heading to East or West.

Example 8: You are flying in the United Kingdom. When turning from 150°M through South onto a heading of 220° using the Magnetic Compass, because it will over-indicate the amount of turn, you should continue the turn beyond a compass indication of 220 (say by 10°) and then level the wings and allow the compass to settle down.

Example 9: You are flying in Scotland and accelerating from 80 kt to 150 kt on an easterly heading. Even though, by reference to a point on the horizon, you are still heading East, the needle of the Magnetic Compass will swing in a clockwise direction and indicate an apparent turn to the North. Once you attain a steady speed and allow the Compass to settle down, it should indicate the correct heading again.

THE DIRECTION INDICATOR,
(also known as DIRECTIONAL GYRO or HEADING INDICATOR).

It is usual to have a gyroscopic Direction Indicator (usually abbreviated as **DI** or **DG**, or maybe **HI**) fitted in the instrument panel of light aircraft.

Being a gyro-based instrument, its indication is steady compared to that of the Magnetic Compass but, due to the fact that the Earth is rotating (at 15° per hour) and the Direction Indicator's axis is fixed in space by the gyroscope, the Direction Indicator has to be re-aligned with a known reference direction at regular intervals.

The Magnetic Compass is used as the reference for the Direction Indicator and so, when aligned with the Compass, the DI will indicate the heading of the aircraft in °Magnetic.

Fig.3-22. The Gyroscopic 'Direction Indicator'.

IMPORTANT: Do not align the DI with the Magnetic Compass if you are changing speed or direction, as the Magnetic Compass will be experiencing acceleration or turning errors, i.e. keep the wings level and maintain a constant speed when aligning the DI with the Compass.

One of the advantages of a Direction Indicator is that it is not subject to turning or acceleration errors. Its accuracy depends upon it being correctly aligned with Magnetic North, so this must be done when the Magnetic Compass is indicating correctly.

RELATIVE BEARING.

It is usual to define the direction of an object from an aeroplane in terms of its *relative bearing*, i.e. its direction relative to the nose (or Heading) of the aeroplane.

A Relative Bearing of an object from an aeroplane is its angular distance from the aircraft's heading measured clockwise from the nose of the aeroplane from 000°REL through to 360°REL.

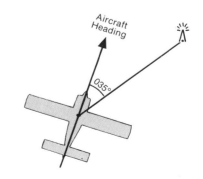

Fig.3-23. The Radio Mast Bears 035° Relative From the Aeroplane.

To Convert A Relative Bearing To A Magnetic Bearing (and vice versa): we simply add the Relative Bearing of the object to the *Magnetic Heading* of the aircraft to obtain the *Magnetic Bearing* of the object from the aeroplane.

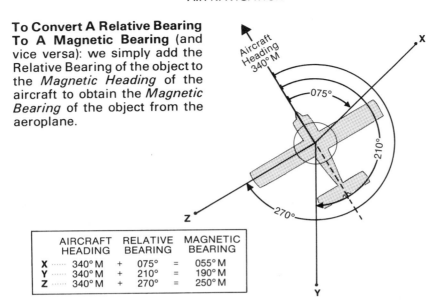

AIRCRAFT HEADING	RELATIVE BEARING	MAGNETIC BEARING
X ...... 340° M	+ 075°	= 055° M
Y ...... 340° M	+ 210°	= 190° M
Z ...... 340° M	+ 270°	= 250° M

Fig.3-24. Relative Bearings and their Conversion to Magnetic Bearings.

Aircraft Magnetic Heading	±	Relative Bearing of object from aircraft	=	Magnetic Bearing of object from aircraft

If the answer works out to be in excess of 360°, then this means you have gone more than once around the complete circle. To achieve a usable answer simply deduct 360°, e.g. 372° is the same direction as 012°.

These are two different ways of describing the position of an object seen from the aeroplane:

- the **Relative Bearing** is related to the nose (HDG) of the aeroplane; and
- the **Magnetic Bearing** is related to Magnetic North.

You will come across relative bearings at a later stage in your development as a Pilot when you study Radio Navigation Aids in preparation for obtaining an Instrument Meteorological Conditions (IMC) rating. In Radio Navigation:

- a fixed-card radio compass uses relative bearings;
- a Radio Magnetic Indicator (which has a radio compass needle superimposed upon a compass card that indicates directions relative to *Magnetic North)* uses *Magnetic Bearings.*

☐ **Exercises 3 — Direction** will now be straight-forward for you.

4

WIND-SIDE OF THE NAVIGATION COMPUTER

The Slide Navigation Computer is a wonderful invention that allows a Pilot to handle navigation problems involving the *Triangle of Velocities* in a fast and accurate manner. The three vectors in the triangle can be marked on the plotting disc so that they appear in the same relation, one to the other, as in flight, making it easier to visualise the situation and check that the vectors have been applied correctly.

Components of the *'Wind-Side'* are:

(1) A circular, rotatable **Compass Rose** (or azimuth) set in a fixed frame which is marked with an **Index** at the top.

(2) A transparent plastic **Plotting Disc** attached to the rotatable compass rose, marked with a **Centre-dot**.

(3) A **Slide** plate printed with concentric *speed arcs* and radial *drift lines.* This plate slides through the frame and compass rose assembly, hence the term 'Slide' navigation computer which is often used to refer to this type.

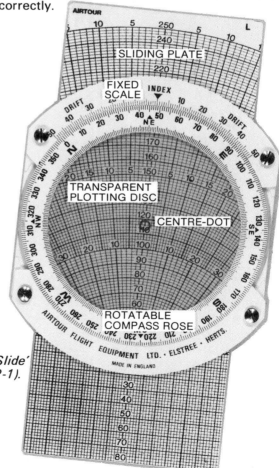

Fig.4-1. Wind-Side of the 'Slide' Navigation Computer (CRP-1).

45

THE TRIANGLE OF VELOCITIES.

Before you can use the navigation computer effectively, you must understand the Triangle of Velocities which, of course, has three sides. The first two are:

- the motion of the aeroplane through the air, i.e. **Heading/True Air Speed;**
- the motion of the air over the ground, i.e. **Wind Velocity** (direction and speed).

When these two are added together, the third side of the triangle, which is their resultant effect, is:

- the motion of the aeroplane over the ground, i.e. **Track/Ground Speed.**

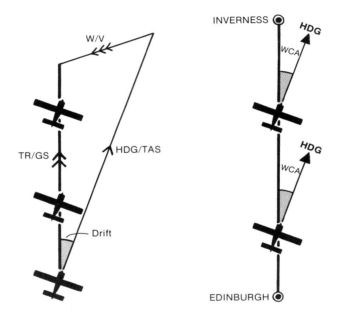

Figs.4-2a & b. The Triangle of Velocities;   Wind Correction Angle.

Note that **the wind always blows the aeroplane from its Heading to its Track.** In other words, the wind vector must start at the HDG/TAS vector and end at the TR/GS vector. If you have this firmly fixed in your mind, then computer solutions will follow easily and correctly.

A wind from the right will carry an aeroplane onto a Track that is to the left of its Heading. This is known as left drift or port drift. The Drift Angle is measured from HDG to TR. In the above illustration, 10° port drift is shown.

To achieve a particular Track, say between two towns, the aeroplane must be steered into-wind on a Heading that allows for the drift. In the above illustration, to achieve the Track shown, the aeroplane is being steered on a steady Heading 10° to the right of Track. This can be described as a **Wind Correction Angle** of 10° right. The Wind Correction Angle is measured from TR to HDG and is, of course, equal and opposite to the Drift Angle.

Each of the three vectors in the Triangle of Velocities has two aspects: **magnitude** (size) and **direction**. This means that in the Triangle of Velocities there are six components:

VECTOR	MAGNITUDE	DIRECTION
HDG/TAS	**TAS**	**HDG**
W/V	**Wind Speed**	**Wind Direction** (from)
TR/GS	**GS**	**TR**

Typical navigation situations facing a Pilot involve knowing four of these six elements and finding the other two. It is as simple as that!

MARKING THE VECTORS ON THE PLOTTING DISC.

If you can sketch a Triangle of Velocities with the three vectors placed properly, then the wind-side of the computer will cause you no difficulties at all.

Whilst you are still learning how to use the computer, it is a good idea to mark each of the vectors with their arrowheads on the plotting disc to ensure that the Triangle of Velocities is portrayed correctly. Marks on the plotting disc can be removed quite easily at the end of each problem with a moist finger.

Once you become familiar with the use of the computer, however, the actual drawing in of each vector becomes unnecessary, and just one single mark (known as the *Wind-mark*) to illustrate the extent of the Wind Velocity is all that is needed.

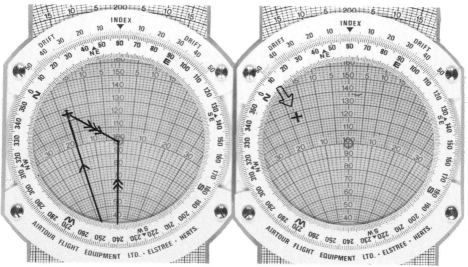

Fig.4-3. Initially Show the Vectors;   *Later You Need Only Show the Wind-Mark.*

WORK TOTALLY IN °TRUE (OR TOTALLY IN °M).

It is most important that, when working out the vector triangle, the directions are all related to the one datum. In the United Kingdom, it is traditional for Private Pilots to work in °True. You may work in °Magnetic; the eventual results are identical but, whatever you do with the wind-side of your computer, ensure that you stay either **totally in °True** or totally in °Magnetic. Do not mix °T and °M in the one Triangle of Velocities!

Our initial examples are worked in °T to match common UK practice.

CHOICE OF METHOD.

The navigation computer is such a fine instrument that each problem can be solved in a number of ways, each method producing the correct results. Pilots, being individuals, choose the method that suits them best, and you will find a variety of methods in common use.

We recommend that you consult your Instructor, establish his or her preferred method, then go ahead and learn this and neglect the others. Later in your training you may like to consider the other methods but, in the early stages at least, use one method only.

The greatest use of the navigation computer is made at the flight planning stage on the ground prior to flight, when the Pilot already knows:
• the Track in °T, measured on an aeronautical chart;
• the Wind Velocity in °T/kt, found on the weather forecast; and
• the True Air Speed that the aeroplane will achieve.

The wind-side of the computer can then be used to calculate:
• the Heading to steer; and
• the Ground Speed that will be achieved.

The **Flight Planning Problem** can be summarised as:

      Known: TR, W/V, TAS.

      Find: HDG, GS.

The author's preferred method for 'Wind-Side' calculations is one that finds HDG and GS in a very efficient manner. We consider it first as **Method (A).**

Method (B) is another commonly used approach to solving the Triangle of Velocities, and is known as the *'Wind-mark-down'* method. It is considered second.

You should now proceed to the method recommended by your Instructor. (Both methods cover identical problems.)

Use of the Wind-Side:
METHOD (A)

Check that this is the Way your Instructor works.

The Normal Flight Planning Situation
on the Ground Prior to Flight.

EXAMPLE A1: To Determine HDG and GS when Flight Planning.

Known: Required Track 150°, measured off chart.
True Air Speed 100 kt, known, or calculated from expected RAS/CAS.
W/V 360°T/30, stated on forecast.
Magnetic Variation 5°W, shown on chart.

Find: HDG and GS.

NOTE: An efficient means of recording navigation data is to use a Flight Log, a typical one of which is illustrated below. The known information can first be entered as shown, with the results of your calculations following at a later stage.

FROM/TO	TEMP °C	F L	TAS kt	WIND °T/kt	TRACK °T	DRIFT	HDG °T	VAR	HDG °M	GS kt	DIST nm	TIME min
			100	360/30	150			5°W				

Fig.4-4.

Step (1): Place the W/V on the Plotting Disc.
(Wind direction and wind speed are known, i.e. both aspects of the W/V vector are known.)

• Rotate the compass rose until the wind direction 360 (North) is under the Index; and
• Mark the start of the W/V vector 30 kt **above** the Centre-dot.

Since the Track is known, show the W/V blowing **towards the Centre-dot**, i.e. the wind vector will come **from** direction 360° and end at the Centre-dot. Marking the starting point of the wind 30 kt above the Centre-dot is most easily achieved by first setting one of the labelled wind arcs under the Centre-dot, and then placing the Wind-mark 30 kt above it.

At this early stage in your training, mark in the full W/V, showing the three arrowheads of the W/V vector pointing down towards the Centre-dot. This will give you a very clear picture as the whole Triangle of Velocities is developed.

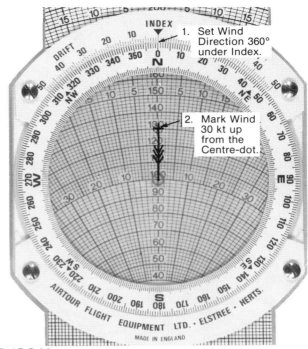

1. Set Wind Direction 360° under Index.

2. Mark Wind 30 kt up from the Centre-dot.

Fig.4-5. Wind Velocity 360/30 set on the Computer at the Flight Planning Stage; Example A1, Step (1).

Step (2): Place the TR/GS Vector on the Plotting Disc.

Track is known (having been measured on the chart); Ground Speed is not known. In this case, only one aspect of the TR/GS vector is known – its direction, but not its magnitude.

- Rotate the compass rose until the required TR of 150°T is under the Index.

(We cannot position the appropriate Ground Speed arc under the Centre-dot because we do not yet know its value.)

3. Set TR 150° under Index

Fig.4-6. Example A1, Step (2) completed.

Step (3): Place the HDG/TAS Vector on the Plotting Disc.

True Air Speed is known, but the Heading is not. In this case, only one aspect of the HDG/TAS vector is known – its magnitude.

- Move the slide and place the TAS 100 kt speed arc under the Wind-mark (which is the starting point of the W/V vector).

(This is where a clear understanding of the Triangle of Velocities is most important! The end of the HDG/TAS vector is where the W/V begins.)

Fig.4-7. Example A1, Step (3).

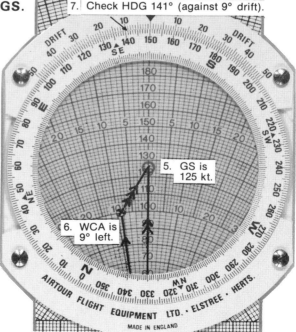

4. Set TAS 100 kt under Wind-mark.

Step (4): Read-Off the Answers for HDG and GS.

- The GS of 125 kt appears under the Centre-dot.

- From the drift lines, the Wind Correction Angle is 9° to the left of the Track. This means to achieve TR 150°T, the aeroplane must be pointed 9° into-wind and flown on a HDG of 141°T to allow for the 9° of right (starboard) drift.

NOTE: The arithmetic (for determining HDG 141 from TR 150 and a Wind Correction Angle of 9° into-wind) can be checked on the scale near the Index.

7. Check HDG 141° (against 9° drift).

5. GS is 125 kt.

6. WCA is 9° left.

Fig.4-8. Ex.A1 – ANS: HDG 141°T, GS 125 kt.

NOTE: If **Magnetic** Heading is required, it is simply a matter of applying Variation. If VARN is 5°W, then 141°T is 146°M (Variation West, Magnetic Best).

FROM/TO	TEMP °C	F L	TAS kt	WIND °T/kt	TRACK °T	DRIFT	HDG °T	VAR	HDG °M	GS kt	DIST nm	TIME min
			100	360/30	150	9°R	141T	5°W	146M	125		

Fig.4-9.

EXAMPLE A2: Another Problem to Find HDG and GS.

Given a True Air Speed of 174 kt, a forecast W/V of 240°T/40 kt, and a desired Track of 290°T, calculate the True Heading required and the Ground Speed that will be achieved. What is the Magnetic Heading if Variation in the vicinity of the flight is 6°W?

Known: TAS 174 kt;   **Find:** HDG and GS.
Required
TR 290°T;
W/V
240°T/40.

FROM/TO	TEMP °C	F L	TAS kt	WIND °T/kt	TRACK °T	DRIFT	HDG °T	VAR	HDG °M	GS kt	DIST nm	TIME min
			174	240/40	290			6°W				

Fig.4-10.

Step (1): Place the W/V on the Plotting Disc.

Both wind speed and wind direction are known.

Since the required TR is known, we show the W/V blowing down from the Index towards the Centre-dot.

- Set wind direction 240 under the Index.
- Mark in the wind strength 40 kt above the Centre-dot.

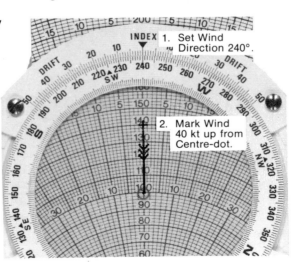

INDEX 1. Set Wind Direction 240°.

2. Mark Wind 40 kt up from Centre-dot.

Fig.4-11. Example A2, Step (1).

Step (2): Place the TR/GS Vector on the Plotting Disc.

TR is known;
GS is **not** known.

- Rotate the compass rose until the required TR 290°T is under the Index.

(We cannot position the appropriate speed arc under the Centre-dot because we do not yet know the GS.)

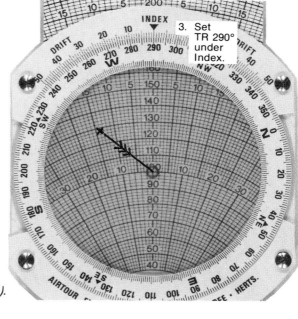

Fig.4-12.
Example A2, Step (2).

Step (3): Place the HDG/TAS Vector on the Plotting Disc.

TAS is known;
HDG is **not** known.

- Move the slide to place the TAS 174 kt under the Wind-mark, which is starting point of the W/V vector (since the W/V vector commences where the TAS/HDG vector ends).

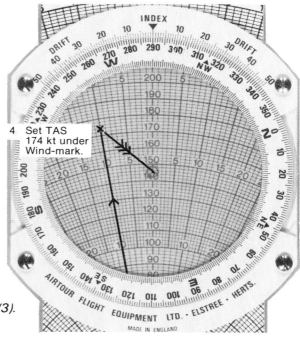

Fig.4-13.
Example A2, Step (3).

53

Step (4): Read-Off the Answers for HDG and GS.

- The Wind Correction Angle of 10° left can now be read-off the drift lines, i.e. the aeroplane must be steered 10° into wind (i.e. left of the desired Track to allow for the 10° right, or starboard, drift). In this case, to achieve the desired Track of 290°T, the aeroplane must be steered on a Heading of 280°T.
- The Ground Speed 145 kt lies under the Centre-dot.

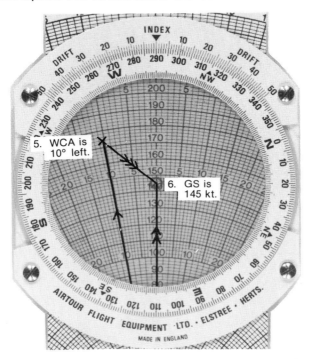

Fig.4-14. Example A2 almost completed: HDG 280°T, GS 145 kt.

Magnetic Variation in the area is 6°W, so HDG 280°T is 286°M.

ANS: HDG 280°T, Variation 6°W, HDG 286M;
     GS 145 kt.

FROM/TO	TEMP °C	FL	TAS kt	WIND °T/kt	TRACK °T	DRIFT	HDG °T	VAR	HDG °M	GS kt	DIST nm	TIME min
			174	240/40	290	10°R	280	6W	286	145		

Fig.4-15.

**EXAMPLE A3: A Slightly Unusual Flight Planning Problem —
Finding the HDG/TAS to Achieve a Particular TR/GS.**

Occasionally you may want to achieve a particular Ground Speed, for instance to arrive overhead the destination at a particular time. The example here is a modification of the previous example.

What True Air Speed is required to achieve a Ground Speed of 120 kt in Example A2 above?

Known: TR 290°T, W/V 240°/40 kt, GS 120 kt.

Find: TAS and HDG.

FROM/TO	TEMP °C	FL	TAS kt	WIND °T/kt	TRACK °T	DRIFT	HDG °T	VAR	HDG °M	GS kt	DIST nm	TIME min
				240/40	290			6W		120		

Fig.4-16.

Step (1): Place W/V on the Plotting Disc.

• Set wind direction 240° under the Index.

• Place Wind-mark 40 kt above the Centre-dot, wind blowing down.

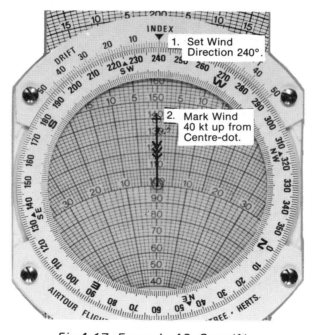

Fig.4-17. Example A3, Step (1).

Step (2): Place the TR/GS Vector on the Plotting Disc.

In this case both TR 290°T and GS 120 kt are known.

- Rotate the compass rose and set TR 290°T under the Index.

- Set GS 120 kt under the Centre-dot.

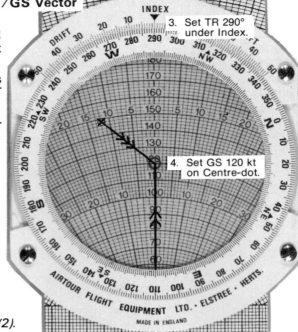

3. Set TR 290° under Index.

4. Set GS 120 kt on Centre-dot.

Fig.4-18.
Example A3, Step (2).

Step (3): Read-Off the TAS, and determine the HDG from the Drift.

- Read-off TAS 150 kt under the Wind-mark.

- Read-off drift of 12°, therefore HDG is 12° left of TR. HDG is 278°T.

NOTE: The wind is from the left, so the Wind Correction Angle is 12° left of the desired Track to allow for the expected 12° right (starboard) drift. Your arithmetic can be checked against the small scale near the Index.

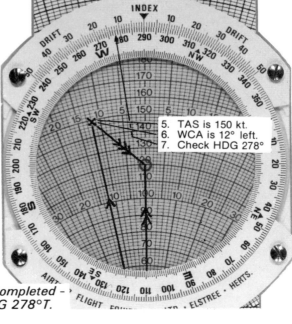

5. TAS is 150 kt.
6. WCA is 12° left.
7. Check HDG 278°

Fig.4-19. Example A3, completed –
ANS: TAS 150 kt, HDG 278°T.

ANSWER: TAS 150 kt, HDG 278°T.

FROM/TO	TEMP °C	FL	TAS kt	WIND °T/kt	TRACK °T	DRIFT	HDG °T	VAR	HDG °M	GS kt	DIST nm	TIME min
			150	240/40	290	12R	278	6W	294	120		

Fig.4-20.

☐ Now complete **Exercises 4 — Wind-Side-1.** These are typical Flight Planning calculations carried out prior to flight.

Calculating The Wind Velocity In Flight

After obtaining two position fixes en route, it is possible to determine the **actual** W/V, which can then be used in your further calculations rather than the less accurate forecast wind.

The two position fixes enable you to determine the Track Made Good (TMG) and the Ground Speed achieved during the time you have maintained a reasonably steady Heading and True Air Speed.

When in-flight, the Pilot knows:
• the Heading maintained using the Compass or Direction Indicator;
• True Air Speed;
• the Track Made Good (TMG) by observation of the ground and map;
• the Ground Speed by comparing distance covered with the time it takes.

These are four of the six items in the Triangle of Velocities and, using them, you can find the other two – Wind Direction and Wind Speed (i.e. Wind Velocity).

This problem can be summarised as:

    Known: HDG/TAS and TR/GS.

      Find: W/V.

Remember that in the UK it is usual for Private Pilots to work in °True.

EXAMPLE A4: Finding the W/V In Flight.

Known: HDG 143°M, Variation 5°W, (HDG 138°T), TAS 120 kt.
TR 146°T, GS 144 kt.

Find: W/V.

NOTE: Another way of asking the same question is to give HDG 138°T and starboard drift 8° (rather than TR 146°T).

FROM/TO	TEMP °C	F L	TAS kt	WIND °T/kt	TRACK °T	DRIFT	HDG °T	VAR	HDG °M	GS kt	DIST nm	TIME min
			120		146		138	5W	143	144		

Fig.4-21.

Step (1): Place the TR/GS Vector Under the Centre-dot.

- Rotate the compass rose and set Track 146°T under the Index.
- Set GS 144 kt under the Centre-dot.

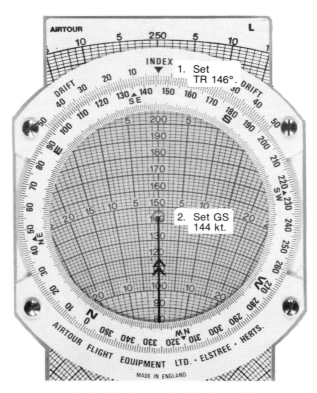

Fig.4-22. Example A4, Step (1).

Step (2). Place the HDG/TAS Vector on the Plotting Disc.

From HDG 138°T and TR 146°T, the Drift is 8° to starboard (right); the HDG is 8° to the left of TR (i.e. the Wind Correction Angle is 8° left).

- Mark-in the HDG direction as the 8° drift line to the left of Track.

- Mark the TAS where the 120 kt speed arc intersects the drift line; this now indicates the HDG/TAS vector.

The W/V blows the aircraft from HDG to TR.

*Fig.4-23.
Example A4, Step (2).*

3. Mark WCA 8° Left.

4. Mark TAS 120 kt.

Step (3): Determine the W/V.

- Rotate the compass rose until the Wind-mark is on the Index line with the arrows pointing down towards the Centre-dot. The direction the wind is blowing from, 360°T, is now indicated under the Index.

- Read-off the wind strength of 30 kt. (Setting a definite speed arc under the Centre-dot, 100 kt in this case, makes the wind strength easier to read.)

ANS: W/V 360°T/30 kt.

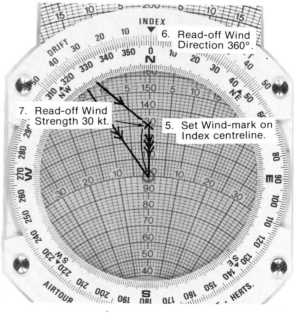

6. Read-off Wind Direction 360°.

7. Read-off Wind Strength 30 kt.

5. Set Wind-mark on Index centreline.

Fig.4-24. Example A4, Step (3).

FROM/TO	TEMP °C	F L	TAS kt	WIND °T/kt	TRACK °T	DRIFT	HDG °T	VAR	HDG °M	GS kt	DIST nm	TIME min
			120	360/30	146	8R	138	5W	143	144		

Fig.4-25.

☐ Now complete **Exercises 4 — Wind-Side-2.**

Finding The TMG and GS In Flight

The usual means of determining Track Made Good and Ground Speed is by visually fixing your position over ground features. On a flight over water or featureless terrain or in poor visibility, however, where you are unable to fix your position, it is possible to estimate a 'Dead Reckoning' Track and Ground Speed using:

- Heading from the Compass (corrected to HDG in °True using Variation if required);
- TAS (calculated from the Rectified/Calibrated Air Speed if necessary);
- W/V (speed and direction, known from the forecast or previous calculations).

EXAMPLE A5.
    Known: HDG 057°M, TAS 120 kt, W/V 115°T/40, VAR 7°W.
    Find: TR/GS.

FROM/TO	TEMP °C	F L	TAS kt	WIND °T/kt	TRACK °T	DRIFT	HDG °T	VAR	HDG °M	GS kt	DIST nm	TIME min
			120	115/40			050	7W	057			

Fig.4-26.

Since the HDG is known, but the TR is not, the HDG/TAS vector will be set under the Centre-dot and the W/V will emanate from here. In this case, therefore, with the wind direction set under the Index, the wind will start at the Centre-dot and blow down the slide, hence the Wind-mark will be shown down from the Centre-dot.

Step (1): Place the Wind Velocity Vector on the Plotting Disc.

- Rotate the compass rose until the wind direction 115°T is under the Index.

- Mark the end of the W/V vector 40 kt **below** the Centre-dot.

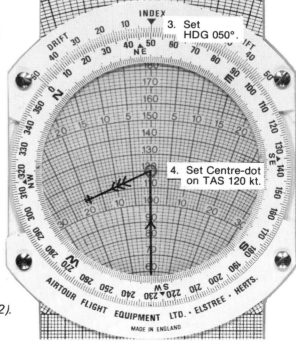

1. Set Wind Direction 115°.

2. Mark Wind 40 kt **below** Centre-dot.

Fig.4-27.
Example A5, Step (1).

Step (2): Place the HDG/TAS Vector Under the Centre-dot.

- Set HDG 050°T under the Index.

- Move the slide so that TAS 120 kt is under the Centre-dot.

3. Set HDG 050°.

4. Set Centre-dot on TAS 120 kt.

Fig.4-28.
Example A5, Step (2).

Step (3): Read-Off the GS and Drift.

The *HDG/TAS* vector is now set under the Centre-dot and the *W/V* vector acts out from the Centre-dot. The Wind-mark on the outer end of the W/V vector lies over the *TR/GS* vector.

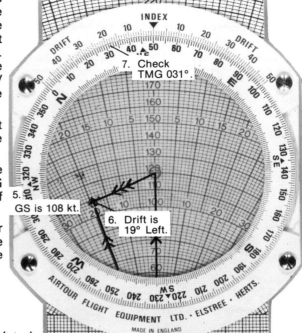

- The GS of 108 kt appears under the wind dot.

- The drift lines indicate 19° of drift left of HDG 050°, giving a TMG of 031°T.

(You can check your arithmetic against the small scale near the Index.)

Fig.4-29.
Example A5, completed.

ANS: Drift 19° left (port), TR 031°T; GS 108 kt.

FROM/TO	TEMP °C	FL	TAS kt	WIND °T/kt	TRACK °T	DRIFT	HDG °T	VAR	HDG °M	GS kt	DIST nm	TIME min
	120		115/40	031	19L	050	7W	057	108			

Fig.4-30.

☐ Now complete **Exercises 4 — Wind-Side-3.**

NOTE: If you are satisfied with this Method of using the Wind-Side of your Computer then it is not necessary to work through the next part (Method B), the calculations of which are a repeat of what you have already just done.

You should, however, complete the final part of this chapter which shows how to work out **Wind Components**, as this is important information for take-off and landing operations on runways where the wind is not blowing directly along the runway (often the case).

Use of the Wind-Side: METHOD (B)

Confirm with your Flying Instructor if this is his or her preferred method, which is commonly called the *'Wind Down' method*, because:
- the wind direction (**from** which it blows) is placed under the Index;
- the Centre-dot is used as the starting point of the W/V vector; and
- the Wind-mark, in this case representing the end of the W/V vector, is drawn in beneath the Centre-dot (i.e. **down** from the Centre-dot).

Since the W/V blows the aeroplane from its Heading to its Track, and the Heading vector ends where the W/V vector starts, the Heading/TAS vector should be placed up the centre of the slide so that it ends at the Centre-dot.

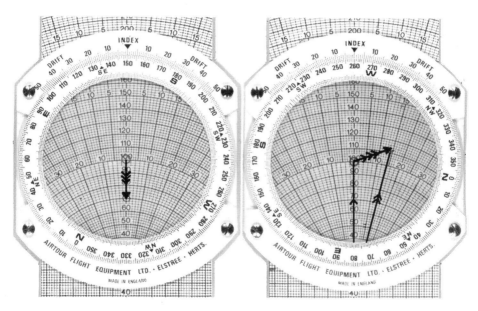

Fig.4-31.

The simplest type of problem to solve using the 'Wind-mark down' Method is the in-flight situation of knowing the HDG, TAS and W/V, and then having to find the TR and GS. This situation could arise on an over-water flight, or a flight over barren terrain or in poor visibility, where it is difficult to obtain two position fixes to determine TR and GS. HDG is found from the compass, TAS is calculated from the Indicated Air Speed, and forecast W/V (in °T) is used.

Remember that **all** working on the computer must be totally in °T, or totally in °M. Do not mix them! In the UK, it is usual for Private Pilots to work in °T, so this will mean converting the compass reading into °True, using Magnetic Variation, (and Deviation if required).

To Find Track And Ground Speed In Flight

This is EXAMPLE B1.

Known: HDG 050°T, TAS 120 kt, W/V 140°T/30 kt.

Find: TR, GS.

In practice, you would probably enter this data on a Flight Log to keep it neat and orderly.

FROM/TO	TEMP °C	F L	TAS kt	WIND °T/kt	TRACK °T	DRIFT	HDG °T	VAR	HDG °M	GS kt	DIST nm	TIME min
			120	140/30			050					

Fig.4-32.

Step (1): Place the W/V on the Plotting Disc.

- Rotate the compass rose until the wind direction 140°T is under the Index.

- Set the Centre-dot (in transparent window) on an easily noted value (100 in the illustration) and mark the end of the W/V vector 30 knots *down* from the Centre-dot.

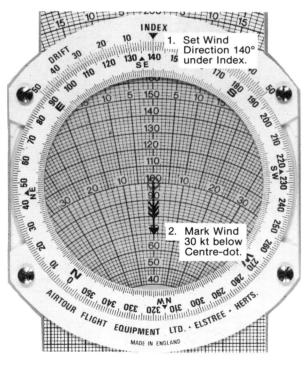

Fig.4-33. Example B1, Step (1).

Step (2): Place the HDG/TAS Vector Under the Centre-dot.

- Rotate the compass rose until the HDG 050°T is under the Index.

- Move the slide so that the TAS 120 kt is under the Centre-dot.

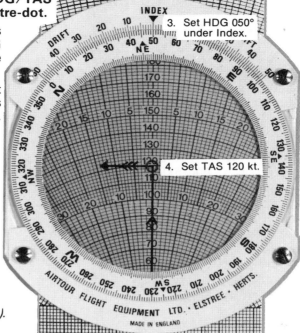

Fig.4-34.
Example B1, Step (2).

Step (3): Read-Off the Ground Speed and Drift, then Calculate Track.

- The Wind-mark now lies over the Ground Speed 123 kt.

- The Wind-mark lies over the 14° drift line, i.e. the wind blowing from the right will cause a HDG of 050°T to result in a Track of (050 – 14 =) 036°T.

(Note that your arithmetic can be checked against the small scale near the Index.)

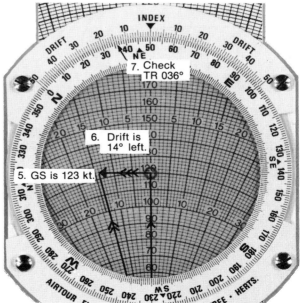

Fig.4-35. Example B1, Step (3) – ANS: GS 123, TMG 036°T.

ANS: GS 123 kt, TMG 036°T added to the Flight Log.

FROM/TO	TEMP °C	F L	TAS kt	WIND °T/kt	TRACK °T	DRIFT	HDG °T	VAR	HDG °M	GS kt	DIST nm	TIME min
			120	140/30	036		050			123		

Fig.4-36.

☐ Now work through **Exercises 4 — Wind-Side-3.**
(Exercises Wind-Side-2 and -1 will follow shortly.)

To Find The Wind Velocity In Flight

EXAMPLE B2.

This is a typical in-flight situation, where HDG and TAS are known, and two position fixes allow you to determine the Track Made Good and the Ground Speed.

Known: HDG 160°T, TAS 145 kt; TMG 168°T, GS 157 kt.

Find: W/V (direction and strength).

FROM/TO	TEMP °C	F L	TAS kt	WIND °T/kt	TRACK °T	DRIFT	HDG °T	VAR	HDG °M	GS kt	DIST nm	TIME min
			145		168		160			157		

Fig.4-37.

NOTE: The same question could have been asked in a slightly different manner, HDG 160°T and drift 8° right being given, rather than TR 168°T.

Step (1): Place the HDG/TAS Vector Under the Centre-dot.

- Rotate the compass rose until the HDG 160°T appears under the Index.

- Move the slide until TAS 145 kt is under the Centre-dot.

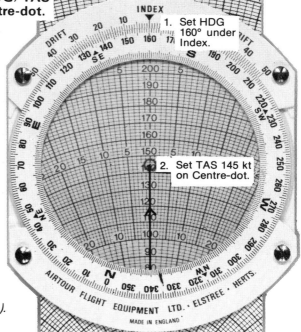

1. Set HDG 160° under Index.

2. Set TAS 145 kt on Centre-dot.

Fig.4-38.
Example B2, Step (1).

Step (2): Place the TMG/GS on the Plotting Disc.

- Mark in the 8° right drift line, since the drift is 8° to the right, calculated from the HDG 160°T and the TMG 168°T.

- Mark the point along this line where the GS is 157 kt. This point is the end of the TR/GS vector.

(The wind has blown the aeroplane from the Centre-dot to this point marked on the plotting disc.)

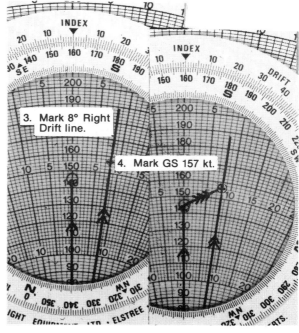

3. Mark 8° Right Drift line.

4. Mark GS 157 kt.

Fig.4-39.
Example B2, Step (2).

Step (3): Read-Off the W/V.

- Rotate the compass rose until the wind dot appears directly down from the Centre-dot.

- The direction that the wind is blowing from appears under the Index, i.e. 045°T.

- The wind strength of 26 kt can be read from the distance beneath the Centre-dot. (You can adjust the slide to make reading this easier.)

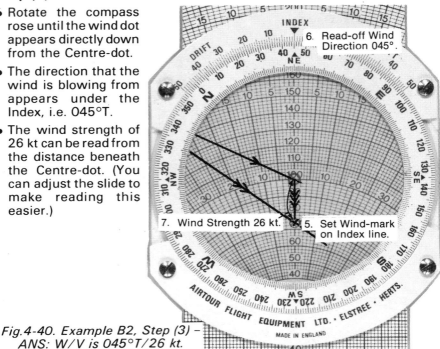

6. Read-off Wind Direction 045°.

7. Wind Strength 26 kt.

5. Set Wind-mark on Index line.

Fig.4-40. Example B2, Step (3) – ANS: W/V is 045°T/26 kt.

ANS: W/V is 045°T/26 kt.

FROM/TO	TEMP °C	FL	TAS kt	WIND °T/kt	TRACK °T	DRIFT	HDG °T	VAR	HDG °M	GS kt	DIST nm	TIME min
			145	045/26	168		160			157		

Fig.4-41.

☐ Now do **Exercises 4 — Wind-Side-2.**

The Flight Planning Situation

EXAMPLE B3: Find HDG and GS, knowing TR, TAS and W/V.

This is the typical situation prior to flight. Since it is at the flight planning stage when the navigation computer is used most, **you must become very adept at this sort of problem.**

From the aeronautical chart, you can measure the desired track (and distance). The wind is known from the forecast. The aeroplane's performance in terms of True Air Speed is known, or can be found from the Flight Manual or Pilot's Operating Handbook.

Known: Desired Track 295°T, TAS 97 kt, Forecast W/V 320°T/25.

Find: HDG and GS.

FROM/TO	TEMP °C	FL	TAS kt	WIND °T/kt	TRACK °T	DRIFT	HDG °T	VAR	HDG °M	GS kt	DIST nm	TIME min
			97	**320/25**	**295**							

Fig.4-42.

Step (1). Place the W/V on the Plotting Disc.

- Rotate the compass rose until the direction from which the wind is ·blowing is under the Index, i.e. 320°T.

- Put a Wind-mark 25 kt **down** from the Centre-dot.

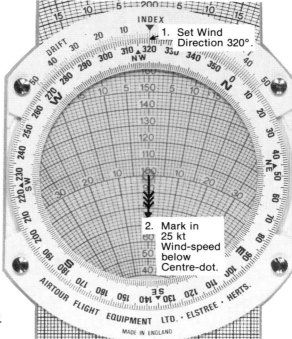

1. Set Wind Direction 320°.

2. Mark in 25 kt Wind-speed below Centre-dot.

Fig.4-43.
Example B3, Step (1).

Step (2): Place the HDG/TAS Under the Centre-dot.

Since the W/V starts at the Centre-dot and blows away from it, the end of the HDG/TAS vector should be placed under the Centre-dot.

- Move the slide until TAS 97 kt appears under the Centre-dot.

- Set **approximate** HDG 295°T under the Index.

NOTE: When we come to set the HDG under the Index, we are faced with a problem – we do not know the HDG!

To get started, use the desired Track as an approximate HDG; i.e. assume that the HDG is approximately 295°T and rotate the compass rose until 295°T appears under the Index.

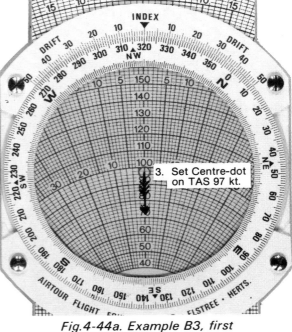

Fig.4-44a. Example B3, first part of Step (2).

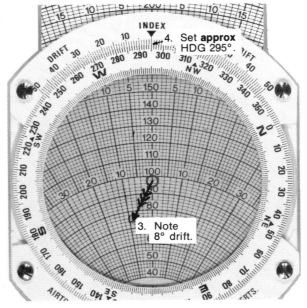

Fig.4-44b. Example B3, second part of Step (2).

70

Step (3): Make Adjustments to the Approx HDG to Allow for Drift.

The W/V dot lies over the 8° left drift line, so, on a HDG of 295°T, the aeroplane should achieve a Track 8° to the left of this.

Since the Desired Track is 295°, the aeroplane should be headed approximately 8° to the right of this to allow for the left drift, i.e. on a HDG of 303°T, with a Wind Correction Angle of 8° right.

- Rotate the compass rose until 303°T appears under the Index, and check the Drift (and calculate the Track).

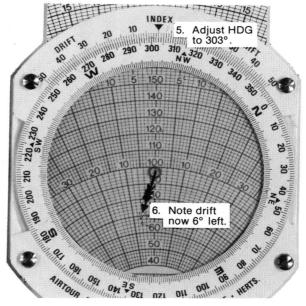

Fig.4-45a. Example B3, Step (3)(a).

(As can be seen, the Drift is now indicated to be only 6° (and not the original 8°), so adjust the HDG to allow for only 6°, i.e an adjusted HDG is 301°T.)

- Set the adjusted HDG 301°T under the Index.

By checking the position of the Windmark, we see that this minor *'jiggle'* of the compass rose has not appreciably altered the 6° drift. (In other words, the adjusted HDG and the expected 6° left (port) drift will allow us to achieve the Desired Track of 295°T.)

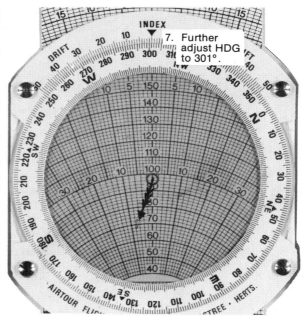

Fig.4-45b. Example B3, Step (3)(b).

Step (4): Read-Off the HDG and GS.

- The HDG 301°T appears under the Index.

- The GS 73 kt appears under the Wind-mark.

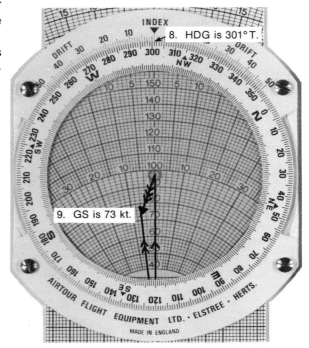

8. HDG is 301°T.

9. GS is 73 kt.

Fig.4-46. Ex.B3, Step (4) – ANS: HDG 301°T, GS 73 kt.

ANS: HDG 301°T, GS 73 kt.

FROM/TO	TEMP °C	F L	TAS kt	WIND °T/kt	TRACK °T	DRIFT	HDG °T	VAR	HDG °M	GS kt	DIST nm	TIME min
			97	320/25	295		301			73		

Fig.4-47.

NOTE: Because there have to be some adjustments to the initial HDG by rotating the compass rose a few degrees this way and that, the above method is sometimes known as the *jiggle* method, as well as the *Wind-mark-down* method. It still gives accurate answers.

To solve a slightly unusual flight planning problem such as 'What TAS is required to achieve a Ground Speed of 80 kt?', the same procedure as above can be used, except that the Wind-mark is placed over the appropriate GS arc, and then the TAS and HDG can be read-off under the Centre-dot.

☐ Now do **Exercises 4 — Wind-Side-1**.

EXAMPLE B3: (ii) The Flight Planning Calculation Repeated a Different Way, (but still with the 'Wind-Mark Down').

This further *wind-mark down* method avoids having to *jiggle* the compass rose when calculating HDG and GS at the flight planning stage. Check with your Instructor if this is his preferred method.

    Known: 320°T/25 kt, TAS 97 kt, TR 295°T.

      Find: HDG and GS.

FROM/TO	TEMP °C	F L	TAS kt	WIND °T/kt	TRACK °T	DRIFT	HDG °T	VAR	HDG °M	GS kt	DIST nm	TIME min
			97	320/25	295							

Fig.4-48.

Step (1): Set the W/V Vector on the Plotting Disc Using the Square Grid.

Rotate the compass rose until the wind direction 320°T appears under the Index.

- Set the zero point of the square grid under the Centre-dot.

- Put a wind-mark 25 kt down from the Centre-dot.

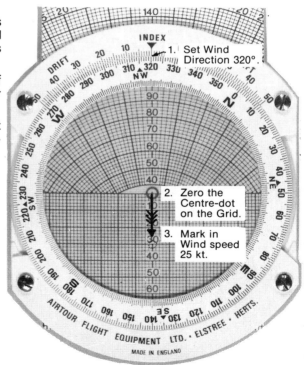

1. Set Wind Direction 320°.

2. Zero the Centre-dot on the Grid.

3. Mark in Wind speed 25 kt.

Fig.4-49. Example B3(ii), Step (1).

Step (2): Set Track, and Mark in Crosswind Line.

- Rotate the compass rose until the TR 295°T appears under the Index.

- Run a vertical line down through the Wind-mark, which is a 10 kt crosswind component. It is this crosswind component from the right that causes the left drift.

Fig.4-50. Example B3(ii), Step (2).

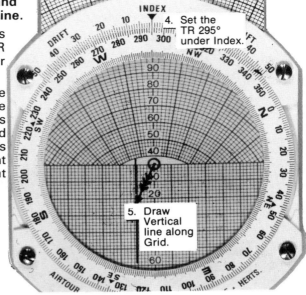

Step (3): Set HDG/TAS on the Plotting Disc.

- Move the slide and place TAS 97 kt under the Centre-dot. Note that the crosswind effect line does not parallel the drift lines at this stage.

- Rotate the compass rose until the crosswind effect line is parallel with one of the drift lines.

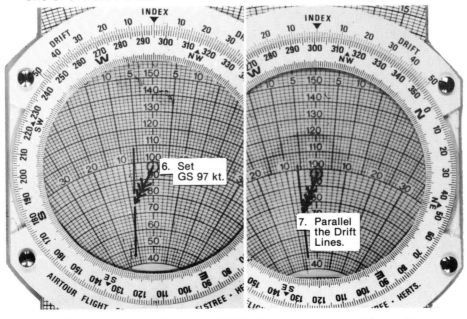

Figs.4-51a & b. Example B3(ii), the two stages of Step (3).

Step (4): Read-Off HDG and GS.

HDG/TAS lies under the Centre-dot. The TR/GS vector ends where the W/V vector ends.

• Read-off HDG 301°T under the Index.

• Read-off GS 73 kt under the Wind-mark.

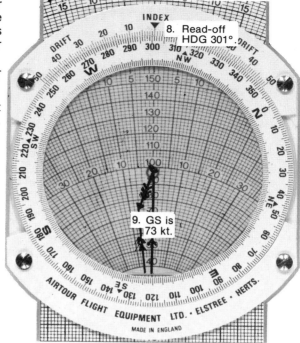

Fig.4-52. B3(ii), Step (4) – ANS: HDG 301°T, GS 73 kt.

ANSWER: HDG 301°T, GS 73 kt.

FROM/TO	TEMP °C	FL	TAS kt	WIND °T/kt	TRACK °T	DRIFT	HDG °T	VAR	HDG °M	GS kt	DIST nm	TIME min
			97	320/25	295		301			73		

Fig.4-53.

□ Use this method to complete Exercises 4 — Wind-Side-1.

WIND COMPONENTS

Quite often a wind needs to be broken down into its two components:
- the **headwind or tailwind** component; and
- the **crosswind** component.

This is especially the case when taking-off and landing, because:

1. For performance reasons, you often need to know the headwind or tailwind component to determine the take-off or landing distance required.

2. For reasons of safe handling of the aeroplane, you always need to know (at least approximately) the crosswind component on a particular runway that you intend using. (The crosswind component is very important and each aeroplane has a maximum crosswind limit specified in its Flight Manual. This crosswind limit should never be exceeded.)

Winds found on Forecasts, and which are most likely to be used for flight planning purposes, are given in degrees True, whereas the wind in Take-off and Landing reports broadcast by Air Traffic Control are given in degrees Magnetic, so that they can be easily related to Runway Direction, which is always in °M. This applies to the direction of the wind given to you by the Tower, or as broadcast on the Automatic Terminal Information Service (ATIS).

A runway whose centreline lies in the direction 074°M will be designated RWY 07. A runway whose centreline lies in the direction 357°M will be designated RWY 36. A wind of 350°M/25 kt would favour RWY 36, which is almost directly into-wind. RWY 07 would experience a strong crosswind from the left; the Pilot should determine just how strong before using this particular runway.

Since both wind direction and runway direction are measured from the same datum (Magnetic North), there is no need to convert into degrees True for your computer manipulations. When using your computer, work either totally in True or **totally in Magnetic.**

Elsewhere in The Air Pilot's Manual, when discussing Take-Off and Landing Performance, we illustrate a simple way of determining wind components mentally. Here we show you how to do it using the **square grid** on your navigation computer.

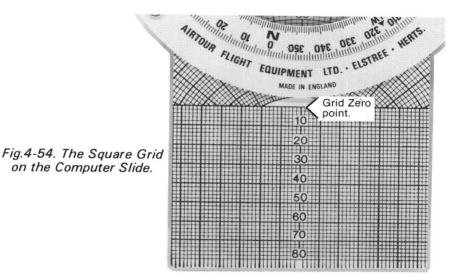

Fig.4-54. The Square Grid on the Computer Slide.

Grid Zero point.

Example: What crosswind and headwind components exist on Runway 18 if the wind broadcast by the Tower is 120°M/30? (Runway 18 means that the runway direction is approx 180°M.)

Step (1): Set-Up the W/V on the Square-Grid.

- Set the zero point of the square grid under the Centre-dot.
- Rotate the compass rose and set wind direction 120° under the Index.
- Put a Wind-mark 30 kt down from the Centre-dot.

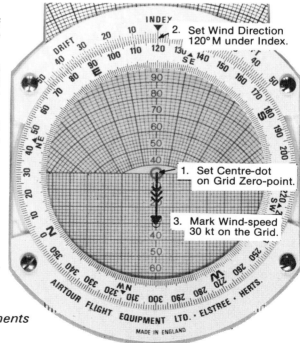

2. Set Wind Direction 120° M under Index.

1. Set Centre-dot on Grid Zero-point.

3. Mark Wind-speed 30 kt on the Grid.

Fig.4-55. Wind Components Example, Step (1).

Step (2): Set the Runway Direction.

• Rotate the compass rose until the runway direction 180°M is under the Index.

Fig.4-56. W/C Example, Step (2).

Step (3): Read-Off the Headwind and Crosswind Components.

• Drop a vertical line to the Wind-mark. The length of this line is the headwind component, 15 kt.

• The horizontal distance of this line from the Centre-dot is the crosswind component, 26 kt.

Fig.4-57. W/C Example, Step (3) – ANS: H/W 15 kt, X/W 26 kt.

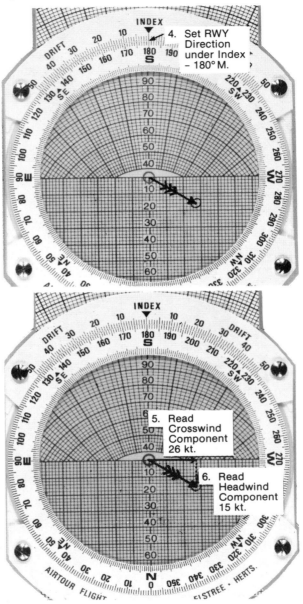

4. Set RWY Direction under Index – 180° M.

5. Read Crosswind Component 26 kt.

6. Read Headwind Component 15 kt.

NOTE: If, when the RWY direction is set under the Index, the end of the wind vector is above the horizontal line through the Centre-dot, then there is a tailwind component and it is advisable to consider changing runways.

The precise strength of the downwind component can be found by placing the reciprocal to the runway direction under the Index (360 in the above case), which allows you to find what is a headwind component for a take-off in that direction.

☐ Now, finally, **Exercises 4 — Wind-Side-4** please.

5

CALCULATOR-SIDE OF THE NAVIGATION COMPUTER

The Calculator-Side of the Navigation Computer looks a little complicated at first, but once you become familiar with it you will find its use very straightforward. A little work now learning how to use it will be repaid many times over as it simplifies your calculations and saves you lots of time.

The Calculator-Side is very useful in solving quickly and accurately the numerous small calculations which are involved with air navigation and also other aspects of operating an aeroplane.

Fig.5-1. Calculator-Side of the 'CRP-1' Navigation Computer.

There are various types of computers that differ one from the other in minor ways on the calculator-side. The one we find to be most suitable for Private (and even Commercial) Pilots is the type used in the previous chapter – the *Airtour CRP-1*.

As you go through this chapter we suggest that you have your computer close by and follow our examples through.

NOTE: Use of the computer for solving the Altitude and Airspeed problems on the small scales in the mid-area of the calculator-side is covered in Chapter 2 (Speed) and Chapter 6 (Time). In this chapter we cover what can be done with the two outside scales, which form a **'Circular Slide Rule'**.

THE CIRCULAR SLIDE RULE.

Multiplication and Division, if it is simple, can be performed mentally, or, if more complicated, by electronic calculators – or by the use of *'logarithms'*. A logarithm is one of a series of numbers, set out in tables, which make it possible to work out problems by adding and subtracting numbers, instead of multiplying and dividing. A Slide Rule is just a pictorial means of using logarithms.

To avoid the need for Pilots to carry long, straight slide rules, a Circular Slide Rule has cleverly been devised. It is very fast, never has flat batteries, is accurate enough for our purposes, and small enough to fit into a flight case.

The Circular Slide Rule has two scales:
• the inner rotary scale; and
• the outer fixed scale.

Both scales are marked off with logarithmic graduations, making it possible to multiply and divide simply by the physical addition or subtraction of lengths of the graduated scales. The numbers on the scales are marked-off in order from 10 all the way around the scale to 100, but the larger the number the closer it is to its neighbour.

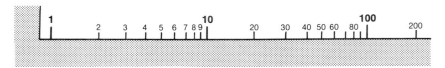

Fig.5-2. A Simple Logarithmic Scale.

If you look at your circular slide rule you will see that the numbers 1, 10, 100, 1000, 0·1, 0·001, etc, are completely interchangeable and are all labelled at the one point as 10. Similarly, 5, 50, 500, 0·5, 0·005 are interchangeable and are all labelled at the one point as 50.

A Slide Rule Can Be Read to Three Significant Figures.

Slide rules and navigation computers are fairly small in size, and so the accuracy to which you can read them depends upon your eyesight. Most scales on a slide rule allow you to **read to an accuracy of three digits.**

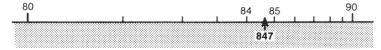

Fig.5-3. This Scale reads 847.

Now when we read the scale we do not know if these 3 significant figures should be written as, for example:

847
84·7
8·47
0·847
8,470
84,700,000.

To know where to place the decimal point requires us to estimate the approximate answer to whatever the question was, which we can do by quick mental arithmetic. The mental calculations give us a very approximate answer (allowing us to place the decimal point correctly), the slide rule manipulations give us that answer accurate to 3 significant figures.

NOTE: When using the slide rule facility of the computer, it is good practice to always follow the procedure:
• rough mental calculation;
• slide rule manipulation to obtain three significant figures;
• place the decimal point (determined by the rough calculation).

As well as allowing you to place the decimal point, the rough mental calculation is a check that your computer manipulations were at least approximately correct and your answer not grossly in error. Doing the mental check first seems to result in fewer errors, and is also good practice for the many times in flight and on the ground when mental calculations are valuable to a Pilot.

Multiplication on the Circular Slide Rule.

Example 1: Multiply 3·25 x 4·29.

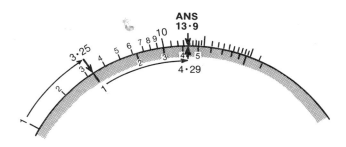

Fig.5-4. The Multiplication 3·25 x 4·29 = ?
on the Circular Slide Rule.

Step (1): Rough Mental Calculation:
  • 3 x 5 = 15.
Step (2): Computer Manipulation:
    • Treat 10 on the outer scale as the starting point and find 3·25;
    • Set 10 on the inner scale below 3·25 on the outer (or 32·5 or 325 or 3,250).
    • Find 4·29 on the inner scale and mark directly above it, i.e. 139.
Step (3): Place the Decimal Point:
    • Determine position of decimal point by referring to our earlier rough calculation 3 x 5 = 15, so the answer is 13·9. It is not 1·39 or 139.
    Answer: 3·25 x 4·29 = 13·9

Division on a Circular Slide Rule.

Example 2: The division 36/12 is an easy one to begin with. We simply need to subtract the logarithm of 12 from the logarithm of 36.

Fig.5-5. The Division 36/12 on the Circular Slide Rule.

Step (1): Rough Calculation:
- 36/12 = 3. (This is so easy we do not need the computer.)

Step (2): Computer Manipulation:
- Treat 10 on the outer scale as the starting point; the logarithm of 36 is the distance from 10 to 36 on the outer scale;
- Beneath 36 place 12 (the logarithm of 12 is the distance from 10 to 12 on the inner scale);
- Then locate 10 on the inner scale and looking above it find the Answer 30. Do not confuse 10 with 1:00 which symbolises 1 hr = 60 minutes on some navigation computers. (The log of 12 has thus been subtracted from the log of 36.)

Step (3): Place the Decimal Point:
- To determine the position of the decimal point is easy in this case, because we know that 36 divided by 12 = 3, and so the answer is not 30 or 300 but 3·0.

Answer: 36/12 = 3·0

Combined Multiplication and Division.

Occasionally calculations involve multiplication and division together, and the circular slide rule is ideal for this. The best approach is to commence with a division and follow with the multiplication. This process can be repeated as many times as necessary.

Example 3: Calculate 25 times 15, divided by 5. (Another simple one that can be done mentally, but a good example to begin with.)

Fig.5-6. The Calculation $\dfrac{25 \times 15}{5}$ on the Circular Slide Rule.

Step (1): Rough Check:
- 25/5 = 5 which, multiplied by 15, gives 5 x 15 = 75.

Step (2): Computer Manipulation:
- Carry out the division 25/5 by placing 5 on the inner scale under 25 on the outer scale. (The answer to this appears on the outer scale above the 10 on the inner scale, and the setting does not have to be altered to carry out the multiplication of this answer by 15.)
- Carry out the multiplication by finding 15 on the inner scale and marking the answer above it on the outer scale, i.e. 75. (You will determine the position of the decimal point by carrying out a quick mental check 25/5 = 5, which is multiplied by 15 to give 75·0.)

Step (3): Place the Decimal Point:
- Reference to our rough check confirms that the decimal point is placed to give 75·0.

Answer: 75·0

Example 4: Calculate $\dfrac{25 \cdot 7 \times 3 \cdot 96}{5 \cdot 12}$

Step (1): Rough Calculation: $\dfrac{25 \times 4}{5} = 20$

Step (2): Computer Manipulation:
- Set 25·7 on the outer against 5·12 on the inner.
- Against 3·96 on the inner read-off on the outer the result 199.

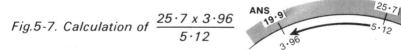

Fig.5-7. Calculation of $\dfrac{25 \cdot 7 \times 3 \cdot 96}{5 \cdot 12}$

Step (3): Place the Decimal Point:
- From our mental calculation, the decimal point should be placed thus: 19·9.

Answer: 19·9.

A Different Way of Expressing a Similar Problem.

$D = \dfrac{25 \times 4}{5}$ may be expressed slightly differently as a ratio:

$\dfrac{D}{4} = \dfrac{25}{5}$ and find D.

The rough mental check indicates that D is (approximately) 20.

The set-up on the circular slide rule is as shown in Fig.5-8.

The Answer is of course 20·0.

It could be the answer to the question
– if an aeroplane travels 25 nm in 5
mins, how far would it travel in a
further 4 mins?
ANS: 20 nm.

*Fig.5-8. Finding Ratios on
the Circular Slide Rule.*

Or it could be the answer to the question: if an aeroplane burns 25 litres of
fuel in 5 minutes, how many litres would the aeroplane have burned at the
same rate in 4 minutes?
ANS: 20 litres.
Or it could be the answer to the question: if an aeroplane travels 25 nm in 5
minutes, how far would it travel in 40 minutes?
ANS: 200 nm.
Or it could be the answer to the question: if you descend 2,500 feet in 5
minutes, how far would you expect to descend in the next 4 minutes? What
is your rate of descent?
ANS: 2000 ft, and 500 ft/min (1 min is 10 on the inner scale).

These are all very common navigational calculations and the Pilot must be
able to perform them with speed and accuracy.

SOLVING SPEED, DISTANCE, TIME AND RATIO PROBLEMS
ON THE NAVIGATION COMPUTER.

Speed is the ratio of **Distance/Time.** As there are 60 minutes in 1 hour, a
speed of 140 knots is the same as travelling a distance of 140 nm over the
ground in 60 minutes. We can set this up on the circular slide rule by
placing the 60 minutes (sometimes written as 1:00 hour) on the inner *Time*
scale against the 140 on the outer *Distance* scale.

On most computers the **Inner Scale is marked TIME** and the **Outer Scale
DISTANCE** (usually somewhere near the **60** mark). This is important to
keep in mind – that TIME is always on the Inner Scale and
DISTANCE/SPEED on the Outer.

*Fig.5-9. A Typical
Distance-Time Problem on
the Circular Slide Rule.*

The circular slide rule is now set-up to answer many questions, such as:

(a) At a Ground Speed of 140 kt, how far will you travel in 30 minutes?

Rough Check: 30 minutes is half an hour which, at 140 kt, is 70 nm.

Method: Find 30 mins on the inner *Time* scale and read-off the answer
70 nm on the outer *Distance* scale.

(b) At a GS of 140 kt, how far will you travel in 15 mins?

Rough Check: 15 minutes is 1/4 hour which, at
140 kt, gives 140/4 = 35 nm.

Method: Find 15 mins on the inner *Time* scale and then read off the
answer 35 nm on the outer *Distance* scale.

(c) At a GS of 140 kt, how long will it take you to travel 65 nm?

Rough Check: 65 nm is slightly less than ½ of 140 nm which, at 140 kt, will take slightly less than 30 min to cover.

Method: Find 65 nm on the outer *Distance* scale and read off the answer 28 mins (approximately) on the inner *Time* scale.

☐ Now complete **Exercises 5 — Calculator-1.**

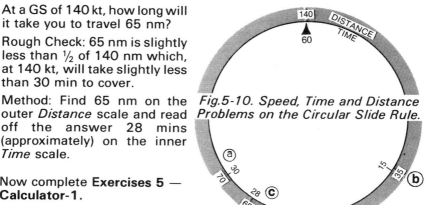

Fig.5-10. Speed, Time and Distance Problems on the Circular Slide Rule.

Further Calculations.

The computer can be used to help us solve many different types of problems involving multiplication, division or ratios. Another sort of calculation we can make is:

Example 5: If we cover 16 nm over the ground in 10 mins, what is our Ground Speed?

Rough Check:
  10 min is 1/6 hour. We cover 16 nm in 10 min, so we will cover 6 times this distance in an hour, i.e. 6 x 16 = 96 nm. The speed is therefore 96 kt.

Method:
1. Set-up 16 nm on the outer distance scale against 10 min on the inner time scale.

2. Against 60 min (1:00 hour) on the inner time scale read-off on the outer distance scale the distance you would travel in that time, which of course is 96 nm, that is the GS is 96 kt.

Fig.5-11. Finding Ground Speed.

ANS: 96 kt.

The computer is now set up to answer lots of other questions relevant to this situation, such as:

(a) How far will the aeroplane then travel in a further 5 minutes?
  ANS: 8 nm.
(b) How long will it take to travel 24 nm?
  ANS: 15 min.

In each case, a rough mental check will confirm that the answers are 8 nm (and not 80 or 0·8) and 15 min (and not 150 or 1·5 min).

☐ **Exercises 5 — Calculator-2.**

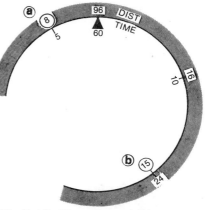

Fig.5-12. Time-Speed-Distance Set-up.

FUEL CONSUMPTION PROBLEMS.

Example 6: If an aeroplane is burning fuel at the rate of 30 litres/hr, what fuel burn-off can you expect in 8 minutes?

Rough Check:
   30 litres per hour is 1/2 litre per minute which, for 8 minutes, will give a burn-off of 4 litres.

Method:
   1. Set 60 min (1:00 hour) on the inner *Time* scale against 30 (litres) on the outer scale.
   2. Against 8 min on the inner *Time* scale read-off 4 (litres) on the outer scale. (Our rough mental calculation indicates that the answer is 4 and not 40 or 400 or 0·4.)
      ANS: 4 litres.

Fig.5-13. A Typical Fuel Consumption Problem on the Calculator.

Example 7: Another Type of Fuel Consumption Problem.

If we have burned 4 litres in 10 minutes, how much will we burn in the next 25 minutes?

Figs.5-14a & b.

Rough Check:
   25 = 2·5 x 10, so expect to use 2·5 x 4 = 10 litres.

Method:
   1. Set-up 10 min on the inner time scale against 4 litres on the outer scale.
   2. Against 25 min on the inner time scale read-off 10 litres on the outer scale.
      ANS: 10 litres (and not 1 or 100 or 1,000).

The circular slide rule is now set-up to answer many other problems relevant to this situation, such as:

(a) What is the rate of fuel consumption in litres/hr? (ANS: 24 litres/hr)

(b) How long would it take to burn 28 litres? (ANS: 70 min)

Example 8: A Further Type of Fuel Consumption Calculation.

If the aeroplane has 26 US Gallons of usable fuel in the tanks, and the average consumption rate is 5·5 USG/hour, what is the safe flight endurance if you wish to land with 1 hour's reserve still intact?

Subtracting the reserve (5·5 USG in this case) leaves 20·5 USG as flight fuel. A rough mental check (20 USG at 6 USG/hr =) 3 and ⅓ hours. By computer, with 60 minutes on the inner scale set against 5·5 USG on the outer, we can read against 20·5 USG on the outer scale the answer of 224 minutes on the inner, i.e. 3 hours 44 minutes.

THE ROUGH MENTAL CHECK IS VERY IMPORTANT.

The rough mental check will avoid gross errors being made. For example, an answer of 22·4 minutes to the above question may not seem in error to a Pilot who does not back up his computer manipulations with mental checks, yet it is in error by a factor of 10. As well as allowing you to place the decimal point correctly, a mental check also allows an approximate check of the numbers involved.

Do not neglect the mental check in order to save time or energy. What is the point of calculating the fuel to be 139 and ordering 1·39 litres or 13·9 litres rather than 139 litres?

It seems a little ridiculous, but rough estimates to back up computer calculations could have prevented a number of accidents, including some involving large jets. Learn the value of mental checks early in your flying career; Professional Pilots make mental checks all the time.

☐ Now complete Exercises 5 — **Calculator-3.**

'OFF-TRACK' PROBLEMS.

Example 9: If an aeroplane is 5 nm off-track after travelling 20 nm, how far off-track will it be after travelling 45 nm?

This is a simple ratio problem of 5/20 = ?/45.

Rough Check:

5/20 = 10/40. Answer will be slightly greater than 10.

Method:

1. Set-up 5 against 20.
2. Find the answer (11·2) against 45.

Fig.5-15.

The computer is now set up to find answers to other problems such as:

(a) If you are 5 nm off-track after travelling 20 nm, how far off-track will you be after travelling a total of 60 nm? (ANS: 15 nm)

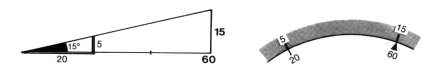

Fig.5-16. An 'Off-Track' Problem.

NOTE: These numbers have a particular significance for us as we will see later on under *the 1-in-60 rule*. If you measure it out you will find that:
• if you are 1 nm off-track in 60 nm, the track error is 1 degree.
• if you are 15 nm off-track in 60 nm, the track error is 15 degrees.
• if you are 5 nm off-track in 20 nm – then (because 5 nm off-track in 20 nm is the same as being 15 nm off-track after 60 nm, as we saw above), the track error is 15 degrees.

Example 10: If an aeroplane is 3 nm off-track after travelling 20 nm, what is its Track Error?

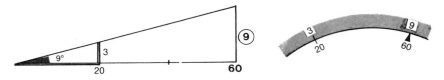

Fig.5-17. 3 nm Off-Track in 20 nm is 9° Track Error using 1-in-60 Rule.

NOTE: The 1:60 method of calculating angles is sufficiently accurate up to about 20°. Its use is explained fully in Section 3 – En Route Navigation Techniques.

□ Now complete **Exercises 5 — Calculator-4.**

CONVERSIONS ON THE COMPUTER.

As a Pilot you will often have to convert from one unit to another unit. Some of the common conversions are labelled on the scales of the circular slide rule to help you, but which ones and precisely how it is done varies from computer to computer so we suggest that you refer to your computer handbook as well as to this manual.

Converting Temperature from Degrees Centigrade to Degrees Fahrenheit.

The standard unit for temperature throughout the world is the degree 'C' (Celsius), except in the United States and a few other places where they still use the °F. Both systems are based on water and its behaviour.

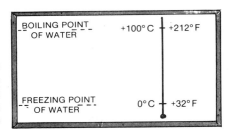

Fig.5-18. Temperature Scales are based on the Freezing and Boiling Points of Water.

The *Airtour CRP-1* has a separate **F/C** scale that allows us to convert very easily from one to the other. The reason for this separate scale is that we cannot convert from Fahrenheit to Celsius, or vice versa, by a simple arithmetical conversion, because the zero on one scale is not zero on the other. 0 degrees C = +32 degrees F.

Example 11: Convert +15°C to °F.

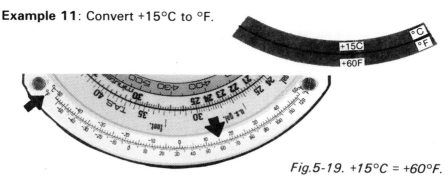

Fig.5-19. +15°C = +60°F.

NOTE: There are formulae that convert °C to °F and vice versa which we consider in our discussions on Meteorology. As you can see, the computer conversion is far easier.

$$°F = \tfrac{9}{5}.°C + 32 \qquad °C = \tfrac{5}{9}.(°F - 32)$$

☐ Now complete **Exercises 5 — Calculator-5.**

CONVERSIONS BETWEEN NAUTICAL MILES, STATUTE MILES and KILOMETRES.

It is an unfortunate fact of life that we have to deal with the same **physical distance** being measured in different units. For most navigational purposes we use the **nautical mile.** In day-to-day life in the United Kingdom longer distances are measured in **statute miles**, which are shorter than nautical miles. A statute mile is an arbitrary distance laid down by Royal Statute during the reign of Elizabeth I.

One of the things that Napoleon was interested in (apart from Josephine) was the metric system, which he introduced into the world, where everything is based on the number 1000. The metric unit of distance is the **metre**, with longer distances being measured in **kilometres** (kilo = thousand).

The metre is 1/10,000,000th (one ten millionth) of the distance from the equator to a pole, which makes the kilometre 1/10,000th of the distance from the equator to a pole, i.e. **the average distance from the Equator to a Pole is 10,000 km.**

The **kilometre** is much shorter than the nautical mile. It is the standard unit for distance in most of Europe and many other parts of the world. The United Kingdom is in the process of slowly changing over from Imperial and Statute standards to Metric standards so, eventually, the kilometre may officially replace the statute mile in day to day life.

Nautical Miles used in Navigation are relevant, however, because of their relationship to the **angular** measurement of Latitude on the Earth. Thus there is a need for us to understand the relationship between these units of distance and be able to convert from one to the other.

Napoleon's attempt to make angular measurement metric was doomed to failure, because geometric shapes like equilateral triangles contain angles which are easy to handle using the 360° system (e.g. an equilateral triangle has three angles of 60°), but which would be complicated in a metric system (three angles of 33·3333333°). Some bosses would also like to see an 8 hour day worked on a metric time system.

The relationship between the Navigational, Statute and Metric units is:

$$1 \text{ nm} = 1·15 \text{ sm} = 1·852 \text{ km (1,852 metres)}.$$

For quick mental checks, we can remember that:
- 1 nm = approx 1·2 sm = approx 2 km;
- approx 0·9 nm = 1 sm = approx 1·5 km;
- approx 0·5 nm = approx 0·6 sm = 1 km.

Our *CRP-1* computer can provide us with accurate conversions. It has indices for *nautical miles, statute miles* and *kilometres* marked in red on the outer scale, making it quite straight forward to convert these units.

To convert from one unit to another:
- as with all computer calculations, carry out a rough mental check; then
- set the known quantity on the inner scale of the computer against its index on the outer scale; then
- against the index of the required unit on the outer scale, read-off the answer on the inner scale.

Example 12: Convert 10 nm to sm and km.

Rough Check: 1 nm = approx 1·2 sm = approx 2 km
10 nm = approx 12 sm = approx 20 km

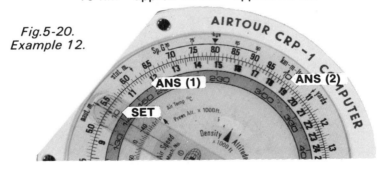

Fig.5-20.
Example 12.

The Answer is:
10 nm = 11·5 sm = 18·5 km.

This same method may be used to convert speeds:

Example 13: Convert 231 kph to mph and kt.

Rough check:
approx 0·5 nm = approx 0·6 sm = 1 km.
231 kph = approx 0·6 x 231 mph = approx 138 mph.
231 kph = approx 0·5 x 231 kt approx 115 kt.

The Answers are: 231 kph = 144 mph
= 125 kt.

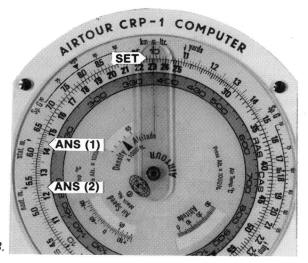

Fig.5-21.
Example 13.

Example 14.: Convert 100 kt to metres/second.

This is slightly more difficult. Make the first conversion from knots (which are nm/hr) to kilometres per hour using the computer, and then work down through metres/hour, to metres/minute, to metres/second.

By computer: 100 kt = 186 km/hr   (to three significant figures)
                = 186,000 metres/hr
                = 186,000/60 metres/minute
                = 3,100 metres/minute
                = 3,100/60 metres/second
                = 51·7 m/sec.

☐ Now do **Exercises 5 — Calculator-6.**

CONVERTING FEET TO METRES AND VICE VERSA.

The Standard unit for Altitude is still the FOOT in most countries – certainly in the *Western* countries, however many *Eastern* countries, such as the USSR, East Germany, etc, use metres. Pilots flying in both these areas need to be able to convert quickly from one system to the other (although the aeroplanes are usually fitted with separate altimeters – one showing feet and the other showing metres).

United Kingdom Pilots visiting countries in Western Europe will find that the topographical charts produced in these countries have the elevation of high ground marked in metres. Some of these charts cover parts of the United Kingdom, but the elevations are still shown in metres. A hill with a spot height marked as 1,000 on a metric chart will be 3,280 feet high. **Beware!**

If you use a chart with heights Above Mean Sea Level marked in metres, but you áre flying an altitude in feet, then you must be able to convert confidently between these two units. For approximate checks, use 1 m = 3·3 ft.

Also, many older pilots (as well as American pilots) may be used to thinking of runway length in *feet* rather than *metres*. If you are contemplating flying in the USA or even if you read American aviation books, conversion of feet to metres and vice versa is necessary. It is also in the syllabus for this examination.

1 METRE = 3·28 FEET approximately.

The conversion is very simple using the red indices for *feet* and *m* on the outer scale of the *CRP-1*.

Example 15: Convert 1000 metres to feet on the computer.

Rough Check:
    1 m = approx 3.3 ft.
 1000 m = approx 3300 ft.
The Answer is 1000 m = 3280 ft.

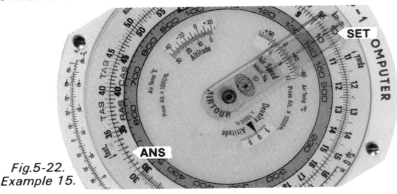

Fig.5-22.
Example 15.

Example 16: Convert 2000 ft to metres.

Rough Check:
       1 ft = approx 1/3.3 m
 2000 ft = approx 2000 x 1/3.3 m
          = 2000/3.3 m
          = approx 600 m
The Answer is 2000 ft = 610 metres.

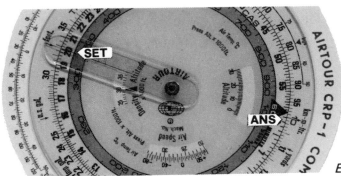

Fig.5-23.
Example 16.

☐ Now do **Exercises 5 — Calculator-7.**

To summarise the relationship between the various units of length:

1 nm = 1·15 sm	**1 nm = 6076 ft**	**1 nm = 1852 metres**

– and of lesser importance:
   1 sm = 5280 ft   and 1 km = 3281 ft (1 metre = 3·28 ft).

VOLUME (in particular, the Volume of Fuel) AND WEIGHT.

In aviation we are faced with three different sorts of volumetric units – the **Imperial Gallon,** the **US Gallon** and the **Litre.** In most General Aviation aircraft the fuel gauges are marked in US Gallons, yet you must order the fuel from the fuel agent in litres. There is a possibility of confusion here, so you must become very confident in converting fuel quantities from one unit to another.

The **weight** of the fuel on board, as well as its volume, is of concern to the Pilot for two main reasons:
• Weight and Balance (i.e. loading of the aircraft); and
• Energy Content of the Fuel (which depends on weight, not volume).

The Pilot must be able, therefore, to convert fuel from a volume to a weight with confidence.

100 octane (or higher) AVGAS weighs only about 0·71 or 0·72 times the weight of an equal volume of water. Scientifically, we describe this by saying that the **Specific Gravity of AVGAS = 0·71 or 0·72.** The precise value depends to some extent upon the temperature and you should consult with your Instructor as to which value to use in your usual flying conditions.

Relative Density is the more modern term and it clearly describes its purpose, which is to compare the density of a particular fluid to the density of water.

Most navigation computers, however, are marked with *Sp. G,* so we will continue to use the term *Specific Gravity.* It means the same thing.

The conversion from one unit of volume to another (Imperial Gallons, US Gallons or litres), or to a weight (kg or lb) is very easily handled on the *CRP-1* computer.

Conversions between Kilograms and Pounds.

For rough calculations, use: 1 kg = approx 2·2 lb.

The index of *kg* is marked in red on the outer scale of the CRP-1 computer, near the 80 mark. The index for *lb* is near the 18 mark on the outer scale.

Example 17: Convert 83 lb to kg.

Rough Calculation:
  1 kg = approx 2·2 lb.
  83 lb = approx 83/2·2 kg = approx 40 kg.

Method:
  • Set 83 on the inner scale against *lb* on the outer scale.
  • Against *kg* on the outer scale, read-off 37·5 on the inner scale, which is the answer in kg.

NOTE: You can use the rotating arm to help you align the numbers with the index.

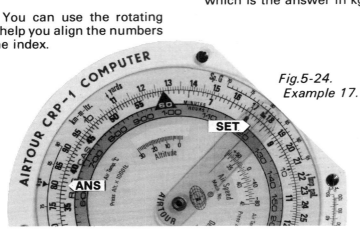

Fig.5-24.
Example 17.

Example 18: Convert 293 kg to lb.

Rough Check:
  1 kg = approx 2·2 lb.
  293 kg = approx 2·2 x 300 lb
         = 630 lb.

Method:
  • Set 293 on the inner scale against *kg* on the outer scale.
  • Against *lb* on the outer scale, read-off answer 648 lb.

Fig.5-25.
Example 18.

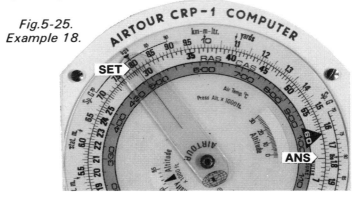

□ Now do **Exercises 5 — Calculator-8.**

Conversions Between US Gallons (USG), Imperial Gallons (IG) and Litres (l).

For rough calculations, the conversion factors are:

> 1 Imp Gal   = 1·2 US Gal   = 4·5 ltr
>
> 0·8 Imp Gal = 1 US Gal   = 4 ltr
>
> 0·2 Imp Gal = 0·25 US Gal = 1 ltr

This calculation is very simple on the *CRP-1*, which has red indices marked on the outer scale for *'US gal', 'Imp gal' and 'Itr'*.

1. Set the known quantity on the inner scale against its index on the outer scale.

2. Read-off the answer on the inner scale against the desired index on the outer scale.

Example 19: Convert 24 US gal to Imperial Gallons and litres.

Rough check:

1 US gal = 0·8 Imp gal	1 US gal = 4 ltr
24 US gal = 0·8 x 24	24 US gal = 4 x 24 = approx 96 ltr
= approx 20 Imp gal	

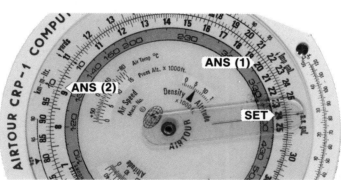

Fig.5-26. Example 19.

ANS: 24 USG = 20 IG = 91 l.

CONVERSIONS OF VOLUME TO WEIGHT.

We need to remember that: **SG of AVGAS = 0·71 or 0·72**

It is useful to know the relationship of volume to weight for water, since it is water that is the standard for Relative Density (i.e. Specific Gravity).

At normal temperatures and pressures:
- 1 litre of water weighs 1 kg;
- 1 Imperial gallon of water weighs 10 lb;
- 1 US gallon of water weighs 8·33 lb.

For a rough check on the volume/weight relationship for AVGAS, use:
- 1 litre weighs 1 x SG kg;
- 1 Imperial Gallon weighs 10 x SG lb.

For US gal, first convert to Imp gal (1 USG = 1·2 IG) and then use 10 x SG to find weight in lb.

The Volume/Weight Calculation on the Computer.

The *CRP-1* computer is advanced in that it has two scales (one graduated in *kg* ond one in *lb*) to cater for fluids of different Specific Gravity. This is useful as SG for AVGAS (used in piston engines) is usually about 0·71 or 0·72, and SG for AVTUR (used in turbine engines) is usually about 0·79.

To convert a Volume to Weight:
- Set the volume on the inner scale against its index on the outer scale;
- Against the given SG (on the *kg* or *lb* scale as desired) read-off the weight on the inner scale.

Example 20: Convert 37 USG of AVGAS (SG 0·71) to weight in lb and kg.

Rough Check:
$$37 \text{ US gal} = 0·8 \times 37$$
$$= \text{approx } 30 \text{ IG}$$
$$= 30 \times 10 \times 0·7 \text{ lb}$$
$$= 210 \text{ lb}$$
$$= 210/2·2 \text{ kg}$$
$$= \text{approx } 100 \text{ kg.}$$

ANS (i): 37 USG (SG 0·71) = 220 lb

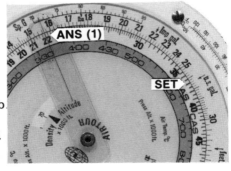

Fig.5-27a. ANS (i).

= 99·5 kg.

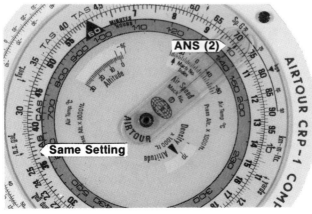

Fig.5-27b. ANS (ii).

☐ You should now be able to complete **Exercises 5 — Calculator-9.**

STANDARD SPECIFIC GRAVITY VALUES.

The density of a fluid will vary with temperature, however for our purposes in light aircraft where only relatively small quantities will be used, we can assume standard SG values for fuel (and oil if required).

AVGAS 100 octane and higher SG = 0·71 or 0·72
less than 100 octane SG = 0·72

You should remember: SPECIFIC GRAVITY OF AVGAS = 0·71 or 0·72

In round figures: 1 litre of AVGAS weighs 0·7 kg; and
1 Imperial gallon of AVGAS weighs 7 lb.

The following SGs do not concern us at Private Pilot level but may be of interest to you:

Jet engines burn AVTUR (kerosene) with SG = 0·79.

Some aircraft load sheets require oil to be considered:

SG (mineral oil)   = 0·90
SG (synthetic oil) = 0·96

6

VERTICAL NAVIGATION

Navigating a car or a ship is basically a two-dimensional activity, i.e. horizontal navigation. Navigating an aeroplane requires a three-dimensional awareness. Vertical Navigation is vital knowledge for a Pilot for three basic reasons:
1. For **Terrain Clearance**, i.e. to ensure that the aircraft will not collide with terrain or fixed obstacles on the ground.
2. For **Traffic Separation**, i.e. to allow Pilots to cruise at an altitude different to that of nearby aircraft, to ensure safe vertical separation.
3. To calculate the **Performance Capabilities** of the aircraft and its engine, so as to operate safely and efficiently.

Vertical Navigation, then, is the guidance of flight in the vertical plane, and includes the science of measuring vertical distances in the atmosphere, known as **Altimetry.**

To measure vertical distance in the atmosphere is not as easy as it sounds. There are errors in the measuring instrument, the altimeter, and compromises in the principle upon which it is built, with the result that **the altimeter presents the Pilot only with approximate vertical information** of his position.

ALTITUDE.
Altitude is the vertical distance of a level, point, or object, measured from Mean Sea Level (MSL). This definition appears in the UK Aeronautical Information Publication (AIP). The abbreviation for *altitude* is ALT.

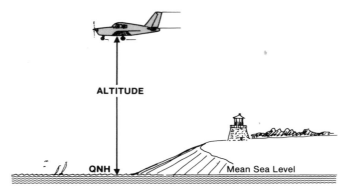

Fig.6-1. Altitude is the Vertical Distance Above Mean Sea Level (AMSL).

For aviation purposes the standard unit of height is the **foot** in the UK and the western world. In other parts, such as Eastern Europe and the Soviet Union, the **metre** is the unit used.

THE BASIC INSTRUMENT –
THE ALTIMETER.

Even after many years, the basic instrument still used to measure altitude is the **Pressure Altimeter.** This is simply a barometer (baro – pressure, meter – to measure) which makes use of the fact that, in the atmosphere, **air pressure decreases as height increases.** This means that the higher you are in the Earth's atmosphere, the lower the pressure – hence the need for most people to wear oxygen masks when they climb Everest or when they fly above 10 000 ft in unpressurised aeroplanes.

There are various types of Pressure Altimeter. The most compact and robust type suitable for installation in an aircraft is the **Aneroid Barometer**, which is similar to those commonly seen hanging in many homes. As the aeroplane goes higher, the atmospheric pressure of the air in which it is flying decreases, and the aneroid, which is an expandable and compressible metal capsule containing a fixed amount of air, is able to expand.

Through a system of linkages (more complicated than that shown, of course), a pointer is driven around a scale. This scale does not read directly in units of pressure, such as millibars (or hectoPascals), but rather in feet. Calculations by the designer have been made to relate the pressure to the altitude, and the scale reads in units of altitude, which, of course, is much more practical for the Pilot. The altimeter indication is known as **Indicated Altitude.**

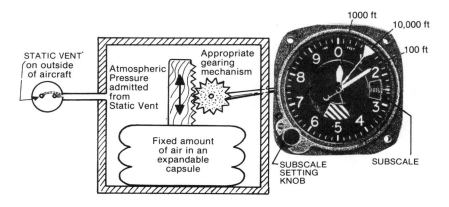

Fig.6-2. The Altimeter is a Pressure Sensitive Instrument.

As the aeroplane climbs, the aneroid expands, driving the pointer to indicate a higher altitude. As the aeroplane descends, the static air pressure in the surrounding atmosphere increases, forcing the aneroid to contract and drive the pointer to indicate a lower altitude.

A number of errors are evident in altimeters and these may be broken into two main types:
1. Errors in the particular altimeter.
2. Errors in the principle upon which altimetry is based, i.e. just how much the pressure in the atmosphere decreases with height.

ERRORS IN THE PRINCIPLE
of How Pressure Decreases with Altitude.

The rate at which air pressure decreases with height varies from time to time and from place to place. The simple barometric altimeter cannot cope with this because it has been calibrated according to a Standard Atmosphere in which a particular height AMSL always corresponds with a particular pressure. Any variation of the actual atmosphere from the *Standard Atmosphere* will cause the altimeter to indicate an altitude different from the **actual** height AMSL of the aeroplane.

The various gases surrounding the Earth and forming its atmosphere are bound to it by gravity. To talk of a Standard Atmosphere is to talk of something that does not exist permanently, since this mixture of gases (or air as we call it) has constantly changing values of:
● pressure;
● temperature;
● density; and
● water content (humidity).

It is, however, necessary to have some sort of measuring stick or *standard,* be it only a theoretical one, against which to **compare** the actual atmosphere in our vicinity.

Lapse Rates.

In the **International Standard Atmosphere,** Pressure, Temperature and Density are defined as reducing at specified rates with an increase in height.

1. The **Temperature Lapse Rate** (rate of fall of temperature with an increase in height) in the ISA is 1·98 degrees C per 1,000 ft up to 36 090 ft, above which the temperature remains constant at minus 56·5°C (at least in the levels up to which commercial aeroplanes fly). For our purposes, **in the ISA:**
   ● temperature falls by 2°C/1000 ft up to 36 000 ft; and
   ● above 36 000 ft, remains constant at –57°C.

2. The rate at which **Pressure** in the theoretical ISA decreases with height varies, but is approximately 1 mb per 30 ft up to about 5000 ft. (This rate drops to about 1 mb per 70 ft at high levels of the atmosphere, but this need not concern us here.) For our purposes, **in the lower levels of the ISA, Pressure decreases by 1 mb(hPa) for each 30 ft increase in altitude.**

3. **Air Density** decreases with height, so that at 20 000 ft the air density is about one-half of its MSL value, one-quarter at 40 000 ft, and one-tenth at 60 000 ft.

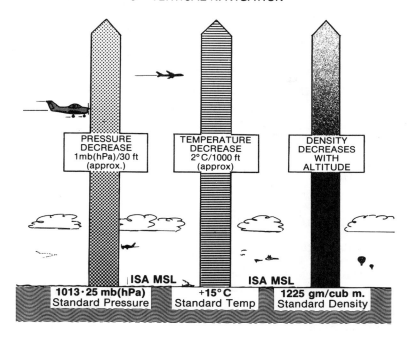

Fig.6-3. The International Standard Atmosphere (ISA).

The Main Use of the International Standard Atmosphere is to Calibrate Altimeters.

This is to provide a mathematical relationship between the **air pressure** measured by the aneroid barometer and the **altitude calibrations** placed on the scale around which the pointer is driven, so that **all** aircraft convert pressure to altitude by a standard method.

PRESSURE ALTITUDE.

Known in some countries as *Pressure Height*, this is the **height in the ISA above the 1013 mb(hPa) pressure datum at which the pressure equals that of the level under consideration.** For example, the ISA pressure at a point 600 ft higher than the 1013 pressure level is approximately 993 mb. If your aeroplane is flying in air whose pressure is 993 mb, then its Pressure Altitude is 600 ft.

NOTE: 1013·25 mb(hPa) is the precise value of *Standard Pressure*. For our purposes, 1013 is sufficiently accurate for ISA MSL pressure. There is a *Q-code* name for Pressure Altitude, **QNE**, but it is rarely used.

Pressure Altitudes are often described in an abbreviated form as Flight Levels, where the final two zeros are omitted. For example, a pressure altitude of 4500 ft (i.e 4500 ft higher than the 1013 pressure level) is also known as Flight Level 45 and written as FL45. Flight Levels are used for cruising at higher levels and are usually separated by at least 500 ft, e.g. FL55, FL60, FL65.

Example 1: 35 000 ft in the International Standard Atmosphere above the Standard Pressure Level of 1013 may be referred to as:
• Pressure Altitude or Pressure Height of 35 000 ft; or as
• Flight Level 350 (where the last two zeros are dropped).

A FLIGHT LEVEL IS A PRESSURE ALTITUDE.

Example 2: 3500 ft in the International Standard Atmosphere above the Standard Pressure Level of 1013 may be referred to as:
• Pressure Altitude (or Pressure Height) of 3500 ft; or as
• Flight Level 35, FL35, (where the last two zeros are dropped).

AIR PRESSURE.

The Earth's atmosphere consists of countless numbers of molecules all moving at high speed and colliding with any object, be it another molecule or the Earth's surface or a person that blocks their path. The force that these molecules exert as they collide gives rise to a **pressure**, i.e. a force per unit area. As these molecules are moving in all directions, the pressure at any point in the atmosphere will be exerted in all directions.

Because of gravity, the ambient pressure at any point in the atmosphere will depend upon the weight of air that is above and pressing down. On a standard day, the column of air pressing down upon the Earth's surface exerts a pressure of 1013 millibars at sea level.

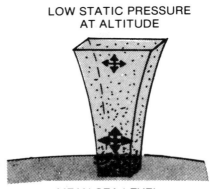

LOW STATIC PRESSURE AT ALTITUDE

MEAN SEA LEVEL
HIGH STATIC PRESSURE

Fig.6-4. Pressure Decreases with Increase of Altitude.

At higher levels in the column of air, the weight pressing down is less and so the pressure will be less. **In the lower levels of the atmosphere** (up to about 5000 ft AMSL), **the pressure drops by about 1 mb for each 30 ft climbed.**

Example 3: If the pressure at MSL is 1013 (to the nearest mb), what is the pressure at 60 ft AMSL?

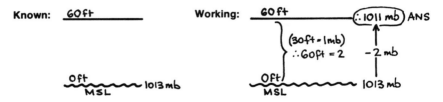

Fig.6-5. A Good Way to do Altimetry Problems – Pictorially.

Example 4: If the MSL pressure is 1013, at what altitude (height AMSL) would you expect the pressure to be 1000 mb?

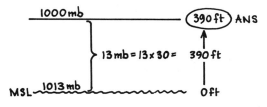

Fig.6-6. Example 4.

☐ Now attempt **Exercises 6 — Vertical Nav-1.**

AIR TEMPERATURE.

The temperature in any one place varies from hour to hour, from day to day, and from season to season. On an *'average day'* in a temperate zone, the temperature at MSL (Mean Sea Level) may be +15°C. By international agreement, +15°C is the Standard Temperature at Sea Level in the International Standard Atmosphere. As we climb, the temperature decreases at about 2°C for every 1000·ft increase in height.

Example 5: What temperature exists at 3000 ft above the 1013 pressure surface (or pressure level) in the International Standard Atmosphere?

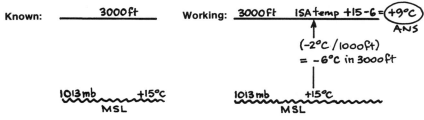

Fig.6-7. Example 5.

Example 6: What temperature exists at 4500 ft in the ISA?

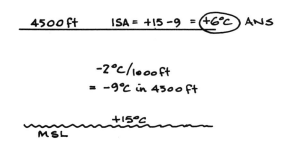

Fig.6-8. Example 6.

Example 7: What temperature exists at 45 000 ft in the ISA? (Beware!)
ANS: –57°C – because in the ISA, temperature is constant at –57°C above 36 000 ft.

Example 8: Calculate what temperature exists at 36 000 ft in the ISA?

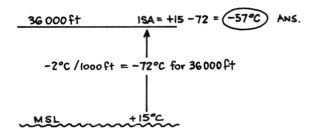

Fig.6-9. Example 8.

Example 9: Calculate the ISA values of temperature and pressure for a pressure altitude of 6000 ft.

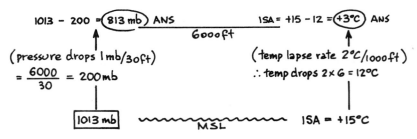

Fig.6-10. Example 9.

Example 10: Calculate the ISA values of temperature and pressure for a Pressure Altitude of –1500 ft, i.e. 1500 ft below the 1013 pressure level.

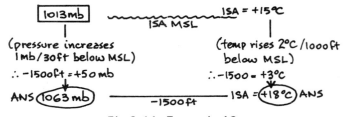

Fig.6-11. Example 10.

NOTE: This sort of calculation for below ISA MSL is sometimes required because:
• there are places on the Earth's surface that are below MSL (e.g. Rotterdam in Holland, the Dead Sea in Jordan, Lake Eyre in Australia); and, more importantly:
• the actual atmosphere is always different to our so-called *standard atmosphere* and negative pressure altitudes are not uncommon.

Example 11: What is the Pressure Altitude of the 990 mb pressure surface?

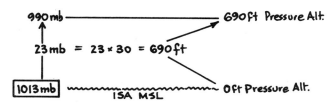

Fig.6-12. Example 11.

☐ Now complete **Exercises 6 — Vertical Nav-2.**

(Even though some of these exercises are very easy, do not avoid them. A sound understanding of Altimetry will stand you in good stead throughout your flying career!)

VARIATIONS IN MEAN SEA LEVEL PRESSURE — QNH

On maps and charts the height of terrain is given as **height Above Mean Sea Level (AMSL)**. It is therefore essential that a Pilot knows the aircraft's height Above Mean Sea Level so that he can relate this with the height of any terrain or obstructions and determine if there is sufficient vertical separation.

So far in our discussion the altimeter has only measured height above the ISA MSL datum of 1013 mb(hPa). In reality, Mean Sea Level pressure varies from day to day, and indeed from hour to hour, as the various HIGH and LOW pressure systems move across the surface of the Earth. If you study the daily weather maps published in newspapers you will notice this.

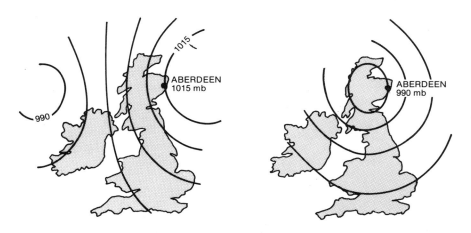

Fig.6-13. Two Different Synoptic Situations.

Consider the situation illustrated in the previous figure. 'Yesterday', a high pressure system of 1015 mb was sitting over Aberdeen. In 24 hours, the pressure system has moved on, and 'today' Aberdeen is experiencing a lower pressure of 990. A profile of the atmosphere over Aberdeen on each of these days is illustrated below.

Fig.6-14. Profile of MSL Pressure Situations –
'Yesterday' and 'Today'.

If the position of the 1013 mb pressure level is related to each of these situations, the following diagrams are obtained.

Fig.6-15. The Standard Pressure Level in Relation to the
MSL Pressure.

Yesterday the 1013 mb pressure level in the actual atmosphere was (1015 – 1013) x 30 = 2 x 30 = 60 ft Above Mean Sea Level (AMSL).	Today the 1013 mb pressure level is (1013 – 990) x 30 = 690 ft Below Mean Sea Level.

Since **height AMSL** is vital information to a Pilot, instead of this unwieldy calculation being required in the cockpit, the design of the altimeter incorporates a small **subscale** and knob geared to the altimeter pointer. **By rotating the knob, the desired pressure datum from which height will be measured is set in the subscale.**

Yesterday we would have set 1015 mb in the subscale to measure altitude (height AMSL).	Today we set 990 mb (today's MSL pressure level) for the altimeter to indicate altitude.

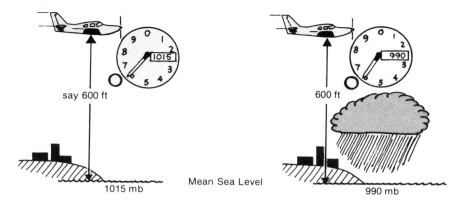

Fig.6-16. When MSL Pressure is Set in the Altimeter Subscale, the Altimeter Indicates Height AMSL for that Pressure Situation.

Altimeter now reads height above the 1015 mb pressure level.	Altimeter now reads height above 990 mb pressure level.

In each case, the altimeter indicates the aeroplane's altitude, 600 ft AMSL.

Q N H.

The Q-code name for the altimeter subscale setting which gives us this altitude is **QNH** (i.e. the MSL pressure level in the **actual** atmosphere). The QNH is the atmospheric pressure corresponding to Mean Sea Level pressure at that place and time. **An altimeter with QNH set on its subscale will indicate altitude, i.e. height AMSL** (definition).

From our example above, we can see that *yesterday* in Aberdeen the QNH was 1015 mb; *today* in Aberdeen the QNH is 990 mb.

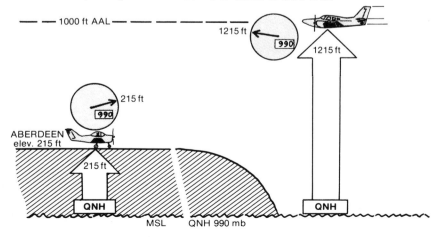

Fig.6-17. 'Today' in Aberdeen the QNH is 990 mb.

The official elevation of a particular aerodrome is that of the highest point on the landing area. Since most aerodromes are fairly level, it gives the Pilot who is taxying an opportunity to check his altimeter prior to take-off. With QNH set, the altimeter of an aeroplane on the ground should indicate aerodrome elevation closely.

The Altimeter Subscale.

The altimeter subscale is controlled by a knob which the Pilot can turn. It is connected to the pointer and mechanically geared in the ratio of approximately 1 mb(hPa) to 30 ft, i.e. **altering the subscale setting by 1 millibar will alter the indicated height by about 30 ft.** Altering the subscale setting by 10 millibars will alter the altimeter indication by about 300 ft.

An **easy means of determining Pressure Altitude** is simply to wind 1013 into the subscale. The altimeter will then indicate the height in the ISA above the 1013 mb(hPa) pressure level – Pressure Altitude.

Example 12: Suppose that the MSL pressure is 1030 (i.e. QNH) and the aeroplane is 600 ft AMSL. With QNH 1030 set in the subscale, the altimeter will indicate an altitude of 600 ft AMSL. The Pressure Altitude can be found (without any calculation) by winding 1013 into the subscale. In this case the pressure altitude is 90 ft.

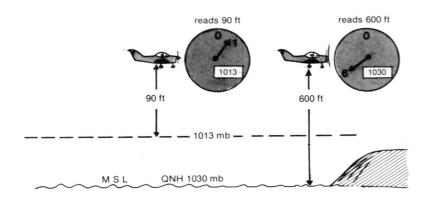

Fig.6-18. Example 12.

Notice that, **if you wind on millibars, you wind on height**, and vice versa.

The correct QNH can be obtained from a number of sources, including Air Traffic Control, Meteorological Forecasts (at least approximately) and your own observations. By *'your own observations'*, we mean that if you are on the ground at an aerodrome whose elevation you know then, after turning the knob until the altimeter indicates the aerodrome elevation, the reading in the subscale will be the current aerodrome QNH.

To illustrate this, suppose you arrive by car at a country aerodrome, elevation 1290 ft, to go flying, and find that the altimeter indicates something quite different to 1290. Simply by turning the knob until the pointers of the altimeter indicate 1290 ft, which is the altitude (height AMSL) of the aircraft, you will have wound the current QNH onto the subscale.

It is obvious that, for the altimeter indication to have any significance, the pilot must be aware of the setting on the subscale.

Example 13: You are flying overhead **Elstree** aerodrome with the current QNH of 1020 set in the subscale, and the altimeter indicating 1500 ft. What Pressure Altitude is that?

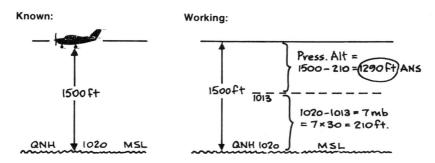

Fig.6-19. Example 13 – ANS: 1290 ft.

Example 14: Your aircraft is sitting on the tarmac at **Compton Abbas** airfield, elevation 810 feet. The altimeter reads 900 ft (i.e. 90 ft too high) with 1015 set on the subscale. What is the airfield QNH (i.e. what is the Mean Sea Level pressure at Compton Abbas at that time, assuming the atmosphere extends down to MSL)?

ANS: with 1015 set in the subscale, the altimeter over-reads the known elevation by 90 ft. By winding-off this 90 ft, we wind-off 3 mb, i.e. QNH is 1012.

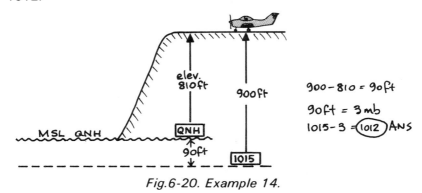

Fig.6-20. Example 14.

☐ Now complete **Exercises 6 — Vertical Nav-3.**

USING THE ALTIMETER TO INDICATE HEIGHT ABOVE AERODROME LEVEL — QFE

It is very convenient for circuit operations if the altimeter can be set to indicate **height Above Aerodrome Level (AAL)**. This means that a 1000 ft circuit at, for example, Leicester airfield (elev 469 ft) can be achieved with the altimeter indicating 1000 ft, rather than 1469 ft if QNH was set in the subscale. It is a satisfactory procedure in the United Kingdom to set QFE in the subscale when flying in the circuit.

On the aerodrome, the altimeter should indicate within +/− 50 ft of Zero with QFE set in the subscale. **QFE is the pressure at aerodrome level.** In flight, the altimeter, with QFE set, will indicate height above the runway. (Having departed the circuit area, however, QFE is of little value, since the surrounding terrain will probably be at a different level to the aerodrome.)

Example 15: You plan to do some circuits at an aerodrome (elevation 749 ft AMSL). On the ground you adjust the subscale of your altimeter until the altimeter indicates 0 feet, which it does with say 996 set in the subscale.

Calculate the current QFE, QNH and Pressure Altitude of this aerodrome, and the altimeter readings you would expect with these subscale settings when the aeroplane is on the ground.

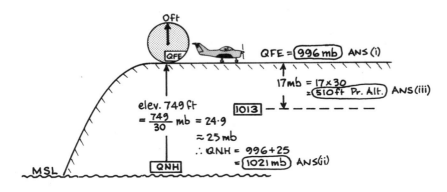

Fig.6-21. Example 15.

Remember that the information your altimeter gives you depends upon what you have set in the subscale.

FOR TERRAIN CLEARANCE, USE QNH.

☐ Now complete **Exercises 6 — Vertical Nav-4.**

FLYING WITH CHANGING SEA LEVEL PRESSURES

Consider the following case of an aeroplane flying from **Land's End** to **Popham,** with the pressure over the south-west of England as shown.

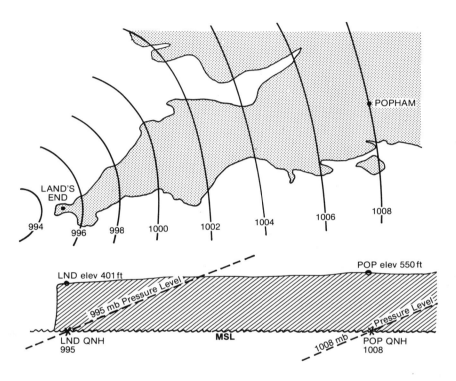

Fig.6-22. Plan and Cross-Section Views of this Synoptic Situation.

We depart Land's End with the Land's End QNH of 995 set on the subscale (i.e. MSL pressure at Land's End), and cruise 3000 ft above this with our altimeter indicating 3000 ft.

Tracking towards Popham, we are flying into an area of higher pressure, and so the 995 pressure level will be gradually rising. If we maintain 3000 ft indicated on the altimeter, with 995 set, we will in fact be climbing with respect to sea level.

Conversely, another aircraft flying in the opposite direction with the Popham QNH of 1008 set on its subscale and cruising at 4000 ft will in fact be gradually descending. Can you spot the two inherent dangers?

Remember that two of the most important tasks for you as a pilot are:
• to avoid hitting the ground unexpectedly; and
• to avoid colliding with another aircraft.

The aircraft coming from Popham, flying from a higher pressure area towards an area of lower pressure, will actually be gradually descending if the altimeter reading 4000 ft continues to have 1008 on the subscale. He will in fact be lower than 4000 ft AMSL, so **terrain clearance could be a problem.** When flying **'From HIGH to LOW, beware below!'** (Danger No.1)

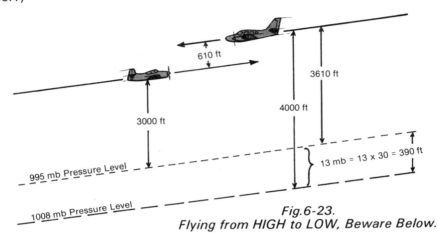

Fig.6-23.
Flying from HIGH to LOW, Beware Below.

The two Pilots may think that they have 1000 ft vertical separation because the altimeter in one aeroplane indicates 3000 ft, and the altimeter in the other indicates 4000 ft. In fact, the vertical separation is only 610 ft, because 4000 ft above the 1008 mb pressure level is only (4000 – 390 = 3610 ft above the 995 pressure level. (Danger No.2).

REGIONAL PRESSURE SETTING (REGIONAL QNH).

The practical solution to both of these problems (terrain clearance and traffic separation) because of changing QNHs is to have all aircraft which are cruising in the same area use the same altimeter subscale setting. For this reason the United Kingdom is divided into Altimeter Setting Regions (ASRs) – (see Fig.A3-4 in Chapter A3 of Vol.2).

Regional QNH can be obtained from:
• all aerodromes with Air Traffic Services;
• any air/ground ATC channel;
• by land line (for pre-flight planning);
• the London and Scottish ATCCs;
• the Manchester Sub-Centre.

When cruising en route, the appropriate subscale setting is the **Regional Pressure Setting,** also known as the **Regional QNH** or the **Area QNH,** the current QNH for that region at that time. Its value will be updated by ATC at least every hour.

The QNH will in fact vary slightly throughout the Altimeter Setting Region, depending upon the pressure pattern. To be on the conservative side, the Regional QNH is the lowest forecast QNH value for that hour, and so will be at sea level or slightly higher. This ensures that the Pilot will be at or slightly higher than the altitude indicated, and not lower.

For example, with Regional QNH set and the altimeter indicating 2000 ft, the aeroplane should be 2000 ft AMSL or slightly higher. No Aerodrome QNH in that Region will be lower than the value of the Regional QNH.

When cruising cross-country, set Regional QNH, and update it when you fly into another region, or whenever ATC communicates an amended value.

ALTIMETRY PROCEDURES ON A TYPICAL CROSS-COUNTRY FLIGHT

In the UK, a typical private cross-country flight in a light aircraft is usually conducted at or below 3000 ft AMSL. Continuing with the example previously started, the flight is from **Land's End** to **Popham**.

1. SET AERODROME QNH or QFE for Take-Off.

With Aerodrome QNH set, the altimeter indicates height **AMSL**, which is useful information both in the circuit area and during the climb-out, especially over high terrain or if ATC requires you to report altitude. On the ground, the altimeter should indicate aerodrome elevation, which at **Land's End** is 401 ft AMSL.

If you choose to set QFE, the altimeter will indicate height **AAL**, and this reading of course has little significance away from the vicinity of the aerodrome. On the ground, with QFE set, the altimeter should indicate close to zero (within +/– 50 ft).

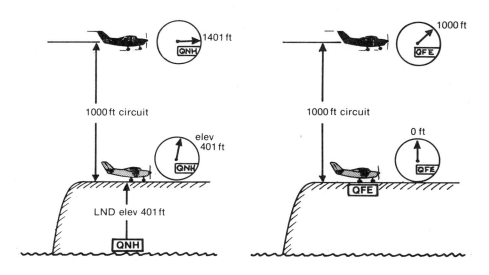

Fig.6-24. Set Aerodrome QNH, or Aerodrome QFE, for Circuit Operations.

2. SET REGIONAL QNH if Cruising Below the Transition Altitude.

Upon reaching cruising altitude 3000 ft, the **Scillies** Regional QNH should be set. Flying so that the altimeter indicates 3000 ft should ensure that the height above mean sea level is 3000 ft or slightly more (since the Regional QNH is always the lowest QNH for the area).

The Regional QNH should be updated as you cross each ASR boundary (shown on aeronautical charts) – in this case passing from the Scillies ASR to the Wessex ASR to the Portland ASR, or whenever the appropriate Regional Pressure Setting is updated by ATC.

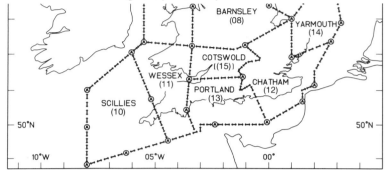

Fig.6-25. Excerpt from the ASR Map.

With Regional QNH set in the subscale, the Pilot can evaluate:
- **Terrain Clearance** – the height of terrain is found from the aeronautical charts;
- **Vertical Separation** from other aircraft.

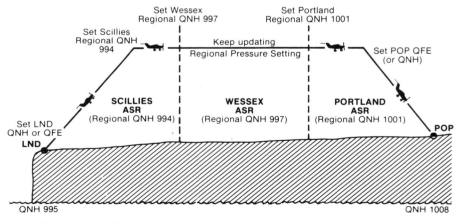

Fig.6-26. Cruising Below Transition Altitude, Set Regional QNH.

NOTE: It is insufficient to assume that errors in horizontal tracking will safeguard you from other traffic in your vicinity operating at or near the same level. Improved tracking aids, such as VOR, Omega, and Inertial Navigation Systems, have made extremely accurate tracking possible.

En Route you may be required, when flying beneath a Terminal Control Area (TMA) or Special Rules Airspace (SRA), to set the QNH of an aerodrome situated beneath that area, to assist in separation from other aeroplanes or to ensure that you do not inadvertently penetrate the Regulated Airspace above you. The Aerodrome QNHs will not differ greatly (if at all) from their Regional QNH.

When transitting a Military Aerodrome Traffic Zone (MATZ) where military aircraft may be operating with QFE set, you may be required to set Aerodrome QFE for separation purposes. Once clear of the MATZ, Regional QNH should be reset on the subscale.

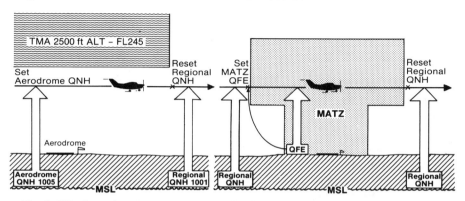

Fig.6-27. Aerodrome (rather than Regional) QNH, or Aerodrome QFE, May Be Required En Route.

3. SET QFE of the Destination Aerodrome, or Aerodrome QNH if preferred, when Approaching the Aerodrome for Landing.

In preparation for joining the circuit, set the aerodrome QFE (or QNH if preferred) for the destination aerodrome as the circuit area is approached. For instance, approaching Popham, you would set QFE 990, or QNH 1008, on the altimeter subscale. (NOTE: In some countries only QNH is used.)

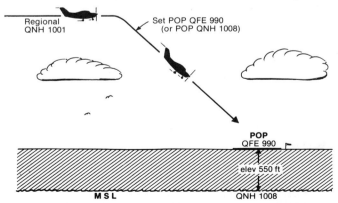

Fig.6-28. Approaching the Circuit, Set Aerodrome QFE (or QNH if preferred).

CRUISING ABOVE THE TRANSITION ALTITUDE

The highest terrain in the United Kingdom is 4406 ft AMSL at Ben Nevis in Scotland, and most of the UK is much lower than this. To avoid the need for continually updating the altimeter setting, it is common practice when flying at levels where terrain is not a problem to set standard pressure 1013 on the subscale. All aeroplanes at these levels, with 1013 set, thereby obtain adequate vertical separation from each other.

The altitude in the climb at which the transition from QNH to 1013 is made is called the Transition Altitude. In the UK, Transition Altitude is generally 3000 ft AMSL. There are some exceptions to this in the vicinity of some major airports, where Transition Altitude may be higher (4000 or 6000 ft AMSL), because traffic density is high and where the high rates of climb and descent of jet aircraft is a consideration.

In other parts of the world where the terrain is much higher, the Transition Altitude is higher. In the United States the Transition Altitude is 18,000 ft; in Papua New Guinea it is 20,000 ft; in Australia it is 10,000 ft.

NOTE: Exceptions, at the time of printing, to the usual UK Transition Altitude of 3000 ft are noted below. You need not remember them, they are included here for interest:
- the London Terminal Control Area, Transition Altitude 6000 ft;
- the Manchester Terminal Control Area, Transition Altitude 4000 ft;
- the Scottish Terminal Control Area, Transition Altitude 6000 ft;
- the Belfast Terminal Control Area, Transition Altitude 4000 ft;
- the Cross-Channel * Special Rules Airspace 4500 ft;
- the Aberdeen * Special Rules Airspace 5000 ft;
- the Leeds and Bradford * Special Rules Airspace 4000 ft;
- the Tees-side * Special Rules Airspace 5000 ft;
- the Honington Military Control Zone 4000 ft.

*3000 ft outside notified hours of operation.

Choice of Altimeter Setting for VFR Flights.

Above the Transition Altitude **outside controlled airspace** VFR flights may cruise with Regional QNH, but it is advisable to use 1013 and cruise on Flight Levels as other aircraft operating on Instrument Flight Rules are required to do so. **In controlled airspace** and above the Transition Altitude, aeroplanes should cruise at Flight Levels (with 1013 set), rather than at altitudes (with QNH set).

THE TRANSITION LAYER.

There would be a possibility of conflict if aircraft cruising at the Transition Altitude were on Regional QNH and aircraft only slightly above it were on the 1013 reference datum. For this reason, there is a layer above the Transition Altitude in which cruising should not occur, to ensure satisfactory vertical separation of at least 500 ft.

In practice, Flight Levels are nominated in 500 ft steps, e.g. FL35, FL40, FL45, FL50, FL55, etc. Since the 1013 mb reference datum may not be at Mean Sea Level, it is possible (indeed most likely) that the actual vertical spacing between a Transition Altitude of 3000 ft and a Transition Level of FL35 will not be 500 ft, as illustrated below.

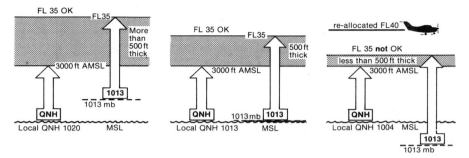

Fig.6-29. Thickness of the Transition Layer Varies with QNH.

As can be seen, the Transition Altitude remains fixed, but the Transition Level moves up or down according to the QNH. If the Regional QNH is less than 1013, FL35 is lower than 3500 ft AMSL and there is less than 500 ft vertical separation between a Transition Altitude of 3000 ft and FL35. So you would need to cruise at FL40 to retain a 500 ft or better vertical separation from an aircraft cruising at 3000 ft on Regional QNH.

If needed, a chart **to convert Altitudes to Flight Levels** (and vice versa) is in the UK Aeronautical Information Publication (AIP RAC 2-4) and is included in the Chapter A3 of Vol.2. of this series. It is also included in Pooley's *Pilots Information Guide.*

To use this chart:
- take a vertical line upwards from the QNH reading along the bottom axis until it meets the appropriate (sloping) Flight Level line; then
- read horizontally across to the equivalent Altitude.

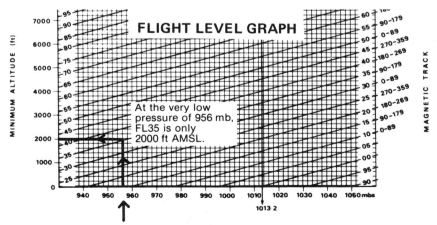

Fig.6-30. Using the Flight Level / Altitude Conversion Chart.

IN SUMMARY.

The **TRANSITION ALTITUDE** is the altitude at, or below which, the vertical position of aircraft is controlled by reference to altitudes, i.e. with Regional QNH set. In the UK, it is usually 3000 ft AMSL.

The **TRANSITION LEVEL** is the Flight Level at, or above which, the vertical position of aircraft is controlled with reference to Flight Levels, i.e. with 1013 set. In the UK, it is usually FL35 (or higher if QNH is less than 1013).

The **TRANSITION LAYER** is the airspace between the Transition Altitude and the Transition Level. It varies in thickness, depending upon the Regional QNH.

SELECTION OF CRUISING LEVELS.

As a Student Pilot, or a basic-PPL holder (i.e. no IMC or Instrument Rating), you will be restricted to flying under Visual Flight Rules (VFR) and as such should always be clear of cloud, satisfy minimum visibility requirements and be in sight of the ground if below 3000 ft AMSL.

It is not mandatory for VFR flights to cruise at any particular altitude or Flight Level, but it is **recommended** (in the UK Aeronautical Information Publication) that VFR flights adopt the IFR cruising level system, known as the Quadrantal Rule, if cruising above the Transition Altitude.

MAGNETIC TRACK	CRUISING FLIGHT LEVEL
000°M to 089°M	FLs in **odd thousands of feet;** FL30, 50, 70, etc.
090°M to 179°M	FLs in **odd thousands plus 500;** FL35, 55, 75, etc.
180°M to 269°M	FLs in **even thousands;** FL40, 60, 80, etc.
270°M to 359°M	FLs in **even thousands plus 500;** FL85, etc.

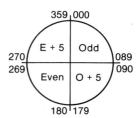

Fig.6-31. The Quadrantal Rule, (advisable to follow, but not mandatory if VFR and outside controlled airspace).

☐ **Exercises 6 — Vertical Nav-5.**

MINIMUM SAFE ALTITUDE, OR SAFETY HEIGHT

Where possible, on a cross-country sortie choose a suitable cruising level that will ensure adequate terrain clearance and vertical separation from other aircraft. The best technique is to:
- determine a **Minimum Safe Altitude** which will ensure adequate terrain clearance; and then
- select an appropriate cruising level, (conforming with the quadrantal rule above 3000 ft AMSL, if applicable).

NOTE: In certain circumstances it may not always be possible to cruise above the calculated minimum safe altitude; for example, due to overlying controlled airspace around a major airport. In such cases extra care to avoid terrain and obstructions should be taken, particularly in minimum visibility, until it is possible to climb above the Minimum Safe Altitude.

To determine a Minimum Safe Altitude or *Safety Height:*
- determine the highest obstacle en route to a set amount either side of track; then:
- add a safety clearance height above this.

There are no hard and fast rules as to how far either side of track you should consider, or how high above obstacles you should fly. Reasonable values are 1000 ft or 1500 ft above the highest obstacle within 5 nm or 10 nm either side of track. This allows for navigational errors. On long tracks or over mountainous areas such as North Wales, 15 or 20 nm might be more appropriate.

To assist you in determining the highest obstacle, it is a good idea to mark in lines 5 nm (or 10 nm) either side of track. Another approach to finding a reasonable extra height to add is to add 10% of the elevation of the highest obstacle plus a further 1500 ft.

Example 16: Elevation of highest obstacle within 5 nm of track is 438 ft AMSL, and within 10 nm it is 798 ft.

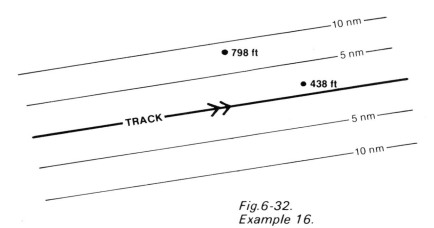

Fig.6-32.
Example 16.

If you decide to use 1000 ft clearance within 5 nm of track, then the Minimum Safe Altitude is 1438 ft, say 1500 ft.

If you decide to use 1000 ft clearance within 10 nm of track, then the Minimum Safe Altitude is 1798 ft, say 1800 ft.

If you decide to use 1500 ft clearance within 10 nm of track, then the Minimum Safe Altitude is 2298 ft, say 2300 ft.

If you decide to use 10% plus 1500 ft clearance within 10 nm of track, then the Minimum Safe Altitude is:

additional height as a safety buffer = 80 (10% of 800) + 1500
= 1580 ft, say 1600 ft.

Minimum Safe Altitude = obstacle 800 ft + safety buffer 1600 ft = 2400 ft.

If you remain above your calculated Minimum Safe Altitude, there should be sufficient buffer to absorb any indication errors in the altimeter (position, instrument and temperature errors) and to stay out of any turbulent areas near the ground, where a downdraft or windshear could be dangerous. In certain circumstances (such as in standing waves downwind of mountain ridges), it may be advisable to add rather more than 10% plus 1500 ft to give sufficient safety margin.

Determining your own Minimum Safe Altitude is a point of airmanship (commonsense). Your Flying Instructor will advise what technique he or she wishes you to use in calculating Minimum Safe Altitudes.

Example 17: Calculate the lowest cruising level, according to the Quadrantal Rule, that will ensure a terrain clearance of 1000 ft within 10 nm of track.

Highest obstacle within area of possible navigation error = 2117 ft.
Track to be flown 177°T.
VAR 6°W.
Regional QNH 1006 mb.
Transition Altitude 3000 ft.

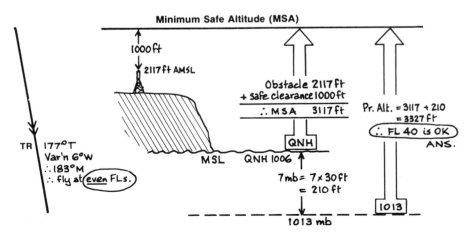

Fig. 6-33. Example 17.

Example 18: Calculate the lowest cruising level, according to the Quadrantal Rule, that will ensure a terrain clearance of 10% of the highest obstacle plus 1500 ft in the above case.

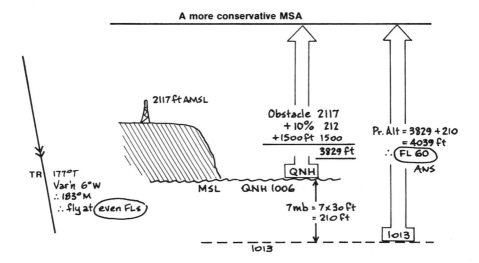

Fig.6-34. Example 18 – Ans: 183M, MSA 4039 ft, FL60.

☐ **Exercises 6 — Vertical Nav-6.**

THE EFFECT OF TEMPERATURE VARIATIONS

So far we have only considered **pressure variations** from the International Standard Atmosphere. **Temperature variations from ISA** play a role not only in Vertical Navigation and Altimetry, but also in **Aeroplane Performance** (covered fully in Vol.4). ISA MSL temperature is +15°C, and the Temperature Lapse Rate is 2°C/1000 ft (decrease with altitude).

PRESSURE ALTITUDES	I.S.A. TEMPERATURES
above 36,000 ft ········	constant at −57°C
36,000 ft ········	−57°C: ISA = +15 − (2 x 36) = +15 − 72 = −57°C
20,000 ft ········	−25°C: ISA = +15 − (2 x 40) = +15 − 40 = −25°C
3,000 ft ·········	+ 9°C: ISA = +15 − (2 x 3) = +15 − 6 = + 9°C
2,000 ft ·········	+11°C: ISA = +15 − (2 x 2) = +15 − 4 = +11°C
1,000 ft ·········	+13°C: ISA = +15 − 2 = +13°C
····· M S L 1013 mb(hPa)	+15°C ·····

Fig.6-35. Temperature Structure in the ISA.

TEMPERATURE DEVIATION FROM ISA.

Suppose that in the actual atmosphere that exists right here and now, the temperature at 2000 ft is, not +11°C as in the ISA, but +16°C, i.e. it is 5°C warmer than in the ISA. This can be expressed as +16°C, a straight out temperature, or as a deviation from the ISA, which in this case is ISA+5. In Aviation it is common practice to use this ISA deviation means of describing temperature.

Example 19: Express –10°C at FL80 as a deviation from the ISA.

At FL 80, i.e. Pr. Alt. 8000 ft ISA = +15 – (2 x 8)
= +15 – 16
= –1°C

Now –10°C is colder than –1°C by 9°C,
and this is expressed as ISA-9 (ANS).

IN COLD AIR, THE ALTIMETER OVER-READS.

The altimeter is basically only a barometer which converts pressure measurements to altitude. It is calibrated according to the International Standard Atmosphere. On a cold day when the air is more dense, various pressure levels at altitude will be lower than on a warm day.

The 913 mb pressure level that equates with a pressure altitude of 3000 ft in the International Standard Atmosphere may be at only 2900 ft. The altimeter, however, because it is calibrated according to the ISA, will indicate this as 3000 ft even though the aeroplane is at 2900 ft. On a day that is warmer than ISA, when the altimeter indicates 3000 ft, the aeroplane may in fact be slightly higher.

This is not significant for separation between aircraft, since all altimeters will be affected identically. It is important for terrain separation, however, so when flying from a high to a low temperature, beware below, because the altimeter will read too high.

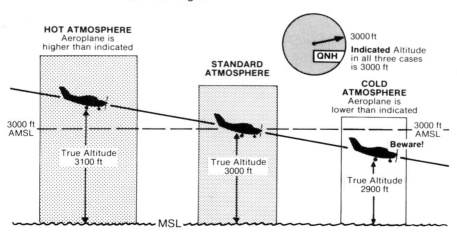

Fig.6-36. When Flying from High to Low Temperature, Beware Below! (same rule as for Pressure).

DENSITY ALTITUDE (or DENSITY HEIGHT).

Density is the mass per unit volume, or if you like, the number of molecules in each unit volume, and is affected directly by variations in Temperature. **Aeroplane Performance** (the speed at which it can fly, and the height to which it can climb) depends, among a number of factors, mainly upon the ambient **Air Density** (denoted by the Greek letter *Rho*). Consequently it is important to be able to calculate **Density Altitude.**

Density Altitude is the atmospheric density expressed in terms of altitude in the International Standard Atmosphere which corresponds to that density.

If, for example, at 1000 ft AMSL in the actual atmosphere the density is the same as the density at 2400 ft in the ISA, i.e. our altitude is 1000 ft AMSL but our density altitude is 2400 ft, the aircraft and engines will perform as if the aeroplane were at 2400 ft.

How To Calculate Density Altitude.

It is impractical for a Pilot to have the equipment necessary to measure air density, so we make use of two pieces of information already available and upon which density depends – **Pressure Altitude** and **Temperature.**

Density Altitude can be calculated by three means:

1. By correcting Pressure Altitude for ISA temperature deviation by 120 ft per 1°C.

2. Graphically, as is done in most Aeroplane Performance Charts, on which both Pressure Altitude and Temperature are the criteria used in entering the graph. Even though Density Altitude itself may not be specified, it is implied by these other two parameters.

3. By using your Navigation Computer.

Example 20: Calculate the Density Altitude at **Huddersfield (Crosland Moor)**, elevation 825 ft, if the current QNH is 999, and the OAT (Outside Air Temperature) +28°C.

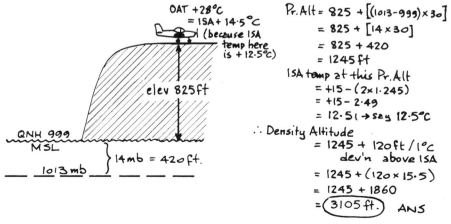

Fig.6-37. Example 20: PA 1245 ft, DA 3105 ft.

NOTE: Even though the aircraft is at less than 1000 ft AMSL, the engines will perform, and the aircraft will fly, as if it were at about 3000 ft in the International Standard Atmosphere, i.e. it will have a much poorer performance. As a good Pilot you should **be aware of poor performance when hot and high.**

Example 21: Calculate the Density Altitude of **Shoreham,** Elevation 6 ft, QNH 1031 mb, OAT –2°C.

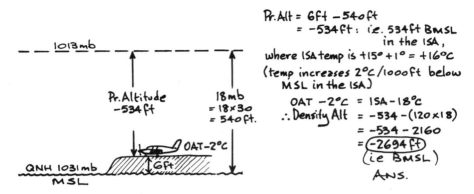

Pr. Alt = 6ft – 540ft
= –534 ft: i.e. 534ft BMSL
in the ISA,
where ISA temp is +15° +1° = +16°C
(temp increases 2°C/1000ft below
MSL in the ISA)
OAT –2°C = ISA – 18°C
∴ Density Alt = –534 – (120 × 18)
= –534 – 2160
= –2694 ft
(i.e. BMSL)
ANS.

Fig.6-38. Example 21: PA –534 ft, DA –2694, i.e. BMSL.

NOTE: A high QNH (i.e. high air pressure) increases density as does the low temperature, with the temperature usually being the critical factor to watch out for. In this particular case of a low aerodrome elevation and a low temperature at Shoreham, we would expect the engines and the aeroplane to perform very well.

Any graph or table in an Aeroplane Performance or Flight Manual that has both **Pressure Altitude** and **Temperature** on it means, in fact, that **Density Height is being allowed for,** and will therefore not have to be calculated directly as above or by computer.

☐ Now, finally for this chapter, complete **Exercises 6 — Vertical Nav-7.**

7

TIME

Time is of great importance to the Air Navigator, and the clock is one of the basic instruments used in the cockpit.

Time enables the Pilot to:
- regulate affairs on board the aeroplane;
- measure the progress of a flight;
- anticipate arrival time at certain positions;
- calculate a safe endurance for flight;
- estimate when weather conditions at the destination are likely to improve; measure rest periods between flights;

.... and so on.

Time is also used to measure the Earth's rotation.

We relate the rotation of our planet Earth to the position of celestial or heavenly bodies, such as the Sun and other stars. By using *Time* we can specify the beginning of Day, Sunrise, Noon, Sunset, commencement of Night, Midnight, Moonrise, Moonset, and so on.

To all navigators – land, sea and air – **time is of vital importance** – and is a subject that must be mastered.

MOTION OF THE EARTH.

To measure the passage of time, we need to relate it to some repetitive event. For our ancestors, and indeed for us, a suitable recurring event is the apparent passage of the Sun across our skies – its highest point in the sky simply indicated by the shadows that it casts being shortest. The Sun appears to cross our skies once in every **day.**

On a longer time scale, we notice the regular passage of the seasons – Spring, Summer, Autumn and Winter – a complete cycle of these being called **one year.**

The **Sun** has been used as a simple clock for thousands of years. Whereas early man thought that it was the Sun which moved around the Earth, we now know that this is not the case. It is, in fact, the rotation of the Earth on its axis that causes the appearance of the Sun travelling across across our skies each day, hence the term *apparent passage of the Sun.*

As man's knowledge increased it was realised that **one day is the approximate time span of one revolution of the Earth on its own axis**
....

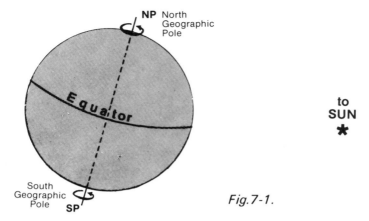

Fig. 7-1.

.... and that **one Year is the approximate time span of one complete orbit of the Earth about the Sun.**

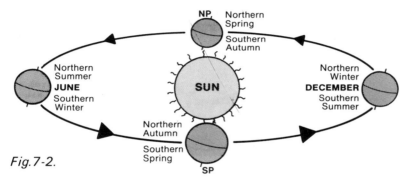

Fig. 7-2.

There is a third fundamental type of Time apart from:
- the rotation of the Earth about its own axis; and
- the orbitting of the Earth around the Sun.

It is:
- Atomic time, whereby atomic vibrations, such as those occurring at very short time intervals in quartz crystals, are used to define the International Atomic Second and calibrate clocks extremely accurately. As this was endorsed internationally only as recently as 1971 you can see that the subject of *time* is still not a closed book. In fact, only in 1985 was the international basis for standard time changed from Greenwich Mean Time (GMT) to Co-ordinated Universal Time (UTC).

Each Day is divided into 24 hours, each hour further divided into 60 equal minutes, and each of these minutes further divided into 60 equal seconds.

To complete one orbit of the Sun, the Earth takes about 365 and ¼ solar days. It is convenient to have a whole number of days in a year, and so we define the Civil Year as 365 days. At the end of each 4 years, when the extra ¼ day each year adds up to one whole day, the extra day is added in to give a **Leap Year** of 366 days. This keeps the calendar reasonably in step with the seasons.

THE MEASUREMENT OF TIME and HOW IT IS EXPRESSED.

To measure time, use is again made of a repetitive event, such as the swinging of a pendulum, or the atomic vibrations within a quartz crystal, to design clocks which measure the hours, minutes and seconds.

Each Day is divided into 24 hours, which begins at midnight (00 hours 00 minutes), and proceeds through midday (1200) to midnight (2400), at which instant the next day begins (0000).

The hours are numbered from 00 hours to 24 hours (rather than 0 to 12 am and 0 to 12 pm), and the 60 minutes of each hour are numbered from 00 min to 59 min. The term *am* means *ante-meridiem,* in the sense that the Sun has yet to pass over your meridian of longitude, i.e. it is still morning; *pm* means *post-meridiem*, the Sun having passed overhead and the time being after noon.

For Flight Planning and Navigation purposes we usually do not refer to the year or the month, but only the **day** of the month as the **date**, followed by the **time** in **hours and minutes.** As most air navigation occurs within a few hours, and only rarely in excess of 30 hours, we can be reasonably confident of which year and month we are talking about, and so there is no need to specify them.

Seconds, which are 1/60 of a minute, are usually too short a time interval for us to be concerned with in practical navigation, hence **it is usual to express date/time as a six figure date/time group.**

Example 1: Express 13th of September, 1986, 10.35 am as a six-figure date/time group.

date	time		
13	10	35	or ANS: 131035
	hr	min	

Example 2: Express 3.21 pm on March 17th, 1987, as a six-figure date/time group.

3.21 pm = 1200 noon
+ 321

1521 on the 24 hr clock   ANS: 171521

In the Six-Figure Date/Time Group:
- The **Date** is a two-figure group for the day of the month from 00 to 31, and is followed by:
- The **Time**, written as a four-figure group on a 24 hour clock – the first two figures representing the **hours** from 00 to 24, and the last two figures representing the **minutes** from 00 through to 59.

To specify the **month**, the six-figure date/time group is preceded by two figures representing the month, and so is expanded into an eight figure time-group. This is often used in NOTAMs (Notices to Airmen).

Example 3: 5.45 pm on September 30th may be written as:
SEP 30 17 45
or 09 30 17 45
or 09301745

In the **eight-figure date/time group**:
- the first two numbers refer to month;
- the second two numbers refer to the date; and
- the last four numbers refer to the time.

☐ Now complete **Exercises 7 — Time-1**.

The RELATIONSHIP between LONGITUDE and TIME.

Fig.7-3.

In one day, the Earth makes one complete rotation of 360° with respect to the chosen celestial body, which is the *'Mean Sun'*. The time of day is a measure of this rotation and indicates how much of that day has elapsed or, in other words, how much of a rotation has been completed. As observers on the Earth, we do not feel its rotation upon its own axis, but rather we see the Sun apparently move around the Earth. In one mean solar day the Sun will appear to have travelled the full 360° of longitude around the Earth.

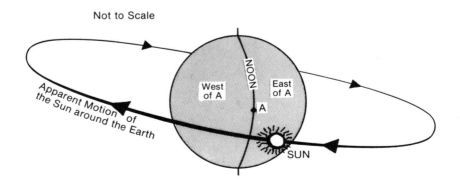

Fig.7-4. Apparent Motion of the Sun Around the Earth.

The angular difference between different longitudes is known as **arc of longitude** and has a direct relationship with Time.

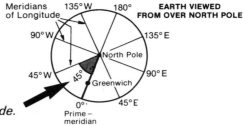

Fig.7-5. Arc of Longitude.

The **arc of longitude** in degrees and minutes of arc is related to the **time interval** in hours and minutes as shown below.

ARC	TIME	
360°	24 hours	: divide by 24
15°	1 hour	: divide by 15
1°	4 minutes	: divide by 4
15′	1 minute	: divide by 15.
1′	4 seconds	

To Convert TIME to ARC:

1. Multiply the hours by 15 to obtain degrees; (1 hr = 15° arc of longitude.)
2. Divide the minutes of time by 4 to obtain degrees (1 min of time = $\frac{1}{4}$° or 15′ arc) and then multiply the remaining minutes of time by 15 to obtain minutes of arc.

Example 4: Convert 9 hr 23 min to arc units.

- 9 hr x 15 = 135°; as 1 hr = 15°
- 23 min / 4 = 5°; as 4 min = 1°
  and the remaining 3 mins of time x 15 = 45′ of arc,
  as 1 min = 15′.

  Adding these, we get 140° 45′.

There is a table in the **Air Almanac** (a book containing, among many other astronomical items, daylight and darkness data), which allows rapid conversion of Arc to Time, and vice versa, thereby avoiding the above calculation. Private Pilots do not require the Air Almanac.

To Convert ARC to TIME:

1. Divide the degrees by 15 to obtain hours, and multiply the remaining degrees by 4 to obtain minutes of time.
2. Divide the minutes of arc by 15 to obtain minutes of time, and multiply the remainder by 4 to obtain seconds of time.

Example 5: Convert 140° 49′ of arc of longitude to time units.

- 140 / 15 = 9 hr, with 5 left over x 4 = 20 min of time, i.e. 140° of arc = 9 hr 20 min.
- 49′ / 15 = 3 min of time, with 4 left over x 4 = 16 sec of time.
- Adding these: 140°49′ = 9 hr 23 min 16 sec (ANS)

□ Now complete **Exercises 7 — Time-2.**

LOCAL TIME.

Time is a measure of the rotation of the Earth, and any given time interval can be represented by a corresponding angle through which the Earth turns. Suppose that the Sun (the celestial reference point) is directly overhead, i.e. it is noon. For every point along that same meridian of longitude, the Sun will be at its highest point in the sky for that day.

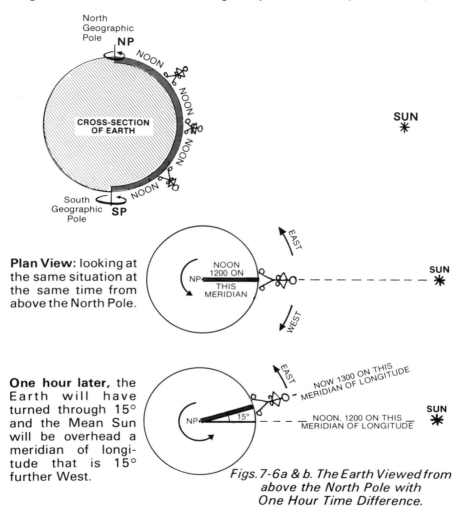

Plan View: looking at the same situation at the same time from above the North Pole.

One hour later, the Earth will have turned through 15° and the Mean Sun will be overhead a meridian of longitude that is 15° further West.

Figs. 7-6a & b. The Earth Viewed from above the North Pole with One Hour Time Difference.

Meridians of Longitude further East are Ahead in Local Time; Meridians of Longitude further West are Behind in Local Time.

Example 6: Place A is 45° of longitude West of Place B. How much earlier or later will noon occur at A compared to B?

45° arc of longitude = 3 hours, and because A is to the West of B, noon will occur **three hours later** at A.

LOCAL MEAN TIME - LMT.

LMT uses the Sun as its celestial reference point, and the local meridian of longitude as its terrestrial (earthly) reference point. Therefore, **all points along the same meridian of longitude will have the same Local Mean Time.**

The Local Mean Time along one meridian of longitude will differ to the Local Mean Time along another meridian of longitude, and this difference will equal the difference (or change) in longitude expressed in time units. **The further East the place is, the further ahead it is in LMT.**

Example 7: If it is noon LMT in Kingston upon Hull (00° 20′ W longitude) with the Sun passing over the 00° 20′ W meridian of longitude, how much earlier or later will it be noon LMT in Blackpool (3°W longitude)?

Kingston upon Hull longitude: 00° 20′ W
Blackpool longitude: 03° 00′ W
difference, or change, of longitude = 02° 40′
which, in time units, is:
2° = 8 mins (as 1° = 4 mins of time)
40′ = 2 min 40 sec (as 1′ = 40 sec of time)
therefore 2°40′ = 10 min 40 sec of time.

Because Blackpool is to the West of Kingston upon Hull, noon at Blackpool with the Sun passing over its meridian will be 10 minutes 40 seconds later than at Kingston upon Hull.

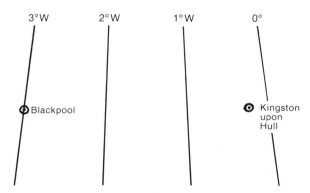

Fig. 7-7. Example 7.

In Air Navigation, the main use of Local Mean Time (LMT) is in extracting data from tables in the Air Almanac on the rising and setting of celestial bodies such as the Sun, Moon and Stars. We can use these tables to determine Sunrise, Sunset, Twilight and so on.

CO-ORDINATED UNIVERSAL TIME (UTC) —
(formerly Greenwich Mean Time).

UTC is the local Mean Time at the meridian of longitude that runs through the observatory at Greenwich, near London. The Greenwich meridian is longitude 0, also known as the **Prime Meridian.** Until recently the international time standard was the well known *Greenwich Mean Time*

(GMT), but this term has now been replaced by **Co-ordinated Universal Time (UTC).** UTC has a more academic definition and is slightly more precise than GMT.

UTC is a *'universal time',* and all aeronautical communications around the world are expressed in UTC. For this reason, Pilots need to be able to convert quickly and accurately from their Local Time to UTC, and vice versa.

Meridians to the East are *ahead* in time, thus:
Longitude East, Universal Least.

Meridians to the West are *behind* in time:
Longitude West, Universal Best.

Example 8: If it is 231531 LMT on the 150°E meridian of longitude running through Sydney, Australia, what is the time in UTC (i.e. in the UK on the Greenwich meridian)?

150° = 10 hours, as 15° of arc = 1 hour
and *'Longitude East, Universal Least'.*

23 15 31 LMT	at 150°E.
– 10 00	arc to time
23 05 31 UTC	(ANS).

NOTE: Australian Eastern Standard Time is based on the 150°E Longitude, which is 10 hours ahead of UTC. Standard Time in Vancouver, British Columbia, Canada, is based on 120°W Longitude and is therefore 8 hours behind UTC.

Example 9: If it is 282340 on the 138°15'W meridian of longitude, express this LMT in Co-ordinated Universal Time (UTC).

Converting arc to time: 138°15' = 9 hr 13 min.
and: *'Longitude West, Universal Best'.*

28 23 40 LMT	at 138°15'W
+ 9 13	arc to time
28 32 53	and of course 32 hr = 1 day + 8 hr
29 08 53 UTC	(ANS)

Example 10: Convert 300825 UTC to LMT at the 138°15'W Meridian.

138°15' = 9 hr 13 min
Longitude West, UTC Best

30 08 25 UTC		
– 9 13	arc to time	9 from 32 (24 + 8),
(ANS) 29 23 12 LMT	at 138°15'W	and carry 1 over into *days* column.

□ Now complete **Exercises 7 — Time-3.**

ZONE TIME.

Obviously Local Mean Time (LMT) is not practical in day to day life, because every different meridian of longitude has its own LMT. When ships are at sea they set their clocks to the LMT of the nearest meridian divisible by 15 (which means that, as 15 degrees = 1 hour, these times will differ from UTC by a whole number of hours).

Even though the ship may not be precisely on that meridian, it means that its clocks will be set to read the same time as the clocks of all the ships in that area or **zone**, and they will not be too far out of step with the Sun – noon at the ship's actual meridian occurring at, or close to, 1200 zone time.

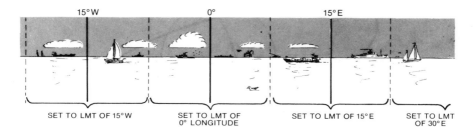

Fig. 7-8. Ships at Sea Set Their Clocks According to the Local Time Zone.

For example, a ship at longitude 145°27′E, when considered in proximity to the nearest meridian divisible by 15, is closest to the 150°E meridian of longitude. It would therefore set the LMT at 150°E on its clocks, and as this Zone Time differs from UTC by (150/15 =) 10 hours, and (longitude *East, Universal Least*) UTC will be 10 hours behind this.

The 150°E Zone is called 'Zone minus 10' because:
- the zone meridian is divisible by fifteen 10 times, and:
- minus 10, because you need to subtract 10 from this Zone Time to obtain UTC (remembering that East longitudes are ahead in time).

Zone Times are not widely used in aviation.

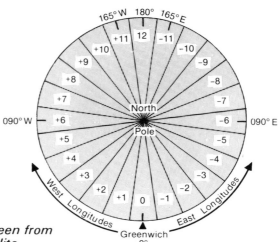

Fig. 7-9. Longitudes as seen from a North Polar Satellite.

THE DATE LINE.

Suppose that the time at the Greenwich meridian is 26 12 00 LMT (i.e. 26 12 00 UTC). Now, if you instantaneously travel **eastwards** from Greenwich to the 180° **East** meridian, the Local Mean Time there is 12 hours ahead of the LMT at Greenwich, that is 26 24 00 LMT at 180°E, or midnight on the 26th LMT at 180°E.

If, however, you travel **westwards** from Greenwich to the 180° **West** meridian, then the time there is 12 hours behind Greenwich, i.e. 26 00 00 or, as it is usually written, 25 24 00 LMT at 180°W, midnight on the 25th. Note that the time is midnight in both cases but, on one side of the 180° meridian it is midnight on the 25th, and on the other side it is midnight on the 26th.

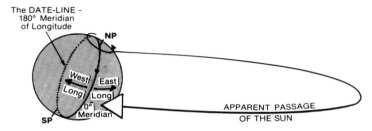

Fig.7-10. The 'Date Line' Runs Basically Along the 180° Meridian.

The 180°E and 180°W meridians are of course the one and the same meridian, the anti-meridian to Greenwich, and we have the situation of it being midnight in its vicinity, but on different dates depending upon which side of the 180° meridian that you are on. Making a complete trip around the world, you would lose a day travelling westwards or gain a day travelling eastwards.

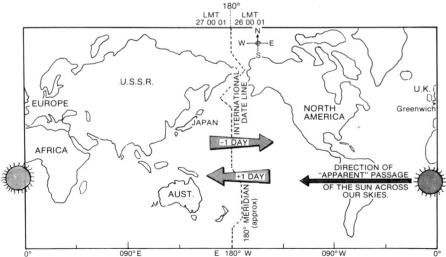

Fig.7-11. Crossing the Date Line Travelling Eastwards – Subtract One Day; Travelling Westwards – Add One Day.

To prevent the date being in error and to provide a starting point for each day, **a Date Line has been fixed by international agreement,** and it basically follows the 180° meridian of longitude, with minor excursions to keep groups of islands together. Crossing the Date Line, you alter the date by one day – in effect changing your time by 24 hours to compensate for the slow change during your journey around the world.

STANDARD TIMES or LOCAL TIMES.

Standard Times operate in a similar fashion to Zone Times in that all clocks in a given geographical area are set to the LMT of a given standard meridian. This is known as **Standard Time** or **Local Time** (not to be confused with Local Mean Time) for that area.

Standard time in the UK is based on the Greenwich Meridian. In other words, 1545 Standard Time in the UK is also 1545 UTC. Standard Time in West Germany is based on the 15°E meridian of longitude, and so is 1 hour ahead of the UK. At 1545 UTC, the time in London is 1545, and in Hamburg it is 1645 West German Standard Time. In Tokyo, which is 9 hours ahead of UTC, it is 2445, i.e. 0045 Japanese Standard Time the next morning.

When involved in flights between different time zones, it is easiest to work entirely in UTC and convert the answer at the end.

Example 11: You depart Prestwick in Scotland on a flight of 3 hours 40 minutes duration to Bremen in West Germany at 0945 UK Standard Time, i.e. 0945 UTC. At what time should your German friends meet you in Bremen?

Departure Prestwick: 09 45 UTC
        Flight Time: 3 40
_____

    ETA Bremen: 13 25 UTC
    arc to time: +1 00   (to convert British to
_____ West German Time)
14 25 MEZ (West German Standard Time).
_____

☐ **Exercises 7 — Time-4.**

LIGHT FROM THE SUN.

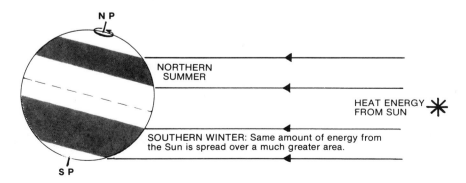

NP

NORTHERN SUMMER

HEAT ENERGY FROM SUN

SOUTHERN WINTER: Same amount of energy from the Sun is spread over a much greater area.

SP

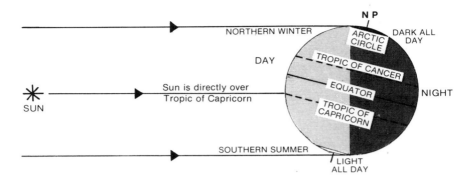

Figs.7-12a & b. The Sun Does Not Shine Evenly on the Earth.

Sunrise occurs when the upper limb of the Sun (the first part visible) is on the visible horizon and **Sunset** occurs when the upper limb of the Sun (the last part visible) is just disappearing below the visible horizon. **Sunlight** occurs between sunrise and sunset.

As we have all observed when waking early (to continue our aeronautical studies), it starts to become light well before the Sun actually rises, and it stays light until well after the Sun has set. This period of incomplete light, or if you like, incomplete darkness, is called **Twilight**, and the period from the start of morning twilight until the end of evening twilight is called **Daylight.**

In the tropics the Sun rises and sets at almost 90° to the horizon, which makes the period of twilight quite short, and the onset of daylight or night quite dramatically rapid.

In the higher latitudes, towards the North and South poles, the Sun rises and sets at a more oblique angle to the horizon, consequently the period of twilight is much longer and the onset of daylight or darkness far more gradual than in the tropics.

At certain times of the year inside the arctic and antarctic circles, the period of twilight occurs without the Sun actually rising above the horizon at all during the day. This is the winter situation.

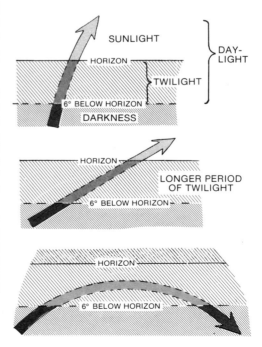

Figs.7-13a, b & c.

Whilst to an observer at sea level the Sun may appear to have set and the Earth is no longer bathed in sunlight, an aeroplane directly overhead may still have the Sun shining on it. In other words, the time at which the Sun rises or sets will depend upon the altitude of the observer.

In fact it is possible to take-off after sunset at ground level and climb to an altitude where the Sun appears to rise again and shine a little longer on the aeroplane. This is especially noticeable in polar regions when the Sun might be just below the horizon, as seen from sea level, for long periods of time (twilight).

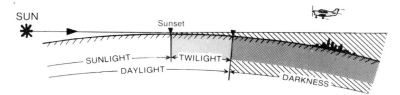

Fig.7-14. An Aeroplane Can Be in Sight of the Sun After It Has Set on the Earth Below.

It is easy to be deceived by brightness at altitude only to find a few minutes later after a descent to near ground level, and possibly under some cloud cover, that it has become very dark. High ground to the West of the aerodrome will also reduce the amount of light from the Sun reaching the vicinity of the aerodrome as night approaches. (An important point to remember when flying!)

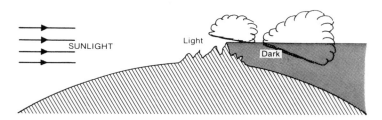

Fig.7-15. Local Sunrise and Sunset is Affected by Terrain.

The times at which Sunrise and Sunset occur depend upon two things:

1. The **Date:** In summer Sunrise is earlier and Sunset later, i.e. the daylight hours are longer in summer. The reverse occurs in winter.

2. The **Latitude:** In the northern summer for instance, place B in the figure below is experiencing Sunrise whilst place A is already well into the day, and it is still night at place C, yet all are on the same meridian of longitude. Because of this they all have the same Local Mean Time (LMT), but are experiencing quite different conditions of daylight due to being on **different latitudes.**

137

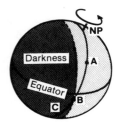

Fig.7-16. Places A, B & C, although on the same Meridian, Experience Different Sunrise and Sunset Times due to being on Different Latitudes.

The Local Mean Time of Sunrise and Sunset on a Particular Date Depends upon Latitude.

The **Air Almanac** (a bi-annual publication of HMSO) contains tables that give Local Mean Time for the occurrence of Sunrise and Sunset at ground level. (The Air Almanac also contains tables for Morning and Evening Civil Twilight, but these are of no significance to Air Navigation in the UK.)

The Local Standard Time of Sunrise and Sunset depends further on the Longitude of the Place.

Sunrise at places on a particular latitude occurs at the same Local **Mean** Time at each place but different places on the same latitude will have a different Local **Standard** Time for the event, **depending on their longitude**. The same applies to Sunset.

Fishguard in Wales and **Ipswich** in Suffolk are both on the same latitude (52°N) but, because their *arc of longitude* difference is 6° (5°W to 1°E), the Sun will rise 6/15 of an hour (24 minutes) earlier at Ipswich than Fishguard, and it will set the same amount later in Fishguard than Ipswich **on Local Standard Time** – be it UTC or, in summer, British Summer Time (BST). Also, the Sun will rise 1/15 of an hour earlier at Ipswich than Greenwich – 4 minutes.

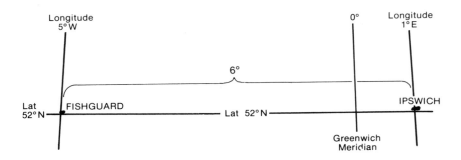

Fig.7-17. Fishguard and Ipswich experience Sunset at the same LMT, but at different Local Standard Times (UTC or BST).

The Local Mean Time for the event (e.g. Sunrise or Sunset), extracted from the Air Almanac tables, is therefore corrected for arc of longitude East or West of the standard meridian – which, in the case of the UK, is (very conveniently) the Greenwich (0°) meridian – to give Local Standard Time.

Fortunately it is not necessary for a Pilot to purchase an Air Almanac every six months because Sunrise and Sunset times are available from ATS Units and Met Offices throughout the UK. These times are already corrected from LMT to UTC or BST, as appropriate, so they can be used with no further conversion needed.

For smaller places the precise times may not be available, so interpolation between localities either side may be necessary to give a good estimate within a few minutes. Common sense dictates to err on the conservative side, especially for sunset.

Sunrise/Sunset tables are published in *Pooley's Flight Guide*.

SUNRISE-SUNSET TABLES

All times are **local**, allowances have been made for British Summer Time — 30 March to 25 October.

		Jersey	London	Cardiff	Manchester	Dublin	Newcastle
Jan	5	0803 1626	0806 1607	0818 1619	0824 1605	0840 1621	0831 1554
	11	0801 1633	0803 1614	0815 1626	0820 1613	0836 1629	0827 1603
	17	0757 1641	0759 1624	0811 1636	0816 1623	0832 1639	0821 1614
	23	0752 1650	0752 1634	0804 1646	0809 1633	0825 1649	0813 1625
	29	0744 1700	0745 1645	0757 1657	0800 1654	0816 1701	0804 1636
Feb	4	0736 1711	0735 1655	0747 1707	0750 1657	0806 1713	0753 1650
	10	0727 1722	0725 1706	0737 1718	0738 1709	0754 1725	0741 1702
	16	0717 1732	0714 1717	0726 1729	0727 1720	0743 1736	0728 1715
	22	0706 1741	0702 1728	0714 1740	0714 1732	0703 1748	0715 1727
	28	0655 1750	0650 1739	0702 1751	0700 1744	0716 1800	0702 1739
Mar	6	0642 1800	0637 1749	0649 1801	0647 1755	0703 1811	0647 1752
	12	0630 1809	0623 1759	0635 1811	0633 1806	0649 1822	0632 1803
	18	0617 1818	0610 1810	0622 1822	0618 1818	0634 1834	0616 1816
	24	0604 1828	0556 1820	0608 1832	0603 1829	0619 1845	0600 1828
	30	0652 1937	0642 1931	0654 1943	0648 1940	0704 1956	0645 1940
Apr	5	0639 1945	0628 1940	0640 1952	0634 1951	0650 2007	0630 1951
	11	0627 1954	0615 1950	0627 2002	0620 2002	0636 2018	0615 2003
	17	0615 2003	0602 2000	0614 2012	0606 2013	0622 2029	0601 2015
	23	0603 2013	0549 2011	0601 2023	0552 2024	0608 2040	0546 2026
	29	0552 2021	0537 2021	0549 2033	0539 2035	0555 2051	0533 2037
May	5	0542 2030	0527 2030	0539 2042	0527 2045	0542	519 2049
	11	0533 2039	0516 2039	0528 2051	0516 2056		509 2101
	17	0524 2047	0507 2049	0519 2101	0506 21		0457 2111
	23	0517 2053	0459 2057	0511 2109	0457		0447 2121
	29	0512 2102	0452 2105	0504 2117			0439 2130
June	4	0507 2108	0447 2112	0459 2124			0433 2139
	10	0505 2113	0444 2117	0456 2129		2146	0429 2144
	16	0504 2116	0443 2120	0455 2132		0457 2152	0427 2148
	22	0505 2117	0444 2122	0456 2134	0439 2142	0455 2156	0427 2150
	28	0507 2117	0446 2122	0458 2134	0442 2142	0458 2158	0429 2150
July	4	0510 2116	0450 2120	0502 2132	0445 2140	0501 2156	0434 2148
	10	0515 2113	0455 2117	0507 2129	0451 2135	0507 2151	0440 2143
	16	0522 2108	0502 2111	0514 2123	0459 2129	0515 2145	0447 2136
	22	0528 2102	0510 2104	0522 2116	0508 2122	0524 2138	0456 2127
	28	0535 2055	0518 2056	0530 2108	0517 2113	0533 2129	0508 2118

SAMPLE ONLY Not to be used in conjunction with Flight Operations or Flight Planning

Fig.7-18. Sample Excerpt of the Sunrise/Sunset Tables in Pooley's Flight Guide.

Flight Operations of light aircraft in the UK, especially by Pilots without a Night rating, are closely geared to the times of Sunrise and Sunset. The earliest time at which a basic-PPL holder can legally fly with passengers is Sunrise minus 30 mins, and he or she must be on the ground again no later than Sunset plus 30 mins, irrespective of the length of twilight time. (This stems from the ANO definition of **Night,** which commences at Sunset plus 30 mins and ends at Sunrise minus 30 mins, both times being taken at surface level.)

NOTE: Good airmanship may dictate to use an earlier time than SS+30 when planning a flight, if, for example, the destination aerodrome has high ground to the West of it, or the weather forecast indicates poor visibility, or cloud cover approaching from the West, as in a Cold Front.

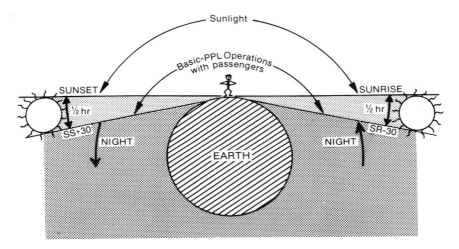

Fig.7-19. In the UK, Official Night Commences at Sunset+30 mins and Ends at Sunrise-30 mins.

Another important consideration related to Sunset is that many smaller airfields in the UK (and throughout Europe for that matter) close at Sunset. This may also apply to the alternate aerodrome(s) chosen for a flight. UK aerodrome operating hours are given in the AGA section of the UK AIP and also in *Pooley's Flight Guide* – the latter having details on most Private Airfields also.

SUMMER TIME.

To take advantage of the longer daylight hours and the better weather in summer, the clocks in many countries are put forward, usually by one hour, to give a new standard time known as *Summer Time.* In the UK this usually occurs between the fourth Sundays in March and October (unless otherwise specified). For example, 1200 UTC becomes 1300 British Summer Time (BST).

British Summer Time = UTC + 1 hour.

A Final Reminder that daylight can end earlier than the published time for a number of reasons, including:
• significant cloud cover;
• poor visibility;
• high ground to the West of an aerodrome.

Remember also that the further South you are the shorter the twilight time.

Make allowances for these when planning a flight that may end near the beginning of 'Official Night' – SS+30. It is good airmanship to plan on arriving **at least** 30 minutes before this time, i.e. at Sunset. Common sense would encourage you to increase this margin on long journeys or on flights where it is difficult to estimate accurately your time of arrival, due to, for example, poor weather forecast en route or at the destination.

☐ Time now to complete **Exercises 7 — Time-5.**

8

THE EARTH

To navigate an aeroplane efficiently from one place to another over long distances or in poor visibility, the Pilot needs to refer to some representation of the Earth. This representation must be smaller in size than the Earth; in other words, it must be a picture of a *'reduced Earth'*.

The simplest and most accurate reduced Earth is a globe, which retains the spherical shape of the Earth and displays the various oceans, continents, cities, and so on. A cumbersome globe is not the ideal navigational tool to have in a cockpit or to carry in a navigation bag, especially if detailed information is required, hence the need for maps or charts that can be folded and put away. The task of the Map-maker is to project a picture of a reduced Earth globe onto a flat surface and make a map or a chart from this.

Maps represent the Earth's surface (or parts thereof) on a *flat* surface; **Charts** show further information or special conditions, possibly using only an outline of geographical features, e.g. the coastline. Since most *maps* that Pilots use show specific aeronautical and navigational data, they are referred to as *charts.*

THE FORM OR SHAPE OF THE EARTH.

The **exact** shape of the Earth's surface is constantly changing. Volcanoes erupt and grow, new islands form and others disappear, landslides and earthquakes cause large land movements, the ocean surface continually changes in height with the tides and, on a very long term basis, the continents gradually move.

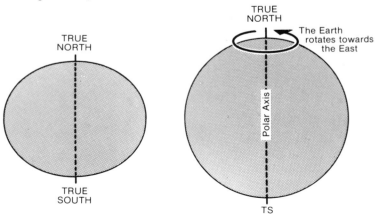

Fig.8-1. The Earth is a Slightly Flattened (oblate) Sphere.

Fig.8-2. The Earth Rotates about its Axis.

The regular geometric shape which the Earth resembles most is a **sphere** but, even when all the surface bumps are ironed out, the Earth is still not a perfect sphere. It is slightly flat at the North and South poles, forming a flattened (or oblate) spheroid, the *polar diameter* being approximately 23 nm less than the *equatorial diameter* (6,865 nm as against 6,888 nm). For the purposes of practical navigation, however, **the Earth can be treated as a Sphere.**

As well as moving in an orbit about the Sun, the Earth rotates on its own axis. This axis of rotation is called the geographic **Polar Axis**, and the two points where this axis meets the surface of the sphere are called:
• the North Geographic Pole – or **True North**; and
• the South Geographic Pole – or **True South**.

If you stand anywhere on Earth and face towards the North Geographic Pole, then you are facing *True North.*

CIRCLES ON EARTH.

A **Great Circle** (GC) drawn on the Earth's surface is one whose plane passes through the centre of the sphere (Earth).

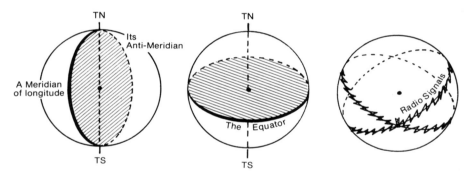

Figs.8-3a, b & c. A 'Great Circle' has the Centre of the Earth as its Axis.

Great Circles have some significant properties, including those below.

1. A Great Circle is the largest circle that can be drawn on the surface of the Earth or on any sphere.

2. The shortest distance between any two points on the surface of a sphere is the arc of a Great Circle.

3. Only one Great Circle can be drawn between two points on the surface of a sphere (unless the two points are diametrically opposed, as are the geographic poles).

Some examples of Great Circles are:
• Meridians of Longitude;
• the Equator;
• the paths that radio waves follow.

A **Small Circle** is any circle on the surface of a sphere that is not a great circle, i.e. the centre of a Small Circle is **not** at the centre of the Earth. Parallels of Latitude (other than the Equator) are Small Circles.

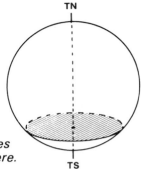

Fig.8-4. The Plane of a Small Circle Does NOT Pass through the Centre of a Sphere.

LATITUDE AND LONGITUDE.

A convenient way of specifying the **Position** of any point on Earth is to relate it to the imaginary lines that form the latitude and longitude graticule (or grid) on the surface of the Earth.

Latitude.

The reference for latitude is the plane of the **Equator,** the Great Circle whose plane is perpendicular (i.e. at right angles, or 90 degrees) to the polar axis.

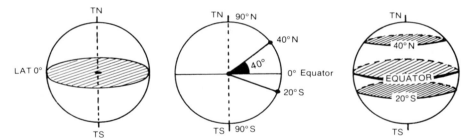

Figs.8-5a, b & c. LATITUDE.

- The **Latitude** of a place is its angular distance in degrees from the Equator, measured at the centre of the Earth and designated either North or South. For instance, Nottingham is at 53°N latitude.

- A **Parallel of Latitude** joins all points of the same latitude and (except for the Equator) is a Small Circle. Nottingham, Bremen in Germany, Torun in Poland, Micurinsk in the USSR, Yellowhead Pass in the Canadian Rockies, Wicklow in Eire, and Stoke-on-Trent in the UK are all about 53° North of the Equator, and therefore the line joining them is called the 53°N parallel of latitude.

- Parallels of latitude are parallel to the Equator and to each other.

- The longest parallel of latitude is the Equator (Latitude 0°). The other parallels, as you move away from the Equator towards the higher latitudes, progressively decrease in size, until the 90° parallels of latitude become just points at the N and S geographic poles.

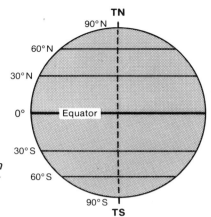

Fig.8-6. The Further from the Equator, the Smaller the Parallel of Latitude.

Longitude.

The basic reference for longitude is the **Greenwich Meridian,** which is also known as the **Prime Meridian.** It is that half of the Great Circle which contains the polar axis (about which the Earth rotates), and passes through the Greenwich Observatory situated near London, as well as the North and South Geographic Poles. The Prime Meridian is designated as *'Longitude 0°'.*

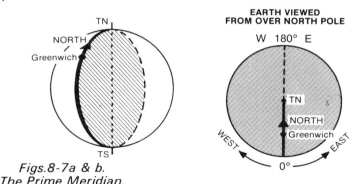

Figs.8-7a & b.
The Prime Meridian.

The other half of the same Great Circle that contains the Prime Meridian runs from the North Geographic Pole to the South Geographic Pole, but on the other side of the Earth to Greenwich. It passes down the Western side of the Pacific Ocean and is known as *'Longitude 180°'.* It can be reached by travelling either East from the Prime Meridian or by travelling the same angular distance (180 degrees) West from the Prime Meridian. Therefore it can be called either '180°E' or '180°W'. It is also called the anti-meridian of Greenwich.

- All of the Great Circles containing the polar axis (and therefore passing through the North and South Geographic Poles) are called **Meridians of Longitude.**

- Meridians of Longitude are specified by their angular difference in degrees *East* or *West* from the Prime Meridian.

145

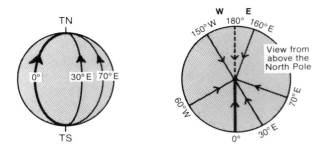

Fig.8-8. The Longitude of a Place is the Angle Between Its Meridian of Longitude and the Prime (Greenwich) Meridian, Measured Eastward or Westward from the Prime Meridian.

SPECIFYING THE POSITION OF A PLACE ON EARTH.

The **Parallels of Latitude** and **Meridians of Longitude** form an imaginary graticule or grid over the surface of the Earth. The position of any point on the Earth can be specified by:

- its **Latitude** – its angular position N or S of the plane of the Equator; together with:
- its **Longitude** – its angular position E or W of the prime meridian.

It is usually sufficiently accurate to specify the Latitude and Longitude of a place in degrees and minutes (one minute being 1/60th of one degree). For extreme accuracy, each minute can be divided into 60 seconds of arc. The symbols used are:
- degrees°;
- minutes'; and
- seconds".

For example, the position of **Belfast (Aldergrove)** in Northern Ireland is: (54°39'15"N, 06°13'30"W). For our purposes (54°39'N, 06°14'W) is sufficiently accurate.

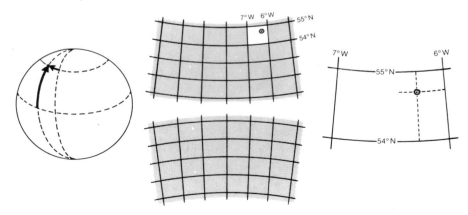

Fig.8-9. The Position of Belfast (Aldergrove) in Northern Ireland is 54°39'N, 06°14'W.

146

NOTE: With the advent of airborne computerised navigation equipment using latitude/longitude reference (e.g. Inertial and Omega systems), some documents (e.g. the UK AIP) show the N or S and E or W prior to the co-ordinate, as this is the order in which *Lat and Long* are entered on such equipment. Also, instead of *seconds* (mentioned above), the *minutes* of the co-ordinates are decimalised. For example, (N52°16·4', W002°45·9'). (The standard is that the N/S co-ordinate has four digits prior to the decimal point, while that for E/W has five. This helps to differentiate them.)

Specifying Latitude and Longitude is the normal method of indicating a particular position on Earth, and is the one that Pilot/Navigators most commonly use at the flight planning stage when they are preparing their maps and flight plan. Once in flight, however, there are other means of specifying the position of the aircraft, such as:
• by position over or abeam a landmark or radio beacon, for instance, 'over Shrewsbury', 'abeam Prestatyn', 'over Lydd VOR'; or
• by range (distance) and bearing from a landmark or radio beacon, for instance, '10 nm on a bearing of 290°T from Dungeness'.

NOTE: The use of place names needs to be confined to places that are likely to be known to the recipient of the message, and which are shown on the commonly used aeronautical charts. In the UK with its high density of population, place names are frequently duplicated and can be misleading.

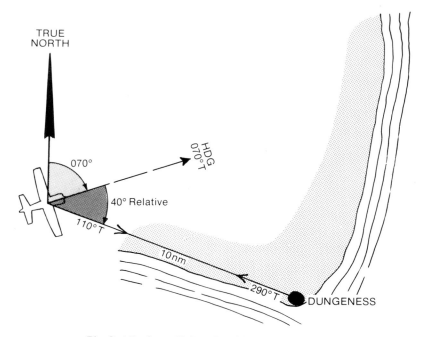

*Fig.8-10. Specifying Position on The Earth
by Relative Bearing.*

DISTANCE ON EARTH.

The standard unit of distance in navigation is the **nautical mile** (nm), which is the length of 1 minute of arc of any Great Circle on Earth (assuming the Earth to be a perfect sphere).

There are 360 degrees in a circle and 60 minutes in a degree, making 60 x 360 = 21,600 mins of arc in a circle. The circumference of the Earth is therefore (60 x 360 = 21,600 minutes of arc, which is 21,600 nm.

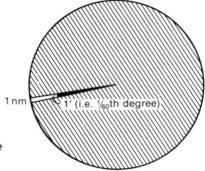

Fig.8-11. 1 nm is the Length of 1 minute of Arc of a Great Circle on the Earth.

• **Latitude** (the angular distance North or South of the Equator) is measured up and down a Meridian of Longitude (which is a Great Circle) and therefore:

---

1 Minute of Latitude at Any Point on Earth = 1 nautical mile (nm).

This is very useful for measuring distances on a chart.

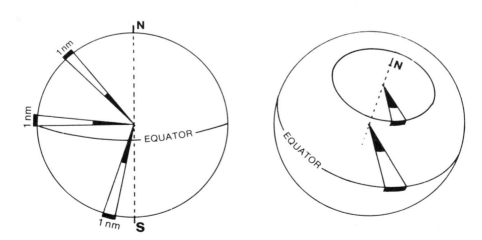

Fig.8-12. 1 Minute of Latitude = 1 nm; 1 Minute of Longitude Varies in Length.

---

1 Degree of Latitude at ANY Point on Earth = 60 nm.

- **Longitude** is measured around the Parallels of Latitude (small circles except for the Equator), and so 1 minute of longitude varies in length depending upon where it is on the Earth's surface.

  The only place where 1 minute of longitude is equal to 1 nm is around the Equator; the higher the latitude, the further away from the Equator the place is, and the shorter the length in nm of 1 minute of longitude in that region.

When using charts, do not be confused by the fact that:

---

we measure 1 minute of latitude (always 1 nm) up or down the side of the chart along a meridian of longitude;

– it is logical when you think about it.

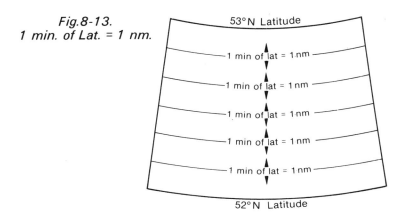

Fig.8-13.
1 min. of Lat. = 1 nm.

53°N Latitude

1 min of lat = 1 nm

1 min of lat = 1 nm

1 min of lat = 1 nm

1 min of lat = 1 nm

1 min of lat = 1 nm

52°N Latitude

THE CONVERSION OF DISTANCES FROM ONE UNIT TO ANOTHER.

There are various systems of units in use around the world, and the Pilot must be able to convert from one to the other.

For conversions :
1 nm = 1852 metres = 6076 feet = 1·15 sm.

The *CRP-1* navigation computer has convenient conversion marks on the outer scale which makes it extremely easy to convert from one unit to another without having to remember the exact ratio figures.

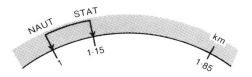

NAUT   STAT   km

1   1·15   1·85

Fig.8-14. The Method of Computer Set-up for Distance Conversions.

ANGLES ON EARTH.

The most fundamental reference from which angles are measured is that of True North, from 000°T, through 090°T, 180°T, 270°T, to 360°T. As can be seen in the illustration below, if an aeroplane follows a long range Great Circle track, the track direction referred to True North will gradually change, i.e. the **Great Circle track** will cross successive meridians at a gradually changing angle.

Sometimes it is convenient to fly a track whose direction remains constant when referred to True North, i.e. so that the track crosses all meridians of longitude at the same angle. This is known as a **Rhumb Line track.**

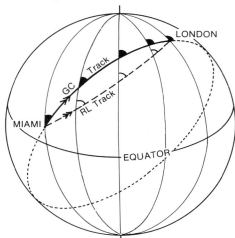

Fig.8-15. The GREAT CIRCLE Track and the RHUMB LINE Track.

The Rhumb Line track and Great Circle track between two places coincide only if the two places lie on either the same meridian of longitude (a Great Circle), the track between them being 180°T or 360°T, or on the Equator (which is also a Great Circle), the track between them being 090°T or 270°T. In practical terms, the GC direction and the RL direction may be considered to be the same over short distances, such as those typically flown within the UK.

The Pilot must always be very clear as to whether he is referring direction to **True** North or to **Magnetic** North, the difference between the two being the Magnetic Variation, as discussed in Chapter 3 of this manual. In this chapter, we are referring direction to True North.

REPRESENTING THE SPHERICAL EARTH ON FLAT MAPS AND CHARTS.

The *latitude-longitude* graticule is translated onto Maps and Charts by Cartographers (Map-makers) whose major problem is to represent the spherical surface of the Earth on a flat sheet of paper. The process consists of:

• scaling the Earth down to a 'reduced Earth'; and then
• projecting the reduced Earth's surface onto a sheet.

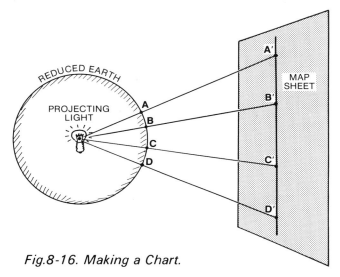

Fig.8-16. Making a Chart.

This process always leads to some distortion, either of areas, distances, angles or shapes. By using certain mathematical techniques when projecting the spherical Earth onto a flat Chart, the Map-maker can preserve some properties, but not all – a spherical orange peel cannot be perfectly flattened out! Some property will always be distorted to a greater or lesser extent depending upon how the points on the surface of the reduced spherical Earth are transferred onto the flat Chart.

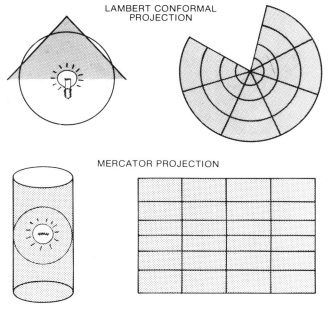

Fig.8-17. A Conical Projection   and   a Cylindrical Projection.

Unlike a sphere, certain other curved surfaces (such as a cylinder or a cone) can be cut and laid out flat; conversely, a cylinder or a cone can be made out of a flat sheet of paper. This is not possible with a spherical surface – try it with an orange peel! By projecting points on the surface of the *reduced Earth* onto either a conical or cylindrical surface (which can then be flattened out to form a sheet), less distortion occurs and a better chart results, compared with a projection onto an already flat sheet like that illustrated in Fig.8-16.

A simple view of map-making is to think of a light projecting the shadows of the latitude-longitude graticule of the reduced sphere onto a cone (Lambert's Conical Projection) or onto a cylinder (Mercator's Cylindrical Projection), the cone or cylinder then being laid out flat to form a chart.

Charts based on conic and cylindrical projections are widely used in aviation, mainly because they:
- **preserve shapes** (of islands, lakes, towns, countries, etc.);
- **preserve angular relationships** – (in mathematical terminology, maps exhibiting this vital property are said to be *conformal* or *orthomorphic*); and
- have a reasonably **constant scale** over the whole chart (for ease of measuring distance).

TOPOGRAPHICAL CHARTS.

Navigating by visual reference to the ground, the Pilot, of course, refers to land features and so a **topographical** chart showing the surface features of the area in detail is of great value. There are various topographical charts available for visual navigation in the United Kingdom, and these (in order of importance) include:
- ICAO Aeronautical Charts, scale 1:500 000 (half-million);
- Topographical Air Charts of the United Kingdom, scale 1:250 000 (quarter-million);
- Operational Navigation Chart series (ONC), scale 1:1 000 000 (one million).

The ICAO and ONC series charts (for those of you who are interested) are based on the Lambert's Conformal **Conic** projection. The chart sheet is formed from a *secant cone* that cuts the sphere representing the *reduced Earth* at two Standard Parallels of Latitude. Just which two parallels of latitude are chosen by the Map-maker depends upon which part of the Earth, and how much of it, he wants to represent on that particular chart.

The Standard Parallels are usually mentioned at the bottom or on the side of the chart – for example, on the 'one to half-million Southern England and Wales' chart (Map Sheet Number 2171CD), the Standard Parallels are stated to be 49°20'N and 54°40'N. There is no distortion along the standard parallels, and very little distortion North or South of them in the UK because of the short distances involved.

The projection for the 1:250 000 Topographical Air Charts of the UK is based on a **cylindrical** projection known as the Transverse Mercator Projection. Whereas the normal Mercator Projection starts with a cylinder wrapped around the Equator with its sides parallel to the polar axis, the Transverse Mercator starts with a cylinder wrapped around a chosen meridian of longitude and its anti-meridian, with the sides of the cylinder at 90° to the polar axis.

The UK 1:250 000 Transverse Mercator Charts are based on the 2°West meridian of longitude, which passes North-South through the middle of the British Isles. When flattened out, this provides a chart with no distortion down the 2°W meridian and, in fact, very little distortion anywhere East or West of this meridian within the UK.

AERONAUTICAL CHART ICAO 1:500 000

Lambert Conformal Conic Projection Standard Parallels 49°20' and 54°40'
Convergence factor 0·78829

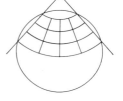

OPERATIONAL NAVIGATION CHART

SERIES	ONC
SHEET	E-1
EDITION	6-GSGS

SCALE 1:1,000,000

Lambert Conformal Conic Projection
Standard Parallels 49°20' and 54°40'

Fig.8-18. Most 1:1 000 000 and 1:500 000 Aeronautical Charts are Based on the Lambert Conformal Conic Projection.

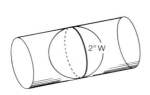

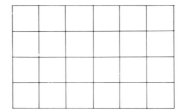

TOPOGRAPHICAL AIR CHART OF THE UNITED KINGDOM

SCALE 1:250 000
TRANSVERSE MERCATOR PROJECTION

Fig.8-19. The UK 1:250 000 Topographical Air Charts are Based on the Transverse Mercator Cylindrical Projection.

Both types of chart covering the relatively small area of the UK have the following properties:
- they are **conformal**: angles and bearings are accurate (absolutely vital);
- **constant scale** over the whole chart in practical terms (i.e. distances are accurate);
- **shapes are preserved** in practical terms;
- **the Track between two places is a straight line** (with there being no significant difference between the Rhumb Line and the Great Circle track between any two places within the UK).

SCALE.

Charts represent a scaled-down view of the Earth, and there are various ways of describing just how much the Earth is scaled down on a particular chart.

**SCALE is defined as the Ratio of the Chart Length
compared to
The Earth Distance that It Represents.**

$$\text{SCALE} = \frac{\textbf{CHART LENGTH}}{\textbf{EARTH DISTANCE}} \quad \textbf{with both in the same unit.}$$

**The Greater the Chart Length for a Given Earth Distance,
the Larger the Scale and the More Detail that can be Shown.**

A large scale chart covers a small area in detail. For example, a UK 1:250 000 (one to a quarter-million) Topographical Air Chart has a larger scale and can show more detail than an ICAO 1:500 000 (one to a half-million) Aeronautical Chart. One centimetre on a 1:250 000 chart represents 250,000 cm on the Earth, whereas, on a 1:500 000 chart, it represents double this Earth distance, i.e. 500,000 cm, hence not as much detail can be shown.

Fig.8-20. Sample Excerpts from 1:250 000;   and 1:500 000.

Scale Can Be Expressed in Various Ways:

(a) as a **Representative Fraction.** For instance, the WAC and the ONC series are 1:1,000,000 charts (one to a million), where 1 centimetre on the chart will represent 1,000,000 cm or 10 kilometres on the Earth, or where 1 nm on Earth is represented by 1 millionth of a nautical mile on the chart. On the ICAO 1:500 000 Aeronautical Charts, an Earth distance is represented by one half-millionth of its length; on the UK 1:250 000 Topographical Air Charts, an Earth distance is represented by one quarter-millionth of its length.

(b) as a **Graduated Scale Line,** which is usually situated at the bottom of the chart. A graduated scale line allows you to measure-off the distance between two points on the chart and match it against the scale line. Make sure that you use the correct scale line (usually nautical miles), since there may be various ones so that nautical miles, statute miles or kilometres can be measured.

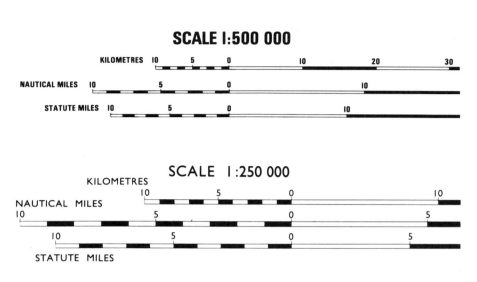

Fig.8-21. Typical Scale Lines.

(c) in **Words** – e.g. '1 cm equals 5 nm', which obviously means that 5 nm on the Earth's surface is represented by 1 cm on the chart.

Even if there is no scale line on the chart, you can always compare the distance between two places on the chart with the latitude scale which runs down the side of the chart, remembering that 1' of latitude = 1 nm, and 1° of latitude = 60 nm.

On conic projections (ICAO 1:500 000), use the latitude scale about mid-way between the two places, because on some charts scale may vary slightly depending upon proximity to the Standard Parallels. In practical terms, however, scale can be considered as constant over all of a 1:500 000 chart.

On the UK Transverse Mercator 1:250 000 charts, the scale is exactly correct at the 2°W meridian, and can be considered as constant to about 300 nm either side of this. Since the UK does not have a large East-West spread, the slight variation in scale is not significant.

To all intents and purposes, therefore, scale may be considered constant at all points on both aeronautical chart series, quarter- and half-million.

CONVERTING CHART LENGTH TO EARTH DISTANCE
(and vice versa).

Whilst the following calculations are not normally performed by a Pilot, they do give you an insight into the making of charts, and you may be examined on them.

Example 1: What Earth distance is represented by a chart length of 5·2 inches on a 1:250 000 chart?

$$1 \text{ inch on the Chart} = 250{,}000 \text{ inches on the Earth}$$

$$= \frac{250{,}000}{12} \quad \begin{array}{l} \text{feet on the Earth} \\ (1 \text{ ft} = 12 \text{ inches}) \end{array}$$

$$= \frac{250{,}000}{12 \times 6076} \quad \begin{array}{l} \text{nm on the Earth} \\ (1 \text{ nm} = 6076 \text{ ft}) \end{array}$$

$$= 3{\cdot}43 \text{ nm on the Earth}$$

$$5{\cdot}2 \text{ inches on the Chart} = 5{\cdot}2 \times 3{\cdot}43 \text{ nm on the Earth}$$
$$= 17{\cdot}8 \text{ nm on the Earth. (ANS)}$$

Example 2: 9 inches on a 1:500 000 chart represents approximately 62 nm. How many kilometres does 9 inches represent on a 1:250 000 chart?

9 in = 62 nm on a 1:500 000 chart,
therefore, on a 1:250 000 chart (i.e. double the scale):
9 in = 62/2 = 31 nm
= 57·5 km (by *CRP-1* computer).

NOTE: Your answer should be accurate to +/− 1 km.

Fig.8-22. Example 2.

☐ Now complete **Exercises 8 — The Earth.**

9

AERONAUTICAL CHARTS

CHARTS FOR VISUAL FLYING IN THE UNITED KINGDOM.

The two main charts for visual navigation in the United Kingdom are:
- the 1:500 000 ICAO Aeronautical Charts (which are the ones most commonly used); and
- the CAA 1:250 000 Topographical Air Charts of the UK (which are suitable for visual navigation only below 3000 ft AMSL).

(**ICAO** stands for International Civil Aviation Organisation – a wing of the United Nations which suggests world aviation standards, in this case for charts, to ensure commonality of presentation between countries.)

Three ICAO 1:500 000 charts cover the whole of the United Kingdom and there are two more at the same scale for the Irish Republic. Because of the larger scale of the 1:250 000 charts, it takes a greater number to cover the same area (18 in fact for the UK). The *one in a quarter-million* charts can, however, show much greater detail than the *half-million* scale.

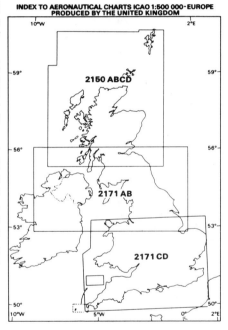

Fig.9-1. 1:500 000 UK Coverage.

The CAA *quarter-million* charts do **not** show aeronautical information regarding Controlled or Special Rules Airspace with a base above 3000 ft AMSL. In general, therefore, they are used only for cross-country flying at or below 3000 ft AMSL, or when operating at low level in a terminal area.

Both series of charts provide a Pilot with:
- **topographical information** (mountains, lakes, rivers, coastlines);
- **cultural information** (cities, towns, motorways, railway lines); and
- **aeronautical information** (Controlled Airspace, Airways, Special Rules Airspace, Prohibited, Restricted and Danger Areas, airfields, radio beacons, etc). The aeronautical information is printed over the top of the topographical and cultural information, generally in blue or magenta (purple).

Use only the current issue of the chart. Reprints occur periodically (usually every one or two years) and the date of the current chart is specified in NOTAMs (NOTices to AirMen). Some items on a chart may change from time to time (for instance, a new radio mast or a new road may be built, airspace may be reorganised) and these changes will be notified to Pilots by NOTAM. Your charts should be amended by hand if required.

It will help if you now refer to some typical charts, and the two that we will use mainly are:

- AERONAUTICAL CHART ICAO 1:500 000, SHEET 2171AB, NORTHERN ENGLAND AND NORTHERN IRELAND (Edition 10, current at the time of printing, was used); and
- TOPOGRAPHICAL AIR CHART OF THE UNITED KINGDOM 1:250 000, SHEET 10, NORTH WALES AND LANCASHIRE.

The charts are self-explanatory. Study them thoroughly and become very familiar with their legends. **As a guide, we will consider the 1:500 000 chart** now, with occasional reference to the quarter million series, where applicable.

NOTE: **The chart excerpts and information in this chapter are for Study Purposes Only.** For actual flight operations ensure you have the latest edition of charts, up-dated by NOTAMs issued since the chart's validity date. Be aware that, once changes are incorporated in the AIP (normally after six months), relevant NOTAMs are cancelled.

TOPOGRAPHICAL INFORMATION shown is that considered to be of most use to the Pilot/Navigator. It is of course impossible to show absolutely everything on a chart, so there may be some details on the ground not shown. Features that are shown on the chart, however, will exist on the ground. For example, an isolated rock may not be considered significant by the Map-maker and therefore will not be shown on the chart. You might spot it on the ground, yet not find it depicted on the chart. If, however, there is an isolated rock shown on the chart, it will certainly exist on the ground. The same thing may be said about cultural features depicted on UK charts, such as Stonehenge or the White Horses; if they are shown on the chart, then they exist on the ground and may be suitable as landmarks for visual navigation.

DRAINAGE and WATER FEATURES (hydrographic features) are usually depicted in blue. Hydrographic features include creeks, streams, rivers, canals, lakes, reservoirs, marshes, shorelines, tidal flats, etc. Just how they are depicted on the chart is explained by the chart legend, but bear in mind that after a flood, for instance, what might be shown as a small stream on the chart may in fact have become a raging torrent. Right throughout aviation, common sense is necessary.

RELIEF. There are various ways of bringing ground contours into relief so that an impression of hills, mountains, valleys, etc, is obtained when you look at the chart. The UK 1:500 000 chart series uses **Contours**, lines joining places of equal elevation above mean sea level, to depict relief. The closer the contour lines are together on the chart, the steeper the ground. The spacing between contour lines is different on the various series of charts.

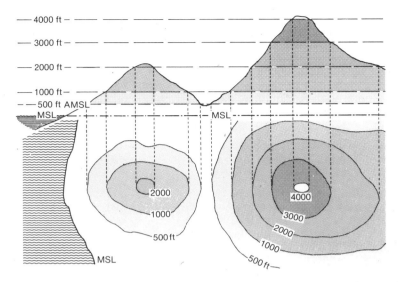

Fig.9-2. Contour Lines Represent Changes in Height AMSL.

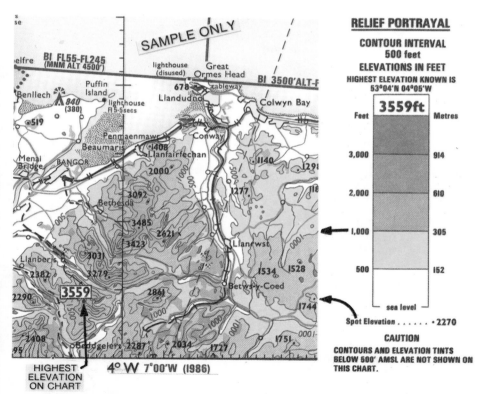

Fig.9-3. Hypsometric Tints to Portray Relief on a 1:500 000 Chart.

Colour or layer tinting is used in conjunction with the contour lines to give even more relief. The colours or tints used for the various ground elevations are shown on a *hypsometric tint* table at the bottom of the chart. (*Hypsometric* means *establishment of vertical heights or elevations*.) The shades of colour generally start with white for low land, then go through light brown and into brown, gradually darkening as the ground becomes higher. Remember that a particular colour may indicate ground elevation up to the level of the next contour above it.

SPOT ELEVATIONS (or spot heights) are shown using a black spot with an adjacent number to indicate the elevation (height AMSL – Above Mean Sea Level) in FEET. These elevations are generally accurate (unless amended by NOTAM).

Spot Elevations are normally used to show local peaks and other critical elevations that are significantly higher than the surrounding terrain. The highest point on each chart (in this case Mount Snowdon in North Wales) has its elevation printed slightly larger than the rest and is displayed in a white rectangle with a black edge. It also rates a mention on the Relief Portrayal table.

HACHURING or **HILL SHADING** is used to give a three dimensional effect on some aeronautical charts. Hachuring consists of very short lines running downhill, and is commonly used to portray bluffs, cliffs and escarpments. Hill shading shows darkened areas on the low side of high ground where you would expect to see shadows with the light coming from the north-west (a graphic standard).

On the CAA quarter-million charts, hill shading and contours are used, but there is, however, no hachuring or hill shading on the the UK half-million series – only contours and layer tints.

Fig.9-4a. Hachuring.

Fig.9-4b. Contours and Hill Shading SAMPLE ONLY on a 1:250 000 in Wales.

160

Be aware that many continental European charts show contours, elevations and spot heights, not in feet AMSL, but in metres AMSL. When flying in France, for instance, you may need to convert feet to metres, or vice versa. This can be done using your navigation computer, or by using the conversion table that is printed on some charts. The charts used in the UK display elevations and heights only in feet.

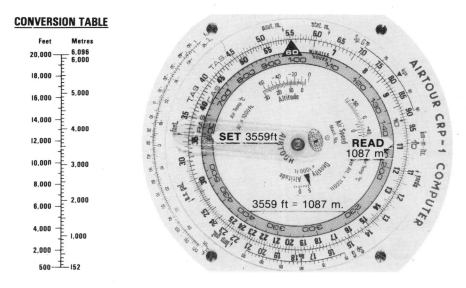

CONVERSION TABLE

Feet	Metres
20,000	6,096 / 6,000
18,000	
16,000	5,000
14,000	
12,000	4,000
10,000	3,000
8,000	
6,000	2,000
4,000	
	1,000
2,000	
500	152

SET 3559ft   READ 1087 m

3559 ft = 1087 m.

Fig.9-5. Convert Height in Metres on European Charts to Feet AMSL.

CULTURAL FEATURES ON THE 1:500 000 CHART.

Cultural Features are of great help to the Pilot/Navigator. It is not possible to show every town or every house on the chart, so a choice is made to show what is significant and of value for visual air navigation. A group of, say, 100 houses is of little significance if it lies in the middle of a city the size of **Manchester** and so will not be specifically depicted on the chart, yet on the moors it may be extremely significant and will be shown.

Roads and Railways can be of great assistance to the visual Pilot/Navigator. Those that will be most significant for air navigation will be clearly shown. Distinctive patterns such as curves, roads running parallel to railway lines and then crossing over, junctions, forks, overpasses, and tunnels, are especially useful. Even the *bed* of disused railway lines can be of navigational value, and these are shown as broken black lines on charts.

Many other useful cultural features, such as the *White Horse, etc*, carved into the ground in various parts of England, may also be shown. Read the legend carefully and become familiar with the symbols (which differ slightly between the various series of charts).

Fig.9-6. Cultural Symbols on the UK 1:500 000 Series

AERONAUTICAL INFORMATION ON THE UK 1:500 000 CHARTS.

Most people are familiar with topographical and cultural information, since these are surface features which are shown on a road map and in an atlas. A Pilot, however, operates in a three-dimensional environment and therefore requires information on the airspace above the surface of the Earth as well.

Aeronautical Information is vital information for a Pilot, showing him not only the position of aerodromes on the ground, but also the division of airspace through which aeroplanes fly, and of course much other information as well. The chart legends explain this information clearly and thoroughly, although sometimes you have to search for the information in the legend and its associated notes. It is a good idea to memorise the most commonly used symbols, e.g. aerodromes, airspace, obstructions, etc. However, **if in doubt, consult the legend.**

Note that, in the case of the 1:250 000 chart, (the low level chart that shows surface features in great detail), only Controlled and Special Rules Airspace with a lower limit at or below 3000 ft AMSL is shown. For flight above 3000 ft altitude, the 1:500 000 chart must be used.

The chart will have all the changes that are effective on the **'AIRAC date'** – the 'Effective Date of Implementation' – which is printed on the chart. Out-of-date charts can be dangerous, so always check that you have the latest edition. Check NOTAMs, UK Air Information Publications (such as the Aeronautical Information Circulars – AICs) and the Chart of UK Airspace Restrictions for any information affecting the chart after the AIRAC date. Note that, once an aeronautical change has been incorporated in the AIP (usually after about six months), the relevant NOTAM or AIC will be cancelled.

Extracts from a Chart Legend are shown below.

SAMPLE ONLY

THIS CHART WILL BECOME OBSOLETE
AFTER APPROXIMATELY 12 MONTHS.
INFORMATION CIRCULARS SHOULD BE CHECKED
FOR PUBLICATION OF NEW EDITION.

VALIDITY OF AERONAUTICAL INFORMATION
Aeronautical information shown on this chart
includes relevant changes notified by:-
UK NOTAMS CLASS II published 26 MARCH 1987
UK NOTAMS CLASS II AIRAC published 26 MARCH 1987
(Effective Date of Implementation for AIRAC changes is
7 MAY 1987)
For changes after 26 MARCH 1987 users should consult
NOTAMs and Air Information Publications.

REFERENCE TO AIR INFORMATION

AERODROME INFORMATION

Aerodrome-Civil ....

Aerodrome-Civil, limited or no facilities ....

Heliport-Civil ....

Aerodrome-Government, available for Civil use. See UK AIP AGA 0-3 ....

Aerodrome-Government ....

Heliport-Government ....

Aerodrome-Disused or Abandoned. Shown for navigational
landmark purposes only ....

Aerodrome Light Beacon .... ☆ FIG ⋯ • ☆ FIR ⋯ •

Site of Intensive Microlight Flying ....
Intensive Microlight Activity also takes place at certain Licensed and Unlicensed
Aerodromes. See UK AIP RAC 5-I.

Glider Launching Site
a. Primary activity at locations ....cables Ⓖ
b. Additional activity at locations ....cables ⊞
Launch cables may be carried to 2000ft AGL. See Legend Note 18.

Numerals adjacent to aerodrome indicate elevation of aerodrome in feet above
Mean Sea Level. Customs Aerodromes are distinguished by a pecked line around
the name of the aerodrome. Active land aerodromes with a runway or landing
strip regardless of surface, of 1829m or over, are indicated by a dot shown in the
centre of the circle symbol.

Aerodrome Traffic Zone (ATZ). See Legend Note I.
Regulated Airspace from the surface to 2000ft above the level of the
aerodrome within a circle centred on the notified mid-point of the
longest runway, radius 2·0NM (RW<1850m) or 2·5NM (RW>1850m).

FOR CURRENT STATUS, AVAILABILITY, RESTRICTIONS AND WARNINGS APPLICABLE
TO AERODROMES SHOWN ON THIS CHART CONSULT AIR INFORMATION PUBLICATIONS
AND AERODROME OPERATORS OR OWNERS. PORTRAYAL DOES NOT IMPLY ANY
RIGHT TO USE AN UNLICENSED AERODROME WITHOUT PERMISSION.

AIRSPACE INFORMATION

Control Zone (CTR)	SFC-2500'ALT
Control Area (TMA and CTA)	
Outer Boundary	3500'ALT-FL245
Inner Boundary	2500'ALT-FL245
Control Area (Airway)	A1 FL65-FL245
Special Rules Zone (SRZ)	SFC-FL65 ●●●●●●●●●●●
Special Rules Area (SRA)	1500'ALT-FL65 ●●●●●●●●●●●

CONTROLLED AND SPECIAL RULES AIRSPACE IS SHOWN WITH A BLUE TINT

ATS Advisory Route (ADR) Centre-line	— DW3 FL50-FL240 —
Low Level Corridor or Special Route	750'ALT-2500'ALT
Radar Advisory Service Zone or Area. See UK AIP RAC 3-6.	— • — • —
Air Traffic Service Unit (ATSU) Area. See UK AIP RAC 3-12.	– – – – –
Flight Information Region Boundary (FIR)	—┴—┴—┴—┴—
Reporting Point: Compulsory .... ▲ On Request .... △	
Shown only for ADRs and certain Recommended Routes.	
Special Access Lane Entry/Exit	LIVER -POOL- E
Notified in UK AIP, subject to specified conditions. E⌐ indicates centre of lane.	
Visual Reporting Point (VRP). Notified in UK AIP.	⌐VRP⌐ NESTON
(Within larger built-up areas location identified by ⊕.)	

SAMPLE ONLY
Not to be used in conjunction
with Flight Operations or
Flight Planning

AIRSPACE AND COMMUNICATION INFORMATION

MILITARY AERODROME TRAFFIC ZONES (MATZs)

Military Aerodrome Traffic Zones (MATZs) have the following vertical limits: SFC to 3000ft AAL within the circle and 1000ft AAL to 3000ft AAL within the stub.

Zone configuration can contain one or two stubs of standard dimensions, a combined stub, one stub of reduced length or no stub at all. In some cases the MATZ circle radius is reduced to 3NM. Often two or more MATZs are amalgamated to produce a <u>Combined Zone (CMATZ)</u>.

STANDARD MATZ
WITH TWO STUBS
AND LARS

Controlling Aerodromes show the MATZ penetration frequency to be used. FOR MATZ PENETRATION PROCEDURES AND RULES REGARDING THE AERODROME TRAFFIC ZONE (ATZ) SEE UK AIP RAC 3-2.

<u>LOWER AIRSPACE RADAR SERVICE (LARS).</u> The abbreviation LARS has been added to the MATZ frequency to identify those MATZ ATS Units participating in the Lower Airspace Radar Service. Other participating Units are identified by the portrayal of a LARS frequency box. The Service, Radar Advisory (RAS) or Radar Information (RIS), is available to all aircraft in unregulated airspace up to and including FL95 within approximately 30NM of each participating ATS Unit. See UK AIP RAC 3-6.

Altimeter Setting Region Boundary (ASR)...............................	HUMBER ASR ⇤⇥ ⇤⇥ ⇤⇥ ⇤⇥ BARNSLEY ASR

Fig.9-7. Some Sections of the 1:500 000 Airspace Legend.

To illustrate how airspace information is depicted on a chart, we have have taken one of the most intense areas of airspace in the UK – that around Manchester and Liverpool.

Fig.9-8. Extract from a 1:500 000 Chart.

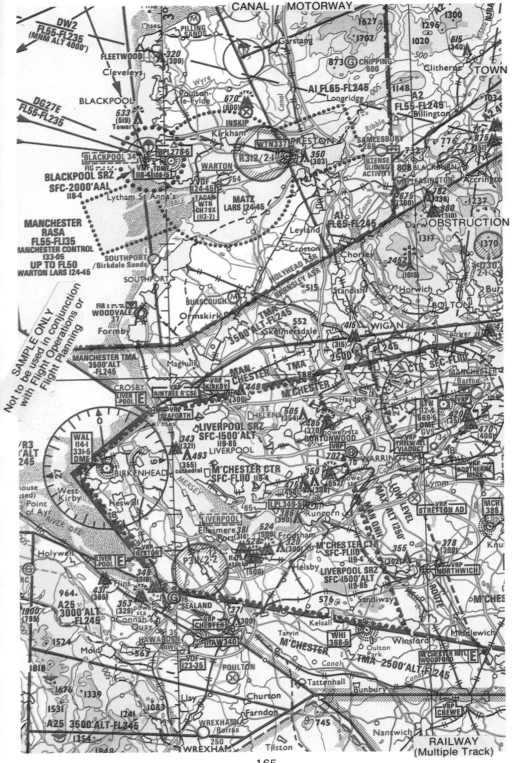

Some items of interest regarding how the airspace is split up, starting near the top of the extract and moving down, are:

- **Airway A1** (a Control Area) extending from FL65 to FL245;
- **Blackpool Special Rules Zone (SRZ)** extending from the surface to 2000 ft AAL, with an operating radio frequency of 118·4 MHz;
- **Warton Military Aerodrome Traffic Zone (MATZ)**, with an operating radio frequency of 124·45 MHz;
- **Manchester Terminal Control Area (TMA)** extending initially from 3500 ft ALT (AMSL) to FL245 and then, as Manchester is approached, from 2500 ft ALT to FL245;
- **Manchester Control Zone (CTR)** extending from the surface (SFC) to FL110, with an operating radio frequency of 119·4 MHz;
- **Liverpool Special Rules Zone**, from the surface to 1500 ft ALT (which partially overlaps the Manchester CTR), and with an operating radio frequency of 119·85 MHz;
- **Special Access Lane** into the Liverpool SRZ, labelled with 'E' near the mouth of the Mersey River.
- Some **Prohibited, Restricted** and **Danger Areas**, designated by the letters **P, R** and **D**, as appropriate, and followed by an identifying number and the altitude limits – examples: **R312/2.1** is Restricted Area number 312, which extends from the surface to 2100 ft ALT (i.e. AMSL), located in Warton MATZ; **P311/2.2**, Prohibited Area number 311, SFC – 2200 ft ALT, located just South of Liverpool.

Information on some of the various aerodromes shown on this extract includes:

- **Blackpool Aerodrome,** Elevation 34 ft AMSL, a civil aerodrome as indicated by its colour, the underlining of the name indicating that permission is required to fly within the Aerodrome Traffic Zone and to land and take-off, and that a communications watch should be maintained (see Legend Note 1). **New chart editions have a revised depiction of ATZs** (see Legend excerpt on P163);
- **Burscough** (8 nm S of Warton), a site at which Intensive Microlight Flying takes place.
- **Poulton** (South of Liverpool), an abandoned or disused aerodrome.

Further information is given in *'LEGEND NOTES',* which should be read carefully. Examples are shown below.

LEGEND NOTES

Note I. UK AERODROMES-FLIGHT WITHIN AERODROME TRAFFIC ZONES-RULES OF THE AIR RULE 35 PARAS (2) AND (3). Aerodromes where Mandatory Rules apply regarding permission to fly anywhere within; to take-off or land anywhere within the respective Aerodrome Traffic Zone and where specified Communication Rules apply are identified on this chart by the portrayal of a Blue Circle with a Blue Tint around the designated runway position. ATZ Services and RT Frequencies are shown on the chart at the top left margin. Notified ATZ operating times are listed at UK AIP RAC 3-2-10. It should be noted that at most Government Aerodromes ATZs exist at all times.

Note 2. MILITARY LOW FLYING SYSTEM: Military low flying occurs in most parts of the UK at any height up to 2000ft above the surface. However, the greatest concentration is between 250ft and 500ft above the surface and civil pilots are advised to avoid this height band whenever possible.
Military Aircraft are considered to be low flying when:-
a. Fixed-wing aircraft, except light propeller-driven aircraft, are flying below 2000ft above the surface.
b. Light propeller-driven aircraft and helicopters are flying below 500ft above the surface. UK AIP RAC 5-I.

Fig.9-9.

- **Hazards To Aviation** information is also depicted. These hazards include certain aerial activities such as parachuting or hang-gliding, as well as permanent obstructions such as radio masts or cables.

Obstructions which reach 300 ft or more Above Ground Level are considered to be hazards to aeroplanes and are therefore shown on charts, the numerals in brackets beside the symbol for the obstruction indicating the height of its top AGL, and the numerals in italics but not in brackets indicating the elevation of the top of the obstruction AMSL. Obstructions 299 ft AGL and lower may not be shown.

Note that, since the first contour is at 500 ft AMSL and obstructions less than 300 ft AGL may not be shown, it is possible to have an obstruction that is just less than 800 ft AMSL not indicated in any manner on the chart.

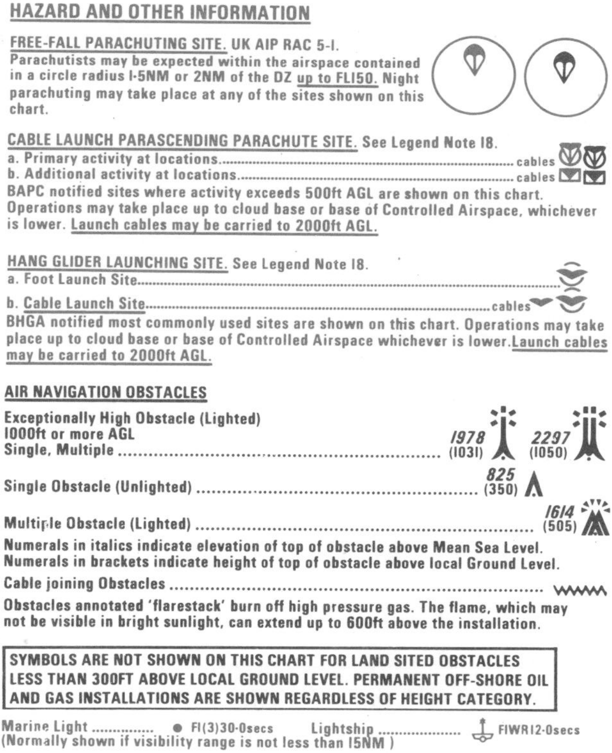

Fig.9-10. Hazard and Other Information on the 1:500 000 Series.

In the chart extract below, a number of hazards to aviation are shown, including:

- an exceptionally high obstruction (lighted), with a top 1676 ft AMSL, itself being 1265 ft high (i.e. height AGL);
- a single unlit obstruction just beside it with a top 825 ft AMSL and 350 ft AGL;
- a further obstruction (unlit) to the NE at Louth, with a top 390 ft AMSL and 300 ft AGL;
- free-fall parachuting at **Sturgate** and **Kirton-In-Lindsey,** with parascending (as an additional activity) at the latter.

167

Several other items on the chart excerpt that could be hazards to aviation, but which are listed elsewhere on the legend, are:

- gliding at **Scampton** and **Kirton-In-Lindsey;** and
- numerous disused or abandoned aerodromes, e.g. Bardney.

NOTE: Much of the area portrayed lies within the **Lincolnshire AIAA** (Area of Intense Aerial Activity), which extends from 2500 ft ALT (AMSL) up to Flight Level 180. A **Lower Airspace Radar Advisory Service (LARS)** is available from Waddington, Finningley, Cottesmore and Binbrook ATS units, on the frequencies shown. These are contact frequencies for flight within the Linconshire AIAA.

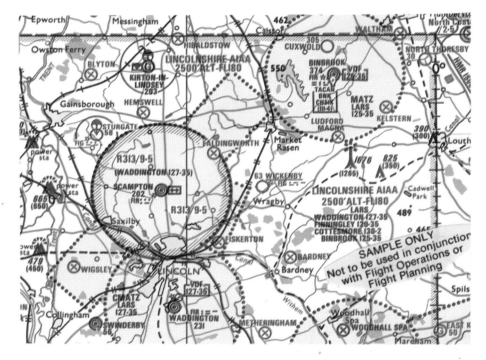

Fig.9-11. 1:500 000 Lincolnshire Excerpt. (NOTE: New Chart Editions have a Revised ATZ depiction – see sample Legend, P163.)

AIRSPACE RESTRICTIONS AND OTHER HAZARD INFORMATION.

These are also listed on the legend. If you refer back several pages to the chart extract for the **Manchester/Liverpool** area, some Airspace Restrictions were outlined (viz R312 and P311).

A DANGER AREA (D) is airspace of defined dimensions within which activities dangerous to the flight of aircraft may exist at specified times, such as the flying of captive balloons, or weapons ranges, possibly with military aircraft towing targets on long cables. Pilots should avoid Danger Areas and, when flying in their vicinity, keep a sharp lookout for military aircraft.

The charts show only those Danger Areas that extend above 500 ft AGL. Many rifle ranges, etc, have upper limits less than 500 ft AGL, so Pilots must satisfy themselves that they are flying clear of such activities.

A PROHIBITED AREA (P) is an airspace of defined dimensions in which the flight of aircraft is prohibited.

A RESTRICTED AREA (R) is an airspace of defined dimensions within which the flight of aircraft is restricted in accordance with certain specified conditions (found in AIP RAC 5-2 if required, or from NOTAMs).

Areas Activated by NOTAM are shown with a broken boundary line.

AIRSPACE RESTRICTIONS AND OTHER HAZARD INFORMATION

AIRSPACE RESTRICTIONS

Prohibited 'P', Restricted 'R' and Danger Areas 'D' are shown with identification number/effective altitude (in thousands of feet AMSL). For periods of activity see 'CHART OF UK AIRSPACE RESTRICTIONS AND HAZARDOUS AREAS (UK AIP RAC 5-0-I) or RAC 5-2/3.
Danger Areas whose identification numbers are prefixed with an asterisk (✳) contain airspace subject to Byelaws which prohibit entry during the Period of Danger Area Activity. See UK AIP RAC 5-I.

For those Scheduled Danger Areas whose Upper Limit changes at specified times during its Period of Activity, only the higher of the Upper Limits is shown on this chart.

Areas activated by NOTAM are shown with a broken boundary line.

UNITED KINGDOM LOW FLYING SYSTEM

GEOGRAPHICAL DETAILS OF MILITARY LOW FLYING ACTIVITIES WITHIN THE UK ARE SHOWN ON 'CHART OF UNITED KINGDOM AREAS OF INTENSE AERIAL ACTIVITY (AIAA) AERIAL TACTICS AREAS (ATA) AND MILITARY LOW FLYING SYSTEM' (UK AIP RAC 5-0-I-I) See LEGEND NOTE 2.

AREA OF INTENSE AERIAL ACTIVITY (AIAA) and AERIAL TACTICS AREA (ATA). See UK AIP RAC 5-I.

Areas are shown with name, vertical limits and where applicable contact frequency/ frequencies. Pilots of non-participating aircraft who are unable to avoid these areas are strongly advised to make use of a Radar Service. Constant vigilance should be maintained whilst flying in areas.

HIGH INTENSITY RADIO TRANSMISSION AREA (HIRTA)

Areas with a radius of 0·5NM or more are shown with name/effective altitude (in thousands of feet AMSL). For further details of these and smaller areas see 'CHART OF UK AIRSPACE RESTRICTIONS AND HAZARDOUS AREAS (UK AIP RAC 5-0-I) or RAC 5-I ....

BIRD SANCTUARIES

Areas are shown with name/effective altitude (in thousands of feet AMSL) ....

OTHER WARNINGS

Areas are shown with name/effective altitude (in thousands of feet AMSL) ....

AIRSPACE RESTRICTION INFORMATION

DANGER AREA CROSSING SERVICE (DACS)

A Danger Area Crossing Service (DACS) is available for certain Danger Areas shown on this chart. The relevant areas (identified on the chart by the prefix †) and the unit contact frequencies to be used are shown below. For availability of the service see UK AIP RAC 5-2 Column 5.

DANGER AREA	UNIT CONTACT FREQUENCY
✳D20I	LONDON MIL VIA LONDON INFO 124·75 MHz or ABERPORTH RANGE CONTROL 122·15MHz
D402 and D403	WEST FREUGH APPROACH 130·05MHz or SCOTTISH MIL VIA SCOTTISH INFO 124·9/133·2MHz
D404	SCOTTISH MIL VIA SCOTTISH INFO 124·9/133·2MHz
D405 and D405A	WEST FREUGH APPROACH 130·05MHz
D4II and D4IIA	WEST FREUGH APPROACH 130·05MHz
D509	WEST FREUGH APPROACH 130·05MHz
D5I3B	BORDER RADAR 132·9MHz

DANGER AREA ACTIVITY INFORMATION SERVICE (DAAIS)

A Danger Area Activity Information Service (DAAIS) is available for certain Danger Areas shown on this chart. The relevant areas (identified on the chart by the prefix §) and the Nominated Air Traffic Service Units (NATSUs) to be used are shown below. Full details of the service are contained in UK AIP RAC 5-I. Pilots are advised to assume that a Danger Area is *active* if no reply is received from the appropriate NATSU.

SAMPLE ONLY

169

DANGER AREA	NATSU
D207	LONDON INFORMATION 124·6MHz
✳D306 and D307	DONNA NOOK 123·05MHz
D308	LONDON INFORMATION 124·6MHz
D314	MANCHESTER APPROACH 119·4MHz
✳D406, D406A and D406B	LONDON INFORMATION 134·7MHz
✳D408A and D408B	LEEMING APPROACH 132·4MHz
✳D409A and ✳D409C	LEEMING APPROACH 132·4MHz
D412	LONDON INFORMATION 134·7MHz
D510	NEWCASTLE APPROACH 126·35MHz or
	CARLISLE APPROACH 123·6MHz also
	✛ SPADEADAM 122·1MHz (RANGE INFO ONLY)
✳D512, ✳D512A and ✳D512B	BORDER INFORMATION 134·85MHz or
	SCOTTISH INFORMATION 133·2MHz
D513, D513A and D513B	BORDER INFORMATION 134·85MHz or
	SCOTTISH INFORMATION 133·2MHz
D607 and D608	SCOTTISH INFORMATION 133·2MHz
	✛ NOT A NATSU.

(marked SAMPLE ONLY)

Fig.9-12. Airspace and Hazard Information.

A MILITARY TRAINING AREA is an area of **upper airspace** of defined dimensions within which intense military flying training takes place. These are above FL245, so will not affect most Private Pilots. There is also, however, some military activity at a low level, below 2000 ft AGL (and especially in the band 250 – 500 ft AGL). Legend Note 2 warns of this.

A BIRD SANCTUARY is airspace of defined dimensions within which large colonies of birds are known to breed. Pilots are requested to avoid these areas, especially during any stated breeding season, and are warned of the high risk of bird strikes. Below is an example of a Bird Sanctuary which exists at the mouth of the Severn River from the surface up to 4000 ft AMSL between September and April.

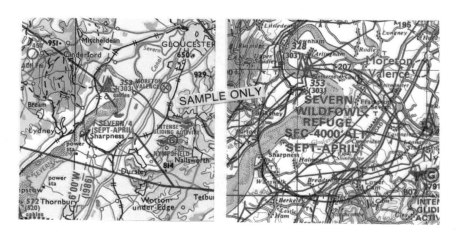

Fig.9-13. Depiction of the same Bird Sanctuary on the Half- and Quarter-Million Aeronautical Charts.

RADIO FACILITIES are also depicted on aeronautical charts, but these will not be significant until you commence training for instrument navigation. Note that the VOR Compass Roses on the chart are aligned with Magnetic North and not True North.

RADIO NAVIGATION AIDS

VHF Omnidirectional Radio Range .... VOR ⊚

Distance-Measuring Equipment .... DME ▫
(Prefix 'T' indicates DME associated and freq paired with ILS
or associated with NDB/NDB(L) Procedure.UK AIP COM 0-4)

Co-located, freq paired VOR/DME .... ◉

UHF Tactical Air Navigation Aid .... TACAN ▽
(VHF freq for Distance Measuring Element is shown in
brackets in TACAN Box.)

Non-Directional Radio Beacon .... NDB and NDB(L) ◎

Other Navigation Aids .... ⊙

VOR COMPASS ROSE
Oriented on Magnetic North

Fig.9-14. Radio Facilities Marked on the 1:500 000 Series.

POSITION INFORMATION.

The **LATITUDE-LONGITUDE graticule** is clearly marked on charts.

- The East-West Parallels of Latitude indicating degrees North or South of the Equator (north in the UK and Europe of course) are labelled at either side of the 1:500 000 chart in 1° intervals (i.e. 60 nm intervals). Each degree is divided into 60 minutes, with marks each 5' and 10', and a full line across the chart at 30'. In the Northern Hemisphere, latitude is measured up from the bottom of the chart.

- The North-South Meridians of Longitude (which gradually converge as they near the North Pole as a result of the 1:500 000 chart being a conical projection) are labelled at the top and bottom of the chart in degrees East or West of the Prime Meridian (in the UK, Longitudes are both East and West). Each degree is divided into 60 minutes, with marks each 5' and 10', and a full line up the chart at 30'. Longitude is measured East or West from the Greenwich Meridian. (Do not confuse the meridian with an isogonal).

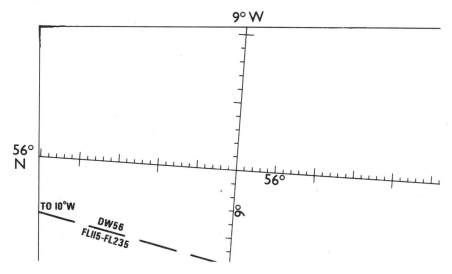

Fig.9-15. Graticule of the 1:500 000 Series.

A HIGH INTENSITY RADIO TRANSMISSION AREA (HIRTA) is an airspace of defined dimensions within which there is radio energy of an intensity which may cause interference or damage to radio equipment in the aeroplane. They are best avoided.

An **AREA OF INTENSE AERIAL ACTIVITY (AIAA)** is airspace of defined dimensions, which is not otherwise protected by Regulated Airspace (Controlled or Special Rules), within which the intensity of civil and/or military flying is exceptionally high, or within which unusual manoeuvres are frequently carried out; for instance, the Vale of York AIAA and the Lincolnshire AIAA.

Airspace Restriction Information is available on the legend of the 1:500 000 chart, and further information can be found in the Aeronautical Information Publication AIP RAC 5-2, and on the Chart of UK Airspace Restrictions and Hazardous Areas, which is included in the AIP. If necessary, the AIP should be referred to on the ground at the flight planning stage.

To obtain information in flight concerning the activity status of a particular Danger Area, the Pilot should call on the appropriate Nominated Air Traffic Service Unit (NATSU) frequency, as listed on the chart legend. (If there is no reply, then assume that the Danger Area is active.)

In the excerpt below is:
- a High Intensity Radio Transmission Area (HIRTA) at **Staxton Wold** extending up to 2000 ft AMSL (**1**);
- a High Intensity Radio Transmission Area (HIRTA) at **Flyingdales**, extending up to 31,500 ft (**2**), and which has special conditions specified in Legend Note 5;
- intense parachuting activity at **Bridlington (3)**;
- generally intense aerial activity throughout the area, since it lies in the **Vale of York** AIAA (**4**).

Other points of interest (though not hazards) on this extract include:
- **London** Flight Information Service frequency 134·7 MHz (**5**);
- Lower Airspace Advisory Radar Service frequencies of 132·4 MHz for **Leeming** and 129·15 MHz for **Linton** (these are contact frequencies within the Vale of York AIAA) (**6**);
- the boundaries of the **Humber, Barnsley** and **Tyne** Altimeter Setting Regions (ASRs) (**7**).

MAGNETIC INFORMATION ON THE 1:500 000 CHART.

ISOGONALS (lines joining places of equal **Magnetic Variation**) are indicated on the 1:500 000 chart by dashed purple-coloured lines. The United Kingdom experiences 'Variation West – Magnetic Best', whilst in Eastern Europe there is 'Variation East – Magnetic Least'. In the area shown in the Vale of York excerpt (Fig.9-16), the Magnetic Variation is 6°W (**8**), i.e. Magnetic North is 6° West of True North.

The **AGONIC LINE** (where True North and Magnetic North are the same direction, and Variation is zero) lies in between the areas experiencing West Variation and those experiencing East Variation. The Agonic line passes through Italy.

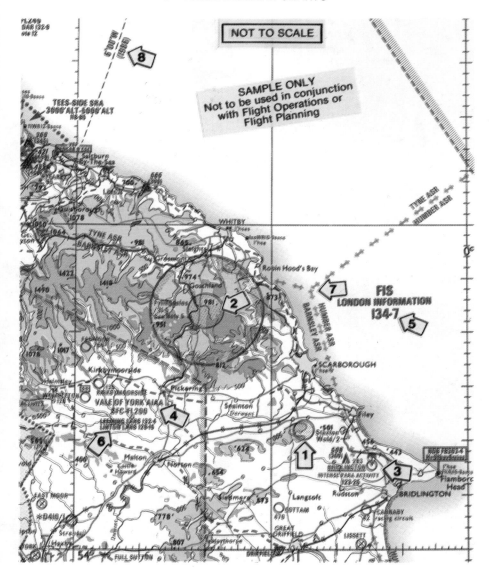

Fig.9-16. Extract of Vale of York AIAA – 1:500 000 Chart.

Because the magnetic poles are gradually moving, the amount of variation at a particular place will also gradually change over a period of years. Every year the isogonic information on the charts is up-dated, and the year of the information shown on the chart.

THE CAA 1:250 000 TOPOGRAPHICAL
AIR CHARTS OF THE UK

Fig.9-17. Excerpt from Sheet 16 – CAA 1:250 000 Series.

The 1:250 000 (quarter-million) Topographical Air Charts are published by the Civil Aviation Authority (CAA) and, because of their larger scale, they show much more detail. This may be useful, especially in busy terminal areas, when you may be operating below 3000 ft AMSL. The 1:250 000 chart shows:

- **Topographical** and **Cultural Information**; along with:
- **Low Level Aeronautical Information (up to 3000 ft AMSL)**, including:
  - all items up to 3000 ft AMSL shown on the 1:500 000 series;
  - Prohibited, Restricted and Danger areas;
  - Control Zones and associated Control Areas;
  - Special Rules Zones and associated Special Rules Areas;
  - Aerodrome Traffic Zones;
  - an approximate runway layout at aerodromes.

CAUTION: The grid of lines prominently superimposed on 1:250 000 charts is a 'National Grid' which is **not** aligned with True North and is not used for normal navigation purposes. When measuring direction on a 1:250 000 chart, be careful that you **align the protractor or plotter with a meridian of longitude**, i.e. with **True North**, and **not** mistakenly use the grid.

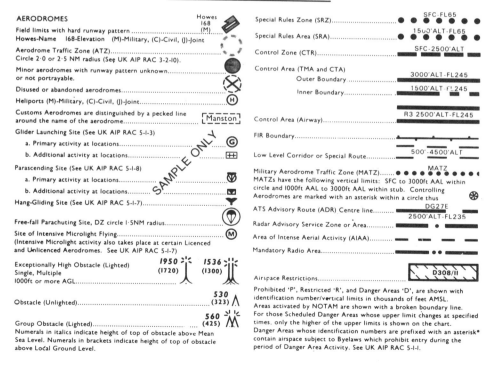

REFERENCE TO AIR INFORMATION

Fig.9-18. Sample Excerpt from the Legend of Air Information on the CAA 1:250 000 Topographical Chart series.

OTHER CHARTS

There are other charts which are not used for position plotting or navigation, but rather to supply specific information. For example:
- the Chart of United Kingdom Airspace Restrictions and Hazardous Areas (AIP RAC 5-0-1); and
- the Chart of United Kingdom Areas of Intense Aerial Activity (AIAA) and Military Low Flying System (AIP RAC 5-0-1.1).

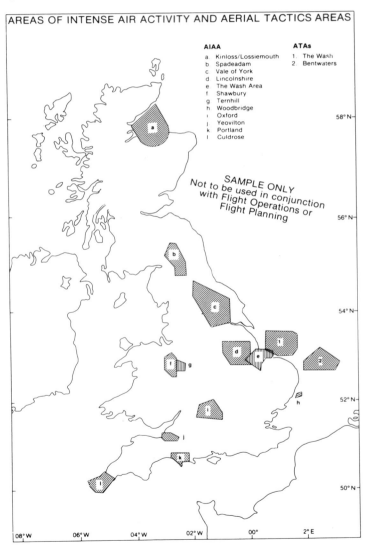

Fig.9-19. UK AIAAs AND ATAs.

Useful information regarding civil aerodromes in the United Kingdom and Ireland can be obtained from *Pooley's Flight Guide.*

EGTB

51 36 40N 00 48 20W	**WYCOMBE AIR PARK (Booker)**	520ft AMSL
2.5 nm SW of High Wycombe.	**BNN 112.30 241 11.7** **LON 113.60 306 14.6**	

c/s 'Wycombe Information'. AFIS 126.55. APRON 121.60.

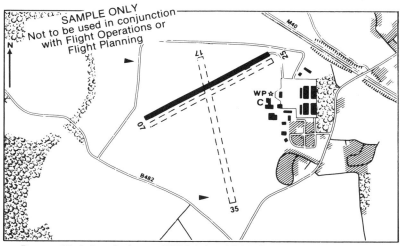

SAMPLE ONLY
Not to be used in conjunction
with Flight Operations or
Flight Planning

Rwy	Dim(m)	Surface	TORA (m)	LDA (m)	Lighting
07/25	735x23	Tarmac	07-735 25-735	07-735 25-735	Thr Rwy LITAS 4° Thr Rwy LITAS 4°
07/25	610x23	Grass	07-610 25-610	07-610 25-610	
17/35	803x28	Grass	17-803 35-803	17-803 35-803	
					IBn 'WP' Gn.

Op. hrs: PPR. 0900-1730 or SS & ¢. **Customs:** 'BAUA'.

Landing Fee: Minimum £5.00 (incl. VAT).

Hangarage: Limited. **Maintenance:** Fixed wing & Helicopter.

Remarks: Operated by Airways Aero Associations Ltd. PPR essential. **Caution** intensive glider launching. Gliders will be flying a circuit opposite to that in use by powered aircraft. Grass areas liable to waterlogging. Variable circuits. Extreme caution when taxying on grass. Permission to land outside scheduled hours not normally given. Joining aircraft are to position to overfly the airfield at 1,200ft. QFE on the runway QDM. When overhead the upwind end of the runway in use, turn in the direction of the circuit and level at circuit height (1,000ft. QFE) on crosswind leg prior to turning downwind.

Restaurant: Restaurant and Refreshments available.

Car Hire: Godfrey Davis. Tel: High Wycombe 36366.

Fuel: 100LL. MOGAS. Jet A1. **Tel:** High Wycombe (0494) 29261/23426.

Fig.9-20. WYCOMBE AIR PARK (Booker) Aerodrome – as shown in Pooley's Flight Guide.

PRIVATE AIRFIELDS AND
LANDING FIELDS

It is important to note that the airfields and landing fields in this section are mostly unlicensed and use is **STRICTLY BY PRIOR PERMISSION ONLY** or by arrangement (¢). Landings are made entirely at pilot's own risk. No extracts or part thereof may be re-published without the Publisher's and Editor's consent in writing.

1 ABOYNE   N5704·50 W00250·00   460 ft. AMSL
1 nm W of Aboyne. (N of River Dee)   **Op. hrs:** PPR
Tarmac strip 09/27, 600 x 5·5m.
Remarks: Operated by Deeside Gliding Club, Waterside, Dinnet. Field grazed by cattle at times. Windsock N of runway. Gliding site – aerotow only.
Landing fee: £2.00. Hotels – Aboyne and Dinnet, both 2 miles.
                                            Tel: Dinnet 033985-339 or 236.

2 ALLENSMORE   N5200 W00250   300 ft. AMSL
4 nm SW of Hereford.   **Op. hrs:** Strictly PPR.
Grass field N/S 550m.
Remarks: Operated by Willox Bridge, Allensmore, Hereford. Contact Mr. Powell. Prior permission advisable. Care must be taken due to animals grazing. Large letter 'A' on white background on hangar roof at N end ~ strip.
Taxi: 0432-51238
Fuel: Nil   idge 098121-203.

SAMPLE ONLY
Not to be used in conjunction or
with Flight Operations or
Flight Planning

3 AVIEMORE (Kincraig)   ·553   850 ft. AMSL
1·5 nm SE of Loch Insh.
Rough grass strip 02/20 ·
Remarks: Operated by   ...ie Williamson, Blackmill, Kincraig, Kingussie, Invernesshire and Cairngo.   Gliding Club. Light aircraft welcome at pilot's own risk, PPR. Beware steeply rising ground to 4000ft. to East of airfield. Glider flying.
Fuel: Nil.   **Tel:** Kincraig 246.

4 BANBURY   N5206·25 W00122·75   530 ft. AMSL
3 nm N of Banbury on A.41.
Two grass strips 15/33, 853m. 09/27, 365m.
Remarks: Operated by F. Spencer, D.F.C., Church Farm, Shotteswell. Prior permission essential. Light aircraft welcome on request and at pilot's own risk. Windsock displayed at North end. No landing fees.
Fuel: Limited.   **Tel:** Wroxton St. Mary 275

5 BERWICK-ON-TWEED (Winfield)   N5445 W00210   170 ft. AMSL
6 nm W of Berwick
Tarmac runways 13/31, 900 x 46m. 06/24, 900 x 46.
Remarks: Operated by M. Fleming & Sons, Winfield, Berwick-on-Tweed. Light aircraft are welcome at all times on PPR. Care must be taken. Windsock displayed. All runway thresholds are displaced, wire fence crosses threshold of runway 24.
Radio: A/G 123·50, c/s Winfield Radio' weekends, & O/R to 0289-86574.
Fuel: Nil.   **Tel:** Whitsome 225 and 236.

6 BRIDGNORTH (Ditton Priors)   N5230 W00234   666 ft. AMSL
6 nm WSW of Bridgnorth. 2 nm NE of spot height 1771ft amsl.
Grass strip (slightly undulating) 07/25, 518 x 18m.
Remarks: Operated by W. E. Lowe, Ditton Farm, Ditton Priors, Bridgnorth, Shropshire. Windsock. Growing crops surround strip. Trees close to South side of runway at approx. half distance. Runway slopes uphill from East. In light wind conditions land uphill and take-off downhill. Light aircraft welcome on request and at pilot's own risk; care must be taken.
Fuel: Nil.   **Tel:** Ditton Priors 240.

Fig.9-21. Further sample of information included in Pooley's Flight Guide.

1:1 000 000 SCALE NAVIGATION CHARTS

As you can imagine charts of this scale (one to one million) cover quite a lot of territory compared to the quarter- and half-million charts. This scale is often used when large distances are involved, to provide Pilots mainly with **topographical information** (mountains, lakes, rivers, deserts, coastlines, etc) and **cultural information** (cities, towns, freeways, country roads, railway lines, etc). Aeronautical information is not shown in detail; aerodromes may be shown, but the division of airspace, other than FIR boundaries and some Restricted Airspace, is not.

There are two major series of 1:1 000 000 aeronautical charts:
● the **Operational Navigation Chart (ONC)** series; and
● the **ICAO World Aeronautical Chart (WAC)** series.

Both series use much the same symbols and are based on the same projection as the half-million charts – the Lambert Conformal Conic projection – consequently angular relationships and shapes are preserved and there is a reasonably constant scale over each chart. Straight Lines closely represent the Great Circle track between two points on ONCs and WACs.

Items such as isogonals, restricted airspace, obstructions, irrigation channels, railway lines and roads, etc, change from time to time, and so they are reprinted regularly – about every two years for busy areas and every five or six years for more remote parts of the world. As with all aeronautical charts, ensure you have the latest edition and study the legend carefully prior to flight.

ONC: 1,000,000 WORLD COVERAGE

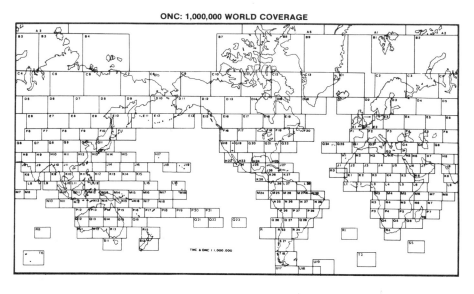

Fig.9-22. ONC World Coverage.

The series most readily available in the UK is the ONC series. It originates from military sources but is available to civil pilots for all but 'sensitive' areas of the world. However, ONCs are not commonly used in the United Kingdom due to the small scale.

The ICAO World Aeronautical Chart (WAC) series originates from civil aeronautical sources. It is widely used in those parts of the world where the 1:1 000 000 scale is better suited to en route navigation, e.g. the Far East, South-East Asia and Australia, due to the large distances involved. Each country producing charts in this series does so according to the ICAO standards.

NOTAM amendments are sometimes issued for WACs, and these are made by hand on the appropriate chart, (and called *Manuscript Amendments*).

As some areas of the world have not been mapped all that accurately (even in the 1980s), there is a small 'Reliability Diagram' at the bottom left hand corner of each WAC that will alert you to the possibility of unreliable information.

Fig.9-23. A WAC Reliability Diagram.

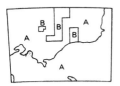

TOPOGRAPHIC BASE
RELIABILITY DIAGRAM

A. Compiled from accurate topographic maps and surveys.

B. Compiled from other available topographic information. Liable to vertical error.

C. Compiled from sketches, reconnaissance, etc.

MEASURING LATITUDE AND LONGITUDE

As a Pilot/Navigator, you sometimes need to determine the latitude and longitude of a place.

To Determine The Latitude Of A Place:

1. Lay a straight-edge East-West through the place, parallel to the parallels of latitude.

2. From the latitude scales running North-South down the page you can read-off the exact latitude. (It should be the same latitude on the scale either side of the place – this ensures that the straight-edge is placed correctly on the chart.)

NOTE: In the Northern Hemisphere the latitude increases towards the North and top of the chart, and the scale lines break up each degree of latitude into 60 minutes, with large marks each 10 minutes. (Make sure that you count from the bottom and up the page, in the direction of increasing latitude.)

To Determine the Longitude of a Place:

1. Lay a straight-edge North-South through the place, parallel to the closest meridians of longitude.

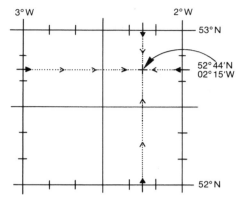

Fig.9-24. Finding the Latitude-Longitude of a Place.

2. From the longitude scales running East-West across the page you can read-off the exact longitude. (It should read the same on the scales above and below the place – this checks that the straight-edge is placed correctly on the chart.)

Plotting a Position.

The reverse problem of plotting a given latitude and longitude on the chart is just as easy:

1. Find the approximate position of the place on the chart.

2. Mark the latitude given on the two nearest latitude scales either side of the position.

3. Mark the longitude given on the two nearest longitude scales North and South of the position.

4. Join the latitude marks and then join the longitude marks – their point of intersection being the desired position.

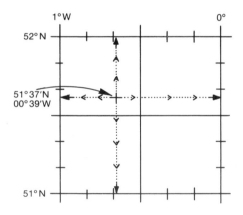

Fig.9-25. Plotting a Known Lat-Long.

NOTE: You are required to be able to specify or mark a position to an accuracy of 1 minute of arc.

RHUMB LINES AND GREAT CIRCLES
ON CHARTS

The **shortest distance between two points** on the spherical Earth is along a **Great Circle** (GC). Radio waves also follow Great Circle paths. Therefore it is convenient for an Instrument Pilot using radio navigation aids to use aeronautical charts designed so that a straight line closely resembles a Great Circle track.

Fig.9-26. Great Circles May Cross Meridians
of Longitude at Varying Angles.

Because the ICAO 1:500 000 Aeronautical Chart series is based on the *Lambert Conformal Conic Projection* (in which the meridians of longitude converge towards the nearer pole), a straight line drawn on these charts closely resembles a Great Circle track and will cross the meridians of longitude at varying angles. Thus a Pilot wanting to fly a Great Circle track would therefore have to navigate along a continually changing track direction. This is not a very tidy procedure if using a Magnetic Compass for heading reference.

It is more convenient for a Pilot, when using a Magnetic Compass or Direction Indicator, if it is possible for him to fly a constant Track Direction. This can be achieved by following a **Rhumb Line** track, rather than a Great Circle track. **A RHUMB LINE crosses all meridians of longitude at the same angle and will appear on the surface of the Earth as a curved line concave to the nearer pole.**

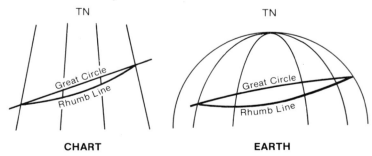

Fig.9-27. A Rhumb Line Track Compared with
a Great Circle Track.

A Rhumb Line track is therefore easier for a Pilot/Navigator to track along, because he can fly a constant Magnetic Heading. The disadvantage is that a Rhumb Line is not the shortest distance between two points on the Earth, but over short distances (such as in the UK and Ireland) this is not significant. A Pilot navigating visually using the Magnetic Compass for heading reference will normally follow the Rhumb Line track, and an Instrument Pilot using radio navigation aids will normally follow their Great Circle track.

NOTE: **Over short distances** (i.e. of less than 200 nm) **the Rhumb Line track and Great Circle track are almost identical** – the RL will be slightly on the Equator side of the GC. The direction of the Rhumb Line track and the Great Circle track are identical at the mid-point en route.

MEASUREMENT OF DISTANCE ON CHARTS

Distance may be measured by various methods and you should be able to achieve an accuracy to within 1 nm by using one of the following methods:

(1) The GRADUATED SCALE LINE, found at the bottom of most charts. Using dividers, or some other means, transfer the distance between the two positions on the chart down onto the scale line.

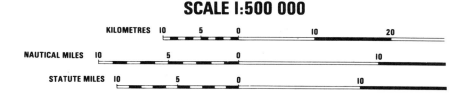

Fig.9-28. A Graduated Scale Line is Included at the Foot of Aeronautical Charts.

(2) The LATITUDE SCALE, which is a graticule found on the side of each chart. At all points on Earth for all practical purposes, 1 minute of latitude = 1 nm.

Using dividers or some other means, transfer the distance between the two positions on the chart across onto the latitude scale. (Because the scale over the whole chart may vary slightly from latitude to latitude, use that part of the latitude scale which is about the same as the mid-latitude of the track that you are considering.)

The number of *minute* divisions then gives you the distance in nautical miles.

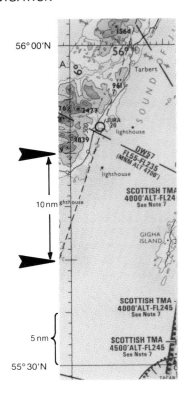

Fig.9-29. Latitude Scales.

(3) By using a correctly graduated SCALE RULE. Navigation Scale Rules (and Plotters) are designed to measure distances on the 1:500 000 and 1:250 000 (and even 1:1 000 000) charts – just make sure that you are reading the distance off the chart against the correct scale line for that particular chart.

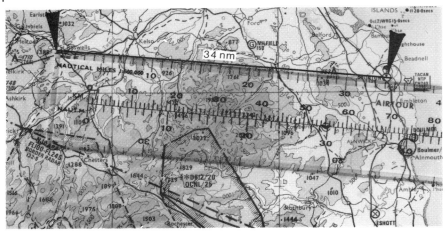

Fig.9-30. Measuring the Distance with a Scale Rule.

MEASUREMENT OF BEARINGS ON CHARTS

If you are to track between two points, then on the chart you will draw the straight line joining them. This will be an approximate Great Circle. Its direction will be the same as that of the Rhumb Line at the mid-meridian of longitude, so **it is common practice to measure direction at the mid-meridian.** This is usually taken as the meridian that the track crosses closest to the half-way mark.

The true direction can be measured against True North at the mid-meridian of longitude by using a **Protractor.**

MEASURING DIRECTION with a PROTRACTOR.

The best way to measure direction with a protractor is to align its north-south axis with True North along the mid-meridian and then to read-off the direction on the outer scale. (You can also measure the direction by aligning the axis of the protractor with the track and measuring the direction against the inner scale.)

Once again it is vital that you have an approximate value in mind prior to using the protractor so that you avoid any gross errors, such as being out by 90° or 180°.

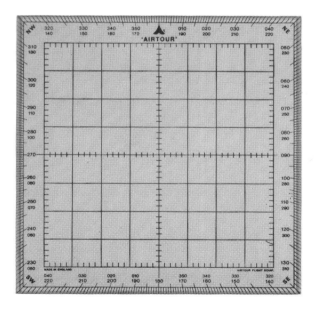

Fig.9-31.
The Square
Protractor is the
Type Commonly Used
in Aviation

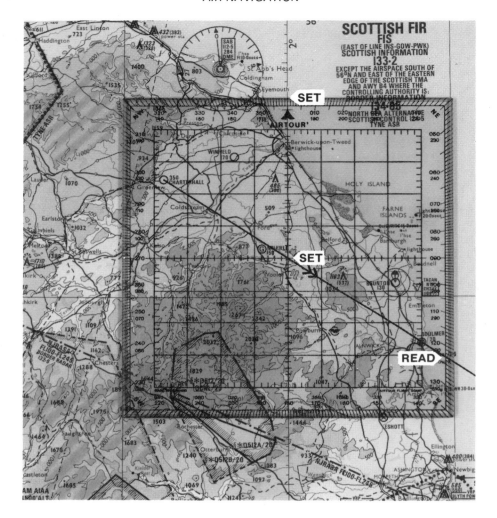

Fig.9-32. Measuring Direction with a Protractor.

MEASURING DIRECTION with a PLOTTER.

A Plotter is a simple device which combines the functions of a Scale Rule and a Protractor. An advantage is that only one instrument is required to measure track and distance, instead of the two. This is significant for doing such measurements in the cockpit.

Prior to any accurate measurements of direction, you should always have an idea of the approximate direction (to, say, 20° or 30°) in mind. This avoids any gross errors.

MEASURING DIRECTION WITH A PLOTTER

1. Place the centre of the plotter over the approximate mid-point of the track (where it crosses the mid-meridian).

2. Align the edge of the plotter with the track line.

3. Align the North-South graticule on the rotatable protractor with the True North/True South latitude-longitude grid of the chart, ensuring that the arrowed lines on the protractor point North!

4. Read-off the TRUE Track against the Course Arrow which points in the direction of travel. The other arrow indicates the reciprocal of the desired track.

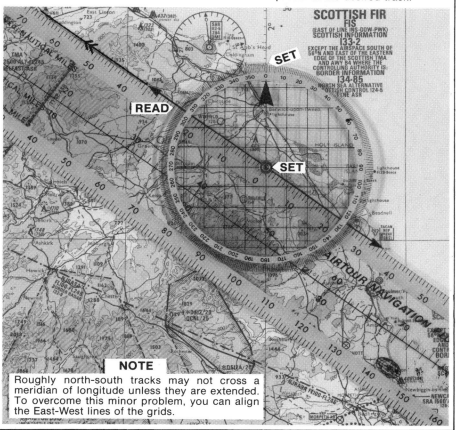

NOTE
Roughly north-south tracks may not cross a meridian of longitude unless they are extended. To overcome this minor problem, you can align the East-West lines of the grids.

Fig.9-33. Measuring Track Direction with a Plotter; (Note the Scales for Measuring Distance).

This concludes the theory of Maps and Charts, and indeed the section on Basic Navigation Theory. Preparation of your charts for a navigational exercise and the techniques of map reading are covered in detail in the sections on Flight Planning and En Route Navigation, which follow.

☐ Now complete **Exercises 9 — Aeronautical Charts.**

Intentionally Blank

2

FLIGHT PLANNING

10. Introduction to Flight Planning 190
11. Pre-Flight Briefing 195
12. Route Selection and Chart Preparation 204
13. Compiling a Flight Log 210
14. The Flight Plan Form 227
Appendix to Ch.13 — Planning the Climb . 293

10

INTRODUCTION TO FLIGHT PLANNING

The aim of **flight planning** is to assist in a safe and efficient flight; good planning will simplify the actual flight and considerably decrease the workload in the cockpit. The more thought and pre-flight preparation given on the ground prior to flight, the more likely that the flight will be completed with ease, safety, confidence and pleasure.

Most Private Pilots act as a sole Pilot/Navigator. Navigational activity is limited by both the confined space of the cockpit and the fact that one's attention must be divided between flying the aeroplane, navigating, and handling radio communications. Passengers may also occasionally require attention. Therefore, it is important to keep the navigational activity in the cockpit to a safe minimum.

Measuring such things as tracks and distances in flight requires the Pilot to be 'head-down' in the cockpit – something best avoided as much as possible. The Pilot/Navigator needs to be constantly looking out of the cockpit, monitoring the flight path of the aircraft and watching for other traffic. The better the flight planning, the easier this is to do.

The Better the Pre-Flight Preparation, The Less the In-Flight Workload.

Flight Planning is pilot-initiated. You play the active role. To do this, and to take your proper responsibility, you must have a sound understanding of the principles involved in good flight planning, and also be aware of your legal responsibilities as Pilot-in-Command. These responsibilities include:
- that you are a suitably licensed Pilot for the particular operation;
- an assessment that the aeroplane is airworthy, and will remain so for the duration of the flight;
- an assessment that the flight will be safe according to the latest meteorological and operational information, including suitability of the aerodromes;
- that sufficient fuel and oil is carried for the flight, plus an adequate reserve to allow for navigational errors and unplanned diversions;
- that the aeroplane is correctly loaded (at or below maximum weights for take-off and landing, Centre of Gravity within limits).

The mental processes required to flight-plan, and the methods used to ensure a successful flight, are simple and based on common sense.

PERSONAL NAVIGATION EQUIPMENT.

The two most vital instruments in visual navigation are the Magnetic Compass and the Clock, so **always carry a serviceable time-piece.** You should also build up a **flight case** or satchel that fits comfortably within reach in the cockpit and contains your navigational equipment.

A typical flight case should contain:
- relevant charts covering at least 50 nm either side of your planned track;
- your navigation computer;
- a scale rule and protractor (or a plotter);
- pens and pencils;
- relevant CAA documents and flight information publications (e.g. *Pooley's Flight Guide*);
- spare Flight Log forms; and
- a pair of good sun glasses.

A kneeboard or clipboard is not a bad idea to hold your papers and charts together in the cockpit.

If a flight is planned some days in advance, much of the preparation can be done well before the flight, however sometimes a flight occurs without advance notice. For a short-notice navigational exercise, where there is no time for preparation the night before, a typical routine is:
- check the availability of an aeroplane;
- check the contents of your flight case;
- obtain the appropriate **weather forecasts** and analyse them;
- obtain the appropriate **NOTAMS** (NOTices to AirMen) and analyse them;
- carry out the **route selection** and **chart preparation;**
- complete a **flight log;**
- consider Search and Rescue (SAR) aspects;
- file a Flight Plan, if required.

Weather forecasts and NOTAMs may be available at your Flying Organisation. If not, obtain them from a Briefing Office or by telephone.

VISUAL FLIGHT.

A Private Pilot with the basic PPL qualification (i.e. no IMC or Instrument Rating) **must** comply with the weather minima stated in the licence privileges **at all times.**

The Visual Flight Rules were discussed in detail in the Aviation Law part of Volume 2, however a reminder of the main requirements for a typical private flight Outside Regulated Airspace (i.e. outside Controlled Airspace and Special Rules Airspace) and at an IAS not exceeding 140 kt is included here, because these requirements may affect your flight planning.

An aircraft may be flown Outside Regulated Airspace under VFR and within the privileges of the Private Pilot Licence **at or below 3000 ft AMSL at 140 kt or less Indicated Air Speed** provided it:
- remains clear of cloud;
- in sight of the surface;
- with at least 3 nm flight visibility with passengers; and
- 1·5 nm flight visibility without passengers.

In addition, a minimum cloud ceiling above all obstacles of 1000 ft is recommended.

NOTE: Refer to AIP RAC 4-6-4 for further enlightenment. Whilst this is a large document and covers very many aspects of flight, some sections make interesting reading for a Private Pilot. There is also a section on this subject in Pooley's *Pilots Information Guide.* Your Flying Instructor will give you guidance.

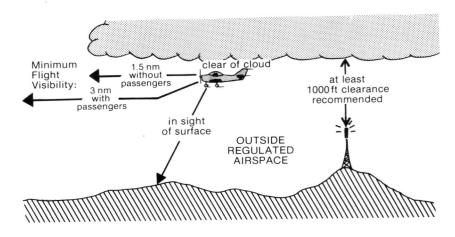

Fig.10-1. Requirements for a Typical Private Flight.

The above criteria are **minimum requirements**, and a Pilot exhibiting good airmanship will increase these according to his experience, abilities and limitations. A flight visibility of 1·5 nm, for instance, allows very little room for error, and an inexperienced Pilot would be well advised to increase his personal minimum. 3 nm flight visibility is a reasonable minimum.

For **en route terrain clearance**, at least 1000 ft above obstacles within 5 or 10 nm of track is desirable. This may not be possible in some congested areas, e.g. where overlying controlled airspace, such as a TMA, temporarily restricts the height at which you can fly.

When considering if the **forecast (or actual) cloud ceiling** at the departure, destination and alternate aerodrome(s) will allow flight in the circuit, the minimum cloud ceiling recommended is the higher of:
• 600 ft above the highest obstacle within 4 nm of the aerodrome; or
• 800 ft above aerodrome level;
(for aerodromes outside regulated airspace).

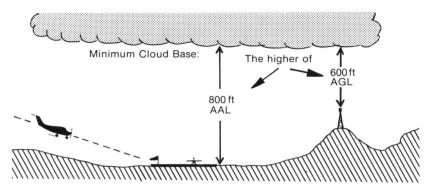

Fig.10-2. In the Circuit of an Aerodrome.

VFR FLIGHT SHOULD OCCUR ONLY BY DAY.

A check that your flight can be carried out with sufficient daylight remaining is a vital consideration prior to flight.

A VFR flight may not depart before the end of Official Night, which is **Sunrise minus 30 mins,** and should be well and truly on the ground by the time Official Night commences – i.e. **Sunset plus 30 mins.** However, you should plan on arriving at the destination aerodrome well before this latest possible time (for basic-PPL holders).

If you are flying locally, at least a 10 minute buffer should be kept and, on longer flights, consider increasing this margin to 20 or 30 minutes. Cloud coverage, mountain shadows and other factors can cause deterioration of the light. Remember that, with a setting Sun, it will be much darker at ground level than in flight. Also, the closing time of your destination aerodrome should be taken into consideration. Many private airfields in the UK close at Sunset.

Operational considerations, therefore, commence right from the beginning of planning a flight.

For example, if flight time to the destination is one hour, and the latest time of day operations at the destination is 1900 UTC, you should plan on arriving there no later than 1850 UTC. This means a latest departure time of 1750 UTC.

If there is some doubt about weather conditions at your planned destination, allow time to proceed to an alternate aerodrome and make a landing, with a buffer period, before SS+30 (last light). Plan your **latest** Time of Departure based on conditions at the destination and alternate aerodromes.

If there is an additional 30 minute flight time from the above destination to an alternate aerodrome, where SS+30 is say 1858 UTC, and you plan to arrive at the alternate no later than 1848, this means that you must plan to depart overhead the destination no later than 1818, and therefore set course from the original aerodrome no later than 1718 UTC. Of course, to use a more sensible buffer than 10 minutes, it would be necessary to depart even earlier than this. **A 30 minute buffer is good airmanship.**

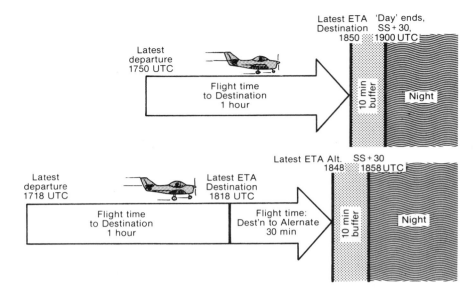

*Fig.10-3. Ascertain the Latest Time of Departure and Use
a Sensible Margin as a Buffer, e.g. at least 10 mins, but maybe 30 mins
shows better airmanship.*

SUMMARY.

The Points to Consider Prior to a Cross-country Flight:

1. How much daylight remains?

2. Is the weather satisfactory en route, and at the destination and alternate aerodromes?

3. Are there any operational problems (e.g. runway works in progress at the destination)?

☐ Now complete **Exercises 10 — Introduction to Flight Planning.**

11

PRE-FLIGHT BRIEFING

Prior to each cross-country flight, the Pilot must carefully consider the weather situation and any operational matters that may affect the proposed flight. A typical pre-flight briefing check list should include consideration of:
- weather information;
- current NOTAMs;
- any changes or additions to operational procedures (UK AIP);
- serviceability of aerodromes (including alternates), and Prior Permission if Required (PPR);
- communications (frequencies on charts, in UK AIP COM, and in *Pooley's Flight Guide*);
- airspace restrictions (see charts, including the normal route chart that you will use, plus the Chart of UK Airspace Restrictions and Hazardous Areas, included in UK AIP MAP);
- any existing or likely hazards to aviation;
- latest time you can land – Sunset plus 30 mins, or maybe the destination and/or alternate(s) close earlier, e.g. at Sunset; (SR/SS times are available from Briefing Offices, and there is a table in *Pooley's Flight Guide*).

THE WEATHER.

Weather forecasts are, of course, a main source of information, but don't be afraid to look at the sky and make your own assessment. If the weather forecast charts or *AIRMET* teletype text forecasts, plus terminal forecasts, are not available at your departure airfield, then you can take advantage of the *AIRMET* recorded telephone service, supplemented as necessary by a call to the appropriate Weather Centre for terminal forecasts and actuals. Note down the details on the published proforma (AIP MET and *Pooley's Flight Guide*). Telephone numbers to use are shown on the *AIRMET Areas* map.

When analysing the destination aerodrome forecast, particular attention should be given to:
- cloud base;
- visibility;
- the presence of fog, thunderstorms, or any other hazards to aviation;
- wind, especially the crosswind component that may exist on any runway.

Remember that the cloud base is given Above Mean Sea Level (AMSL) in en route forecasts, and Above Ground Level (AGL) in aerodrome forecasts.

NOTE: Bear in mind that the Great British weather tends to be quite localised due to geographical influences, principally through hills and mountains, and coastal effects. For this reason it is good to study the weather reports from many places to get a thorough picture.

At this stage we suggest you re-read Chapter C11 of Aviation Meteorology in Volume 2, entitled *Weather Forecasts and Reports*. Examples of chart and teletype forecasts and reports are contained in this chapter, along with details explaining how to read them. **Aerodrome and Area Forecasts are valuable information.**

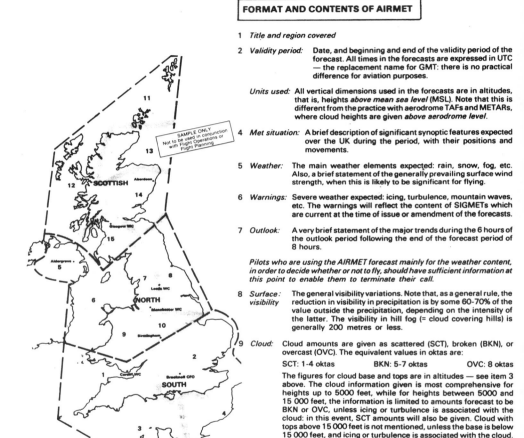

| FORMAT AND CONTENTS OF AIRMET |

1 *Title and region covered*

2 *Validity period:*   Date, and beginning and end of the validity period of the forecast. All times in the forecasts are expressed in UTC — the replacement name for GMT: there is no practical difference for aviation purposes.

    Units used: All vertical dimensions used in the forecasts are in altitudes, that is, heights *above mean sea level* (MSL). Note that this is different from the practice with aerodrome TAFs and METARs, where cloud heights are given *above aerodrome level*.

4 *Met situation:*   A brief description of significant synoptic features expected over the UK during the period, with their positions and movements.

5 *Weather:*   The main weather elements expected: rain, snow, fog, etc. Also, a brief statement of the generally prevailing surface wind strength, when this is likely to be significant for flying.

6 *Warnings:*   Severe weather expected: icing, turbulence, mountain waves, etc. The warnings will reflect the content of SIGMETs which are current at the time of issue or amendment of the forecasts.

7 *Outlook:*   A very brief statement of the major trends during the 6 hours of the outlook period following the end of the forecast period of 8 hours.

Pilots who are using the AIRMET forecast mainly for the weather content, in order to decide whether or not to fly, should have sufficient information at this point to enable them to terminate their call.

8 *Surface: visibility*   The general visibility variations. Note that, as a general rule, the reduction in visibility in precipitation is by some 60-70% of the value outside the precipitation, depending on the intensity of the latter. The visibility in hill fog (= cloud covering hills) is generally 200 metres or less.

9 *Cloud:*   Cloud amounts are given as scattered (SCT), broken (BKN), or overcast (OVC). The equivalent values in oktas are:

    SCT: 1-4 oktas   BKN: 5-7 oktas   OVC: 8 oktas

    The figures for cloud base and tops are in altitudes — see item 3 above. The cloud information given is most comprehensive for heights up to 5000 feet, while for heights between 5000 and 15 000 feet, the information is limited to amounts forecast to be BKN or OVC, unless icing or turbulence is associated with the cloud: in this event, SCT amounts will also be given. Cloud with tops above 15 000 feet is not mentioned, unless the base is below 15 000 feet, and icing or turbulence is associated with the cloud.

10 *Freezing level:*   This is the altitude of the lowest zero degree Celsius isotherm in the region, or part-region.

11 *Airframe icing:*   If severe icing is forecast, this will already have been given under *Warnings*, but is repeated here, along with information on moderate icing if this is expected.

12 *Winds:*

Winds are given in degrees True for 1000, 2000, 5000, 10 000, and 18 000 feet above MSL. Speeds are in knots. Note that, for locations above MSL, the 1000 foot wind will be less accurate than the winds at the higher levels, due to the greater influence of local topographic and other effects.

Surface winds are even more subject to these effects, and will only be given in the forecasts in very general terms, under *Weather*. An estimate of the *surface wind at MSL* may be made by taking the 1000 foot wind, and subtracting 10-20° from the direction (the larger amount for the lighter wind), and reducing the strength by about 1 knot in 5. For *surface winds above MSL*, the reduction from the 1000 foot value will be somewhat less.

Fig. 11-1a. AIRMET Areas map.

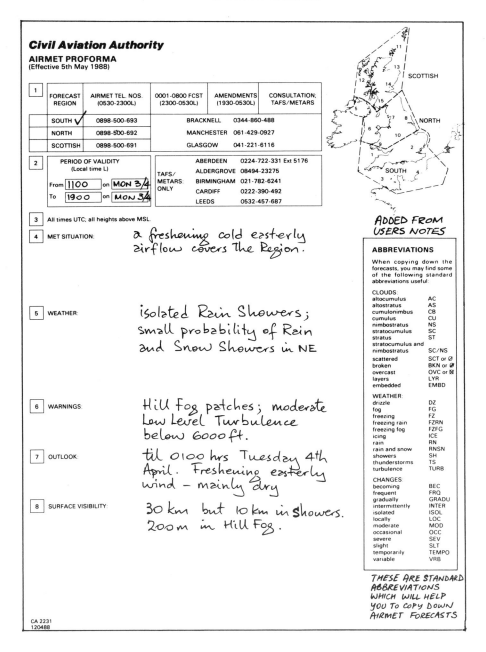

Civil Aviation Authority

AIRMET PROFORMA
(Effective 5th May 1988)

1

FORECAST REGION	AIRMET TEL. NOS. (0530-2300L)	0001-0800 FCST (2300-0530L)	AMENDMENTS (1930-0530L)	CONSULTATION; TAFS/METARS
SOUTH ✓	0898-500-693	BRACKNELL	0344-860-488	
NORTH	0898-500-692	MANCHESTER	061-429-0927	
SCOTTISH	0898-500-691	GLASGOW	041-221-6116	

2

PERIOD OF VALIDITY (Local time L)		TAFS/ METARS ONLY	ABERDEEN 0224-722-331 Ext 5176 ALDERGROVE 08494-23275 BIRMINGHAM 021-782-6241 CARDIFF 0222-390-492 LEEDS 0532-457-687
From	1100 on MON 3/4		
To	1900 on MON 3/4		

3 All times UTC; all heights above MSL.

4 MET SITUATION: a freshening cold easterly airflow covers The Region.

5 WEATHER: isolated Rain Showers; small probability of Rain and Snow Showers in NE

6 WARNINGS: Hill Fog patches; moderate Low Level Turbulence below 6000ft.

7 OUTLOOK: til 0100 hrs Tuesday 4th April. Freshening easterly wind – mainly dry

8 SURFACE VISIBILITY: 30 km but 10 km in showers. 200 m in Hill Fog.

CA 2231
120488

ADDED FROM USERS NOTES

ABBREVIATIONS

When copying down the forecasts, you may find some of the following standard abbreviations useful:

CLOUDS:
altocumulus	AC
altostratus	AS
cumulonimbus	CB
cumulus	CU
nimbostratus	NS
stratocumulus	SC
stratus	ST
stratocumulus and nimbostratus	SC/NS
scattered	SCT or Ø
broken	BKN or ⊘
overcast	OVC or ⊠
layers	LYR
embedded	EMBD

WEATHER:
drizzle	DZ
fog	FG
freezing	FZ
freezing rain	FZRN
freezing fog	FZFG
icing	ICE
rain	RN
rain and snow	RNSN
showers	SH
thunderstorms	TS
turbulence	TURB

CHANGES:
becoming	BEC
frequent	FRQ
gradually	GRADU
intermittently	INTER
isolated	ISOL
locally	LOC
moderate	MOD
occasional	OCC
severe	SEV
slight	SLT
temporarily	TEMPO
variable	VRB

THESE ARE STANDARD ABBREVIATIONS WHICH WILL HELP YOU TO COPY DOWN AIRMET FORECASTS

SCOTTISH
NORTH
SOUTH

Fig. 11-1b. Front side of completed AIRMET Proforma.

NOTAMs.

Operational matters of long standing are published in the UK Aeronautical Information Publication (AIP), whilst recent changes are provided to Pilots as *Notices to Airmen* (i.e. NOTAMs). Urgent NOTAMs Class 1 are distributed via the Aeronautical Fixed Telecommunication Network or by telegram; less urgent Class 2 NOTAMs via the post.

NOTAMs can contain vital information on the serviceability of aerodromes, the activation of Danger Areas, the occurrence of Royal Flights (RF), changes in radio frequencies, etc, etc, and should be read carefully.

UNITED KINGDOM NOTAM

AIRAC	Nos. A62-A74/1985
Effective Date:- 14 March 1985	Information Date: 25 January

National Air Traffic Services
Aeronautical Information Service
Tolcarne Drive Pinner Middlesex HA5 2DU
Telephone 01-866 8781 ext 249 Telex 22807
Telegraphic Address: EGGNYN (Aeronautical) or
NOTOFF Pinner (Commercial)

NOTES:
(i) All times are GMT.
(ii) References are to the UK AIP. This publication should be ANNOTATED IMMEDIATELY. Information, where applicable, should also be used to amend appropriate charts.

PERMANENT NOTAM

COM/RAC

A62 Warton

From 0800 on 14 March 1985, the APP, VDF and RAD frequency will be changed to 124.45 MHz, frequency 122.55 MHz will be permanently withdrawn.

COM 2-1-60 (28 Nov 84)
RAC 3-2-8 (28 Nov 84). SAMPLE ONLY (Tels GRA)
Not to be used in conjunction
with Flight Operations or
Flight Planning

	ROYAL FLIGHTS		SEE RF NOTAM (nr same as REF) FOR DETAILS
RF 108	27 APR		Edinburgh Turnhouse 0905 to Culty Braggan 0930/1345 to Glasgow 1410
RF 117	27 APR		Benbecula 0745 to Edinburgh Turnhouse 0900
RF 118	29 APR		Garrowby Hall 1040 to Scarborough 1100/1145 to RAF Linton-on-Ouse 1210
RF 119+ RF 122	29 APR		RAF Linton-on-Ouse 1215 to Heathrow 1325
RF 120	30 APR		Buckingham Palace 0830 to Isle of Dogs 0840
RF 121	07 MAY		ICKENHAM 1600 to Buckingham Palace 1610

AA NWS		UNITED KINGDOM - MORE THAN ONE FIR/UIR/OCA	
AA 5500	HJ 27 APR	3500ft agl	Release high pressure gas 5500N 0243W (Banks) (GN387/85)
AB 5328	0900-1900 19 MAY	2000ft agl	Air display within Manchester/Barton ATZ 5328N 0223W (IIB81/85+IIB91/85)
AB 5335	0830-1030 1400-1530 18 19 MAY	4000ft agl	Aerobatic display + spot ldg competition 5335N 0303W (RAF Woodvale) rad 3nm (IIB90/85)
AB 5341	HJ 31 MAY 01 02 JUN	5000ft msl	Hot Air Balloon Meet 5341N 0242W rad 2km (& up to 10nm downwind) (Worden Park) (IIB73/85)

Fig.11-2. NOTAMS Should be Checked Pre Flight.

UK FLIGHT PROCEDURES.

Whilst you will be familiar with standard procedures, it may be advisable to revise them and check for any recent changes by reference to AIP RAC (Rules of the Air and Air Traffic Services).

6 VISUAL CIRCUIT REPORTING PROCEDURES

6.1 In order that the maximum use may be made of aerodromes for the purpose of landing and taking off, it is essential that pilots accurately report their positions in the circuit.

6.2 Position reports are to be made as follows:—

a. **Downwind** Aircraft are to report 'Downwind' when abeam the upwind end of the runway.

b. **Base Leg:** Aircraft are to report 'Base Leg', if requested by ATC, immediately on completion of the turn on to base leg.

c. **Final:** Aircraft are to report 'Final' after the completion of the turn on to final approach and when at a range of not more than 4 nm from the approach end of the runway.

d. **Long Final:** Aircraft flying a final approach of a greater length than 4 nm are to report 'Long Final' when beyond that range, and 'Final' when a range of 4 nm is reached. Aircraft flying a straight-in approach are to report 'Long Final' at 8 nm from the approach end of the runway, and 'Final' when a range of 4 nm is reached.

Note:—At grass aerodromes, the area to be used for landing should be regarded as the runway for the purposes of position reporting.

SAMPLE ONLY
Not to be used in conjunction
with Flight Operations or
Flight Planning

7 PROCEDURES FOR ARRIVING VFR FLIGHTS

7.1 An aircraft approaching an aerodrome under VFR where an Approach Control Service is available should make initial RTF contact when 15 nm or five minutes flying time from the aerodrome traffic zone boundary, whichever is the greater. If the aircraft is not equipped with the Approach frequency, communication on the Aerodrome Control frequency will be acceptable. As well as landing information, ATC will pass information on pertinent known traffic to assist pilots of VFR flights to maintain separation from both IFR and other VFR flights.

7.2 If radar sequencing of IFR flights is in progress, ATC will provide VFR Flights with information to enable them to fit into the landing sequence.

7.3 Approach Control will instruct pilots when to change frequency to Aerodrome Control.

11.2 Procedures for Penetration of a MATZ by Civil Aircraft

11.2.1 A MATZ Penetration Service is available from the controlling aerodromes listed at para 11.5 for the provision of increased protection to VHF RTF equipped civil aircraft. Pilots wishing to penetrate a MATZ are requested to observe the following procedures:—

a When 15 nm or 5 min flying time from the zone boundary, whichever is the greater, establish two-way RTF communication with the controlling aerodrome on the appropriate frequency using the phraseology: '......(controlling aerodrome), this is ......(aircraft callsign), request MATZ penetration.'

Fig.11-3. Sample Excerpts from the UK AIP: RAC 3-2.

AERODROMES.

The prime source for information on aerodromes is UK AIP AGA (Aerodromes), as amended by NOTAM. In the case below of SHOREHAM (designator **EGKA**) (UK AIP AGA extract from the Aerodrome Directory), the grass Runway 25 has a Take-Off Run Available (TORA) of 909 metres and a Landing Distance Available (LDA) of 794 m. Although prior permission (PPR) is not required to operate at this aerodrome, Shoreham closes at 1800 UTC in the Winter, and the earlier of Sunset or 2000 in the Summer.

Further information on Local Flying Regulations, Warnings, etc, is given in AGA 3-3, on obstructions in AGA 3-4, on aeronautical ground lights in AGA 4, and on hours of availability in AGA 5. The AGA contents page will direct you to each item. Note that the aerodromes are categorised somewhat by AGA into Customs and Excise Aerodromes, International Aerodromes, etc.

The AIP is too unwieldy for a Pilot to carry in his flight case, however *Pooley's United Kingdom and Ireland Flight Guide* is a good source of aerodrome information and is very easy to carry. (It is produced with the assistance of the CAA and contains similar information to that described above.)

EGKA

50 50 10N 00 17 30W	**SHOREHAM**	6ft AMSL

Immediately W of Shoreham-by-Sea.	**SFD 117.00 291 16.5** **MID 114.00 141 18**

c/s 'Shoreham'. APP 123.15. TWR 125.40. VDF/Hmr 123.15.
NDB 'SHM' 332.

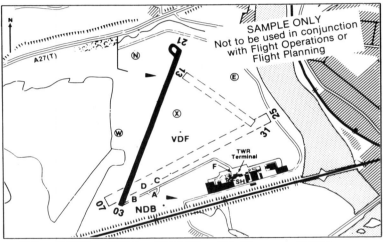

SAMPLE ONLY
Not to be used in conjunction
with Flight Operations or
Flight Planning

Rwy	Dim(m)	Surface	TORA (m)	LDA (m)	Lighting
03/21	824x18	Tarmac	03-824	03-792	Thr Rwy PAPI 3½°
			21-824	21-795	Thr Rwy PAPI 4½°
07/25	909x50	Grass	07-877	07-877	
			25-909	25-794	
13/31	425x30	Grass	13-425	13-425	
			31-615*	31-425	
*Includes 190m starter extension available.					IBn 'SH' Gn

Op. hrs: Winter: Mon-Sat. 08-1800, Sun 09-1800.
Summer: Mon-Sat 0800-SS or 2000, Sun 0900-SS or 2000.

Landing Fee: On application.	**Customs:** see page 34.

Hangarage: Available.	**Maintenance:** Available.

Remarks: Operated by Brighton, Hove and Worthing Joint Municipal Airport Committee. All Rwys except 13 have permanently displaced landing thresholds. PPR to non-radio aircraft. Rwy 13/31 is for use when windspeed exceeds 15Kts.
Note: Helicopter Training Areas E N W X and Taxiway Holding Points A, B, C, D and F on A/D plan above.

Restaurant: Restaurant, Refreshments and Club facilities available.

Car Hire: PDH. Tel: (0273) 684922.

Taxis: Terminal building. Forecourt.

Fuel: 100LL. Jet A1. Diners Card.	**Tel:** (0273) 452303 A.T.C. 452304 Manager.

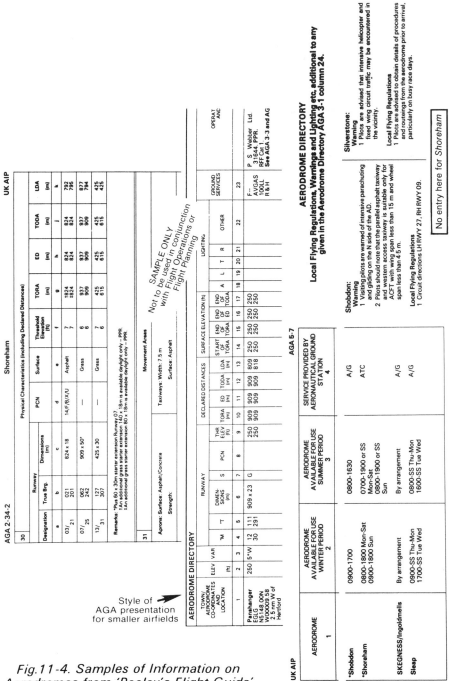

Fig.11-4. Samples of Information on Aerodromes from 'Pooley's Flight Guide' (opposite page) and AIP AGA (above).

COMMUNICATIONS.

The main Flight Information Service and Air Traffic Control frequencies are published on the aeronautical charts. Further information is available in UK AIP COM.

RADIO COMMUNICATION AND NAVIGATION FACILITIES										
STATION	SERVICE	CALL SIGN OR IDENTIFI- CATION	EM	TRANSMITS		RECEIVES		HOURS OF SERVICE WINTER PERIOD	HOURS OF SERVICE SUMMER PERIOD	CO- ORDINATES
				kHz	MHz	kHz	MHz			
1	2	3	4	5	6	7	8	9	10	11
CHICHESTER/ Goodwood	APP	Goodwood Approach	A3E	—	122 45	—	122 45	By arrangement	By arrangement	—
	TWR	Goodwood Tower	A3E	—	122 45	—	122 45	Until 31 Jan 0900-1200 1300-1600 From 1 Feb 0900-1200 1300-1700	Until 30 Sep 0800-1200 1300-1800 From 1 Oct 0800-1200 1300-1600	—
	A/G	Goodwood Radio	A3E	—	122 45	—	122 45	1200-1300	1200-1300	—
Chiltern	NDB	CHT	NONA2A	279	—	—	—	H24	H24	N5137 09 W00030 53
Clacton	VOR	CLN	A9W	—	114 55	—	—	H24	H24	N5150 88 E00108 96
	DME		PON							
	NDB	CLN	NONA2A	669 5	—	—	—	Put into service only when VOR is out of operational use.		N5150 88 E00108 96
Compton Abbas	A/G	Compton Radio	A3E	—	122 70	—	122 70	0900-1700	0800-1600	—

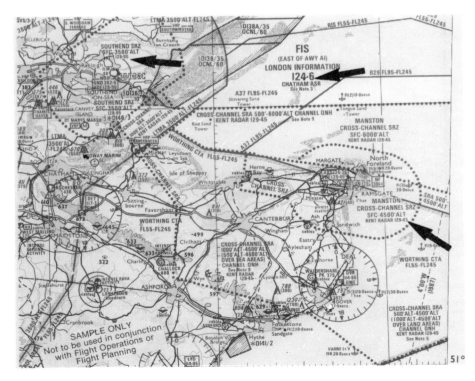

Fig.11-5. Frequencies are Found in AIP COM, and on the Aeronautical Charts Covering the Flight.

AIRSPACE RESTRICTIONS.

Aeronautical charts show how the airspace over the UK is divided into Controlled Airspace, Special Rules Airspace, Danger Areas, etc. Note that the CAA 1:250 000 series of UK charts is only concerned with airspace up to 3000 ft. The ICAO 1:500 000 series and the new 'Airmaster' quarter-million series display airspace up to the base of the UIR – FL245.

It may also be necessary to check the other charts that provide information:
● the Chart of UK Airspace Restrictions; and
● the Chart of UK Areas of Intense Aerial Activity and Military Low Flying system;
which are found in UK AIP MAP.

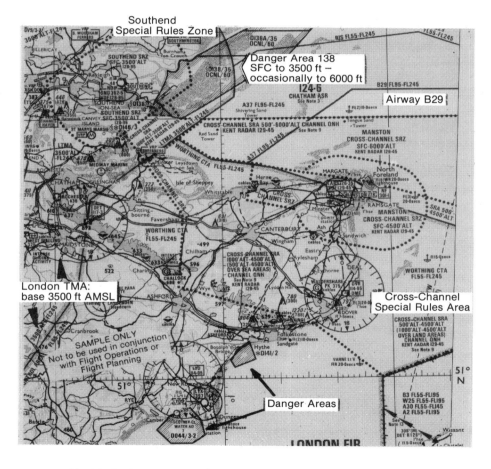

Fig.11-6. Aeronautical Charts Show Airspace Restrictions.

☐ Now complete **Exercises 11 — Pre-Flight Briefing**.

12

ROUTE SELECTION AND CHART PREPARATION

AIRCRAFT PERFORMANCE is a prime consideration in route selection. There is no point planning a **Land's End** direct **John O'Groats** flight in an aircraft whose range is only of the order of 250 nm; nor of planning to cross the Himalayas when the altitude capabitity of the aeroplane is only around 10,000 ft.

TERRAIN is also a major consideration. A single-engined aircraft flying from the west coast of Wales to Manchester might be safer flying around the coastal route than flying direct, which would take it over rugged, mountainous country. Low cloud and high or rising terrain can very quickly create problems for VFR flights.

WEATHER. A line of thunderstorms or an approaching cold front might cause you to plan via a more favourable route. A low cloud base might also cause problems over high terrain. Have a look at the Meteorological Forecast before you finally select a route.

AIRSPACE. A Pilot will always consider **the nature of the airspace** en route, which can be of various types, such as:
● Controlled Airspace;
● Special Rules Airspace (SRA/SRZ);
● Aerodromes (ATZ, MATZ, non-ATZ, CTR);
● Entry/Exit Access Lanes and Low Level Routes;
● Advisory Routes;
● Prohibited, Restricted and Danger Areas;
● Purple (Royal) Airspace;
● Areas of Intense Aerial Activity, or Aerial Tactics Areas;
● Altimeter Setting Region boundaries.

These are all shown on aeronautical charts and/or the UK Aeronautical Information Publication. You can plan your route to take advantage of them where possible, or to avoid them where advisable.

HAZARDS TO AVIATION. There are many things than can be hazardous to aviation, and a Pilot should think about them. The list includes such items as:
● High terrain;
● Obstructions, and their height AMSL;

- High Intensity Radio Transmission Areas;
- Areas for gliding, parachuting, hang gliding, microlight flying, or parascending;
- Bird Sanctuaries;
- any other hazards.

It may be advisable to avoid some of these hazards by some distance.

AVAILABILITY OF GOOD CHECKPOINTS. A route that follows easy-to-identify landmarks or other checkpoints may be preferable to a slightly shorter route on which visual aids to navigation are fewer. Good reporting points are often suggested on aeronautical charts by the manner in which they are depicted. Good visual checkpoints for a VFR flight are:
- prominent and unique mountains, valleys, rivers, etc;
- coastlines, especially points, lighthouses, river mouths, bays, etc;
- towns, cities;
- bridges, overpasses;
- railway lines, transmission lines, crossroads;
- combinations of all of the above, special and unique combinations of roads, railway lines, towns, rivers, etc.

ALTERNATE AERODROME(S). Weather conditions, the doubtful serviceability of your destination aerodrome, or some other reason, may require you to exercise airmanship and carry one or more **Alternates** for your destination. This may force you to fly a different route than the one you would choose if no alternate was included in your pre-flight planning.

NOTE: A useful **UK and Ireland Planning Chart** (on a scale of 1:1 million) is available, which shows (among other things) **aerodrome locations.** The chart is intended for use in conjunction with *Pooley's Flight Guide,* in which chosen aerodromes can be checked for suitability.

Pooley's Planning Chart is also useful in checking distances when flight planning, and en route, to ascertain the coverages of the Lower Airspace Radar Advisory Service (LARS) throughout Britain.

Controlled and Special Rules Airspace up to 3000 ft AMSL is portrayed in magenta.

POOLEY'S FLIGHT PLANNING CHART

UNITED KINGDOM & IRELAND

AERODROMES
HELIPADS
NAVIGATIONAL AIDS
LOWER AIRSPACE RADAR SERVICE
CONTROLLED & SPECIAL RULES AIRSPACE
UP TO 3000' ALT

Air Information up to and including AIRAC NTM 100/1989

1989
POOLEY'S FLIGHT GUIDE

ELSTREE AERODROME, HERTS
Tel: 01-953-4870, 0442-52576

WHAT CHARTS SHOULD I CARRY ?

You will, of course, have been perusing your charts whilst thinking about **Route Selection**, but now that you have decided upon the route that you plan to follow, your charts need to be properly prepared to aid your flight planning measurements and calculations, and later your in-flight navigational work. Remember that a minute's work on the ground might save you some anguish later on when in flight.

Good CHART PREPARATION is Vital.

Carry the appropriate aeronautical charts for your planned flight and any possible diversions (planned or unplanned), i.e. it might be prudent to carry adjoining charts. **They must be current charts.** Coverage of at least 50 nm either side of the planned track is advisable in case of diversions, as is information on aerodromes (found in the UK AIP or *Pooley's Flight Guide*).

After selecting the route, mark it in on your charts and make sure that the route is easily visible in flight. Use of a pencil or something that can be erased easily will allow repeated use of the Chart. Seek the advice of your Flying Instructor as to the best methods.

NOTE: Many Pilots cover their charts with plastic, or even better, purchase them that way. This makes it easier to write on and later to rub out, and prolongs the chart life. It also allows you to keep a log going on the actual chart without making the chart unusable later on. A 'Chinagraph' (or similar) pencil is excellent for marking on plastic-coated charts, and can easily be erased with a tissue. Get into the habit of not using a red Chinagraph for when you commence night flying – red cannot be seen easily in the cockpit at night.

DISTANCE AND/OR TIME MARKINGS ALONG TRACK.

To allow easy in-flight estimation of flight progress starting at each turning point, or checkpoint, put in 10 nm markers. (Some instructors may suggest that you do this by starting at the destination and working backwards, so that the *'odd man out'* is left behind early in each leg, thus making it easy to measure *distance-to-run.* Either method is simple and satisfactory.)

Some people prefer to use time markings, such as your expected position en route every 10 minutes or so, but these change from day to day depending upon the wind, the aeroplane and so on, whereas the 10 nm markings for that route will remain the same. Another approach is to divide each leg up into four; ¼ way, ½ way, ¾ way. This works very well, especially on the short stages common in the UK.

Once again, your Flying Instructor will give you good advice on which method to use.

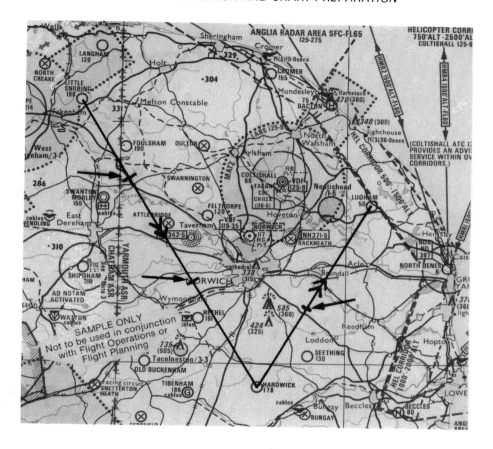

Fig. 12-1. 10 nm Markers on the Chart
Assist Estimation of Distances.

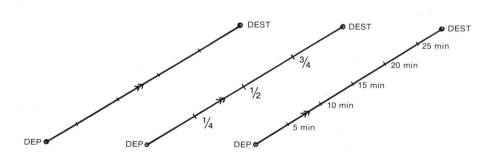

Fig. 12-2. 10 nm Distance Markers, and Other Methods also.

'TRACK-GUIDES' (or FAN-LINES) Can Assist In Estimating Track Errors and Closing Angles.

Navigation in real life never works out precisely as you planned it. Your actual in-flight **Track Made Good** may differ from your **Desired Track** (or Flight Planned Track FPT) marked on the chart. This may be due to reasons outside your control, such as actual in-flight winds differing from those forecast.

To allow for easy estimation of **Track Error** and **Closing Angle**, you may like to mark in lines 10 degrees either side of your desired track. **Estimation** using these *track guides* (sometimes called *fan lines*) is a lot easier in flight than having to use a protractor or plotter.

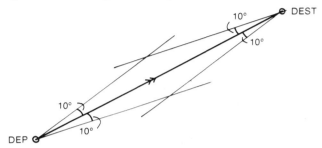

Fig.12-3. 'Track-Guides', or 'Fan-Lines', assist in Estimating Track Error and Closing Angle in flight.

NOTE: These lines are related to the Aircraft's Track, and not its Heading, consequently be clear that **they do not show the Drift** of the aeroplane because drift is related to the aircraft's HDG. *Track-Guides* give you an indication of **Track Error** and enable you to estimate the Closing Angle.

STUDY THE ROUTE PRIOR TO TAKE-OFF.

It is a good idea to study the route drawn on your chart carefully before you depart, especially if you will be flying through congested airspace. Work slowly along the planned track, noting ground features you should see, obstructions, high terrain, Hazardous or Restricted Areas, overlying Controlled Airspace, Areas of Intesive Aerial Activity (AIAAs), etc. Also, look for the radio frequencies of the ATS units that you will use, and, if you wish, note them on your flight log form (discussed in the next chapter).

FOLDING YOUR CHARTS.

The final stage in chart preparation is to fold them satisfactorily for cockpit use. The recommended method of folding charts is shown in the next figure. When folded, arrange your chart so that, in the cockpit with the chart on your clipboard or knee, you can *'fly up the page'*. This means that when you look at the chart, objects that are, for example, ahead and to the right of track should be ahead and to the right of the aircraft when you look out the window. Allow 70 or 80 nm either side of track (1:500 000 scale) to remain visible on the chart. This is a reasonable range for large objects such as mountain ranges, coastlines and so on, that can assist in your navigation.

Step 1) Fold sheet on the long axis, near the mid-parallel,
face out, with the bottom part of the chart upward;
Step 2) Fold inwards near the centre meridian, and
Step 3) Fold both halves backwards in accordion folds.

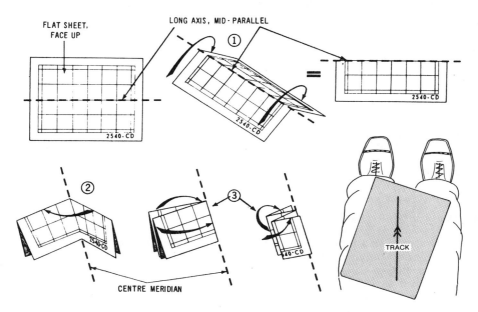

*Fig.12-4. Recommended Chart Folding Procedures; when Folded,
arrange Chart so that you 'Fly up the Page'.*

This may seem like a lot to think about but, in practice, it is quite straightforward. Once you have drawn in the proposed track, each of the above items will be obvious from a close inspection of your chart.

Finally, a further check of the weather forecast and NOTAMs will ensure that the chosen track is suitable from the point of view of cloud on any hills, fog, thunderstorms, and for latest operational information.

☐ Now complete **Exercises 12 — Route Selection & Chart Preparation.**

209

13

COMPILING A FLIGHT LOG

Compiling a Flight Log is a fast and efficient means of planning a cross-country flight. It records the measurements and calculations that you made at the flight planning stage and, once airborne and on your way, provides you with a plan against which you can compare the actual progress of the flight. A Flight Log enables you to predict the **time of arrival** at any point en route, and to calculate the **fuel required**.

There are various forms of Flight Log. Your Flying Training Organisation will provide you with the type that it prefers. We have included a number of commonly used flight logs in this Chapter. What follows here is a brief explanation of typical entries made on a flight log for a flight from **Elstree,** to **Ipswich,** to **Cambridge,** and return to **Elstree.** You might like to work through it carefully, using an aeronautical chart for the London area and your own navigation equipment.

NOTE: The Latitude and Longitude of the various aerodromes involved can be found from the UK AIP (AGA), or from *Pooley's Flight Guide.*

PILOT AND AIRCRAFT.
At the top of the Flight Log, insert your name, the aircraft registration and the date.

PILOT R.STACEY	AIRCRAFT G-ABCD					DATE 3-4-1987			ETD 1430 UTC				
FROM/TO	SAFETY ALT	ALT / TEMP	RAS	TAS	W/V	TR °T	DRIFT	HDG °T	VAR	HDG °M	G/S	DIST	TIME	ETA	HDG °C

Fig.13-1. Put Your Details on the Flight Log.

210

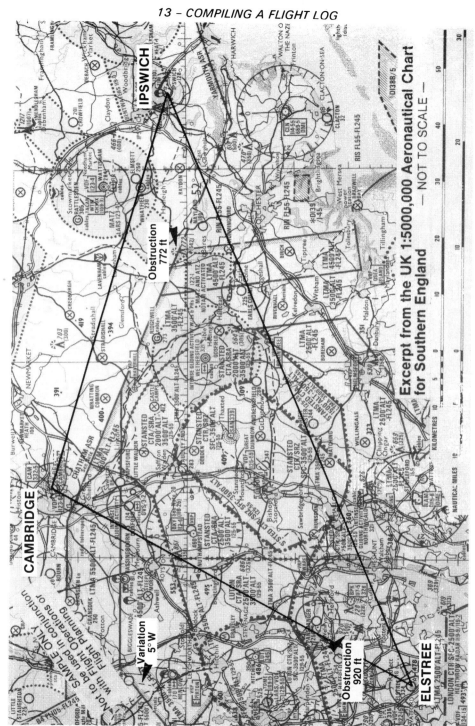

Fig.13-2. Route of the Flight on the 1:500 000 Chart (not to scale).

ROUTE SEGMENTS.

Having marked the planned route on your aeronautical chart:
- insert the Turning Points, Reporting Points, or any other en route points for which you want to calculate specific Estimated Time Intervals (ETIs);
- measure the Tracks and Distances; and
- note the Magnetic Variation.

Insert this information on the flight log.

FROM/TO	SAFETY ALT	ALT TEMP	RAS	TAS	W/V	TR °T	DRIFT	HDG °T	VAR	HDG °M	G/S	DIST	TIME	ETA	HDG °C
ELSTREE															
						069			5W			60			
IPSWICH															
						286			5W			40			
CAMBRIDGE															
						208			5W			38			
ELSTREE															
												TOTAL 138			

Fig.13-3. Tracks, Distances, and Magnetic Variation added.

Measuring the distance is straightforward. First of all it is a good idea to estimate the distance, and then measure it precisely, using either:
- a scale rule, or a plotter, that has **the correct scale marked** on it; or
- dividers, which can then be placed against the appropriate scale line at the bottom of the chart, or else down the latitude scale at the side of the chart, to give you the distance.

Engraving a pencil with 10 nm marks (in the correct scale for the chart) helps in estimations of distance, particularly in flight.

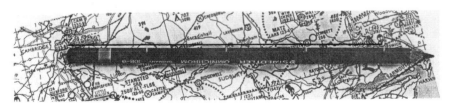

Fig.13-4. A Pencil Engraved (by yourself)
with 10 nm Nicks is Very Useful.

Measuring the Direction requires strict attention, as an error here can cause serious problems in flight. **Always estimate the direction before you measure it.** The track from Elstree to Ipswich is approximately 070°T. This might seem unnecessary to you, but you would be surprised (perhaps shocked!) if you knew the number of times that reciprocal directions have been inserted on flight logs (250°T instead of 070°T in this case, and who knows where the aeroplane would end up).

Having estimated the approximate direction, measure it precisely, using either a Protractor or a Plotter. (Their use was shown at the end of Chapter 9 on Aeronautical Charts.)

A straight line on Lambert's Conformal Conic charts (such as the ICAO 1:500 000 series commonly used in the UK) is an approximate Great Circle. To obtain the Rhumb Line direction, **measure the straight line track at or near the mid-meridian of the route segment**. Whilst this point is not significant on the relatively short legs typically flown in the UK, it is significant on longer legs. (You may fly the Atlantic one day! Magnetic Variation will become very significant then also.)

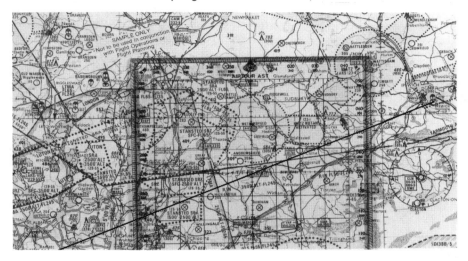

Fig.13-5. The Elstree to Ipswich Leg is 069°T.

Whilst working with the chart, note the **Magnetic Variation** indicated by a dashed magenta line annotated with 5°W, 7°W, or whatever the variation happens to be in that area. Variation is required to convert °T to °M.

Even though most of this chart work can be done well before the flight (at home, for example) in a leisurely manner, you should train yourself to measure tracks and distances fairly quickly so that you can do it efficiently at the aerodrome, or in flight if required.

An unplanned diversion to an alternate aerodrome when airborne, for example, will require an estimate of track and distance, followed by more accurate measurement. Since you will be occupied flying the aeroplane, you must be able to perform such navigational tasks quickly and without error, and in a manner that will not distract you from the main task of controlling the aeroplane's flight path. As a matter of interest, you will probably find it is easier to measure Track and Distance in flight using a Plotter rather than a Protractor and Scale Rule.

DETERMINE SAFETY ALTITUDES, AND SELECT CRUISING LEVELS.

It is good airmanship to determine reasonable Minimum Safe Cruising Altitudes which will provide an adequate vertical clearance above obstacles on and near the planned route. There are various philosophies about how to estimate this Safety Altitude, and you should refer to your Flying Instructor on this point.

Some commonly used procedures for determining Safety Altitude are:
- **take the highest obstacle within 10 nm of track and add 1000 ft;**
- take the highest obstacle within 5 nm of track and add 1000 ft;
- take the highest obstacle within 10 nm of track and add 1500 ft;
- take the highest obstacle within 5 nm of track and add 1500 ft;
- take the highest obstacle within 5 nm of track and add 10% of its height plus 1500 ft;
- take the highest obstacle within 10 nm of track and round it up to the next 500 ft.

As you can see, some methods are more conservative than others.

Calculating a Safety Altitude requires close inspection of the chart area either side of track (made easier if your transparent rule covers 5 or 10 nm on the chart). For the flight originating from **Elstree**, the Safety Altitude is based on a 1000 ft clearance above obstacles within 10 nm either side of track.

The highest obstacle on the first leg is 6 nm north-east of Elstree, at 920 ft AMSL, requiring a minimum safe altitude of 1920 ft to achieve 1000 ft clearance.

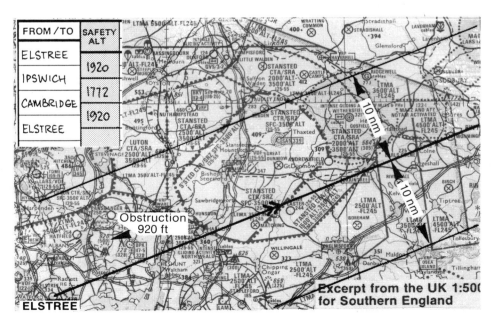

FROM / TO	SAFETY ALT
ELSTREE	1920
IPSWICH	1772
CAMBRIDGE	1920
ELSTREE	

Fig.13-6. Study the Chart and Calculate a Safety Altitude.

NOTE: In some congested areas, (e.g. Manchester, which has an overlying TMA) flights on some routes may be unable to proceed at or above the Minimum Safe Altitude until clear of the restriction (in this case the overlying TMA) – the MSA being fairly high due to a high elevation obstruction near the track. Naturally, practical common sense (airmanship) would strongly suggest to exercise great care in navigation along the route, especially in conditions of minimum visibility, until able to climb to at least the MSA.

Your flying instructor will give you guidance in this.

Remember that contours below 500 ft AMSL and obstructions below 300 ft AGL are not shown on aeronautical charts; in other words, an obstacle that is 799 ft AMSL may **not** be shown, so always keep a sharp lookout, especially in poor visibility.

Having determined the minimum safe cruising altitude for each leg, then select the cruising level which you propose to use. You are constrained:
• on the lower side by the Safety Altitude; and
• on the upper side by perhaps cloud, controlled airspace or a markedly increasing headwind.

Aerodrome Traffic Zones extend up to 2000 ft Above Aerodrome Level (AAL), and Military Aerodrome Traffic Zones extend up to 3000 ft AAL. You may fly through them, of course, but it is good airmanship in some situations to remain clear of an ATZ. There is also no point climbing to a high cruising altitude if your destination is nearby. As a Pilot, you must think about **vertical navigation** as well as horizontal navigation. For this flight, a cruising altitude of 2400 ft has been selected.

Whilst Private Pilots operating to the Visual Flight Rules **may** cruise at altitudes on QNH, they may also choose to fly at Flight Levels based on 1013 mb when cruising above 3000 ft AMSL, to fit in with Instrument Flight Rules traffic observing the Quadrantal Rule.

INSERT METEOROLOGICAL DATA ON THE FLIGHT LOG.

From the weather forecast, insert the wind and the temperature at your selected cruising level. Remember that forecast winds are given in °True. In this case, the wind at 2400 ft AMSL is 270°T/30 kt, and the temperature +10°C.

FROM/TO	SAFETY ALT	ALT / TEMP	RAS	TAS	W/V	TR °T	DRIFT	HDG °T	VAR	HDG °M	G/S	DIST	TIME	ETA	HDG °C
ELSTREE															
IPSWICH	1920	2400 / +10			270/30	069			5W			60			
CAMBRIDGE	1772	2400 / +10			270/30	286			5W			40			
ELSTREE	1920	2400 / +10			270/30	208			5W			38			
											TOTAL	138			

Fig.13-7. Met Data Added to the Flight Log.

CALCULATE THE TRUE AIR SPEED.

The Pilot flies the aeroplane according to the Indicated Air Speed, which is shown on the Air Speed Indicator. To be absolutely precise, the IAS can be corrected to Rectified Air Speed (RAS), to account for small errors in the particular pitot-static system, and a table to do this is in the Flight Manual. At cruising speeds, this error is usually less than 3 kt, and many Pilots consider it unnecessary to refer to the Airspeed Calibration Table like that illustrated below.

For example, at 100 knots Indicated Air Speed (100 KIAS), the Rectified Air Speed will be 98 kt (98 KCAS or KRAS) – hardly significant when you consider the minor fluctuations in airspeed occurring due to gusts, as well as the difficulty in reading the ASI to an accuracy of even +/- 1 kt.

AIRSPEED CALIBRATION
Normal Static Source

CONDITIONS:
Power required for level flight or maximum rated RPM dive.

FLAPS UP										
KIAS	40	50	60	70	80	90	100	110	120	130	140
KCAS	46	53	60	69	78	88	98	107	117	127	136

100 kt IAS = 98 kt RAS

Fig.13-8. Typical Airspeed Calibration for a Particular Aeroplane.

Using IAS (or the slightly more accurate RAS), the important conversion to **True Air Speed** can be made. This allows for the fact that the aeroplane may be flying in air less dense than at sea level, causing the ASI to indicate a speed less than the actual speed of the aeroplane through the air (TAS). In more dense air, the opposite is true, but this is rarely the situation.

The higher the cruising level and the higher the air temperature, the less dense the air, and the greater the TAS for a given IAS. For this flight, cruising at 2400 ft where the air temperature is +10°C, an IAS (or RAS) of 98 kt provides a TAS of 102 kt. (QNH is 1013.)

Enter this onto the flight log.

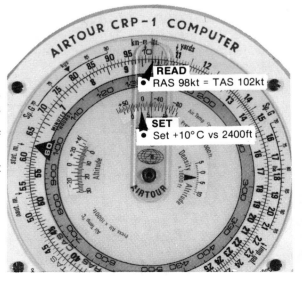

Fig.13-9. Calculate the TAS on the Navigation Computer.

FROM/TO	SAFETY ALT	ALT / TEMP	RAS	TAS	W/V	TR °T	DRIFT	HDG °T	VAR	HDG °M	G/S	DIST	TIME	ETA	HDG °C
ELSTREE															
	1920	2400 / +10	98	102	270/30	069			5W			60			
IPSWICH															
	1772	2400 / +10	98	102	270/30	286			5W			40			
CAMBRIDGE															
	1920	2400 / +10	98	102	270/30	208			5W			38			
ELSTREE															
											TOTAL	138			

Fig.13-10. The Flight Log at this Stage.

CALCULATE HEADING AND GROUND SPEED, using your Navigation Computer.

Set up the Triangle of Velocities on the wind-side of your computer using your preferred technique (refer to Chapter 4 in this manual).

Known: Track 069°T, W/V 270°T/30 kt, TAS 102 kt.
Find: Heading, Ground Speed, and insert them on the Flight Log.

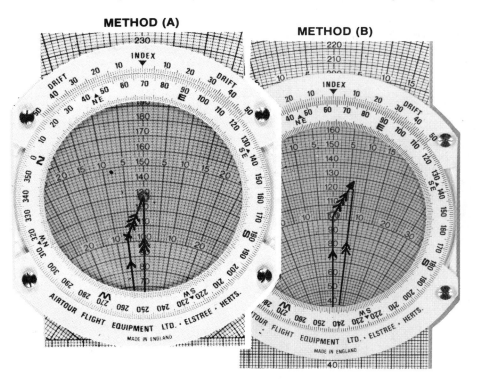

FROM/TO	SAFETY ALT	ALT / TEMP	RAS	TAS	W/V	TR °T	DRIFT	HDG °T	VAR	HDG °M	G/S	DIST	TIME	ETA	HDG °C
ELSTREE	1920	2400 / +10	98	102	270/30	069	−6	063	5W		130	60			
IPSWICH															
	1772	2400 / +10	98	102	270/30	286	−5	281	5W		73	40			
CAMBRIDGE															
	1920	2400 / +10	98	102	270/30	208	+15	223	5W		84	38			
ELSTREE											TOTAL 138				

Fig.13-11. Heading and Ground Speed Calculations added.

CONVERT HEADING TO °Magnetic.

Knowing **Magnetic Variation** (found off the chart), the HDG in °T can be converted to °**M**, which is more useful in the aeroplane since the primary source of directional information is the Magnetic Compass. '**Variation West, Magnetic Best'**. Therefore, HDG 063°T and VARN 5°W, gives HDG 068°M.

When you are in the aeroplane prior to flight, or actually in flight, you can refer to the Deviation Card and convert °Magnetic to °Compass, and enter this on the flight log. As this usually involves less than 3° correction, many Pilots choose not to show it on the Flight Log.

FROM/TO	SAFETY ALT	ALT / TEMP	RAS	TAS	W/V	TR °T	DRIFT	HDG °T	VAR	HDG °M	G/S	DIST	TIME	ETA	HDG °C
ELSTREE	1920	2400 / +10	98	102	270/30	069	−6	063	5W	068	130	60			068
IPSWICH															
	1772	2400 / +10	98	102	270/30	286	−5	281	5W	286	73	40			287
CAMBRIDGE															
	1920	2400 / +10	98	102	270/30	208	+15	223	5W	228	84	38			230
ELSTREE											TOTAL 138				

DEVIATION CARD
FOR

N	30	60	E	120	150
STEER					
001	031	060	089	118	149

FOR

S	210	240	W	300	330
STEER					
181	213	242	271	301	330

ON ☒   RADIOS   ☐ NO

Fig.13-12. Headings in °M and °C added.

CALCULATE THE ESTIMATED TIME INTERVAL FOR EACH LEG.

Using the calculator side of your navigation computer, the **time** taken to cover the distance at the GS calculated above can be determined (see Chapter 5). Prior to using the computer, it is good airmanship to estimate mentally the time so that no gross errors are made.

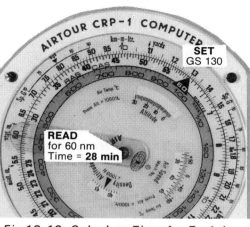

For instance, at a GS of 130 kt, the 60 nm from Elstree to Ipswich will take just under 30 minutes; by computer, an accurate answer of 28 min is obtained. At a GS of 73 kt, the 40 nm from Ipswich to Cambridge will take 33 nm.

Fig.13-13. Calculate Time for Each Leg.

All of the individual Estimated Time Intervals (ETIs) can be added up to give a total flight time. Compare this with the total distance and mentally check if the final results are reasonable.

FROM/TO	SAFETY ALT	ALT / TEMP	RAS	TAS	W/V	TR °T	DRIFT	HDG °T	VAR	HDG °M	G/S	DIST	TIME	ETA	HDG °C
ELSTREE	1920	2400 / +10	98	102	270/30	069	−6	063	5W	068	130	60	28		068
IPSWICH	1772	2400 / +10	98	102	270/30	286	−5	281	5W	286	73	40	33		287
CAMBRIDGE	1920	2400 / +10	98	102	270/30	208	+15	223	5W	228	84	38	27		230
ELSTREE											TOTAL	138	88		

Fig.13-14. Estimated Time Interval for Each Leg added.

FUEL PLANNING.

The amount of fuel that you carry is, of course, extremely important. The **minimum fuel** that should be in the tanks on departure is the amount needed to reach the destination (or an alternate aerodrome) and land, with reserve fuel in intact. The **maximum fuel** that you can carry is *full tanks,* but this may limit the number of passengers or weight of baggage for that flight. It is good airmanship to know what minimum amount of fuel is required for each flight, and to ensure that you have at least this amount on board.

A reasonable 'Fixed Reserve' for most light aircraft operations is 60 minutes, or perhaps 45 minutes, calculated at cruise rate, over and above *Flight Fuel.* This allows for such things as the headwinds en route being stronger than expected, a consumption rate greater than published, minor

AIR NAVIGATION

navigational errors or short diversions. The Fixed Reserve is usable fuel in the tanks that you should **not** plan on using; think of it as an **emergency reserve.**

Whilst fuel is ordered from the fuel agent and shown on the gauges as a quantity (United States Gallons, litres, or Imperial Gallons), it is valuable to know how long this fuel will last in **minutes,** i.e. the endurance. This of course depends upon the consumption rate.

For the flight from Elstree that we are planning, the consumption rate is 7 USG/hour. The flight time has been calculated as 88 minutes, and the required fixed reserve is 45 minutes.

These times can be converted to USG with a simple computer manipulation, and both the time and fuel columns added up to find the **minimum fuel required** in both minutes and US gallons.

CONSUMPTION RATE   7 USG/hr

Stage	mins	US Gal
Route	88	
Reserve	45	
Fuel Required		
Margin		
Total Carried		

Fig.13-15. Beginning of the Fuel Calculations.

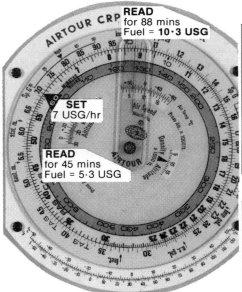

READ for 88 mins Fuel = **10·3 USG**

AIRTOUR CRP

SET 7 USG/hr

READ for 45 mins Fuel = 5·3 USG

CONSUMPTION RATE   7 USG/hr

Stage	mins	US Gal
Route	88 →10·3	
Reserve	45 → 5·3	
Fuel Required		
Margin		
Total Carried		

CONSUMPTION RATE   7 USG/hr

Stage	mins	US Gal
Route	88	10·3
Reserve	45	5·3	add
Fuel Required	133	15·6
Margin		
Total Carried		

Fig.13-16. Calculating Fuel Required.

Any fuel above the minimum required provides a **margin.** If, for instance, 25 USG is loaded, a margin of 9·4 USG over and above the minimum fuel required (15·6 USG) is available. At the consumption rate of 7 USG/hr, this converts to a margin of 80 minutes, providing a total endurance of 213 minutes. This is useful knowledge for the Pilot.

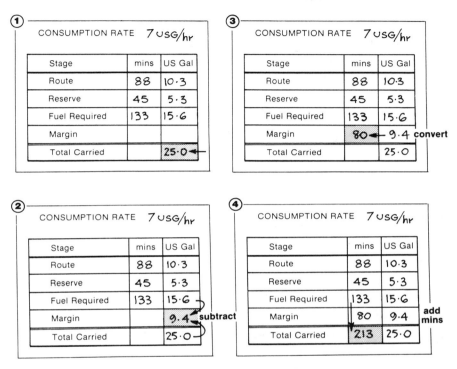

Fig.13-17. The Main Fuel Calculations Completed.

Sometimes you are required to plan for a **flight to an alternate aerodrome** if, for instance, poor weather does not allow you to land at the planned destination. For the flight from **Elstree** to **Ipswich,** with **Cambridge** being carried as an alternate for **Ipswich,** the calculations might appear as shown. The *alternate fuel* is sometimes called *diversion fuel.*

FROM/TO	SAFETY ALT	ALT / TEMP	RAS	TAS	W/V	TR °T	DRIFT	HDG °T	VAR	HDG °M	G/S	DIST	TIME	ETA	HDG °C
ELSTREE	1920	2400 / +10	98	102	270/30	069	-6	063	5W	068	130	60	28		
IPSWICH															
IPSWICH	1772	2400 / +10	98	102	270/30	286	-5	281	5W	286	73	40	33		
CAMBRIDGE															

Fig.13-18. Cambridge, as Alternate for Ipswich.

Stage	min	USG
Destination:	28	3·3
Alternate:	33	3·9
Flight Fuel:	61	7·2
Reserve:	45	5·3
Fuel Required:	106	12·5

If you load a total of 17 USG, then the final fuel calculations will be:

Stage	min	USG
Destination:	28	3·3
Alternate:	33	3·9
Flight Fuel:	61	7·2
Reserve:	45	5·3
Fuel Required:	106	12·5
Margin:	38	4·5
Total Fuel:	144	17·0

Sometimes an allowance for taxi fuel is made (say 1 USG with no time allowance), in which case the fuel table may look like:

Stage	min	USG
Destination:	28	3·3
Alternate:	33	3·9
Flight Fuel:	61	7·2
Reserve:	45	5·3
Taxi:	–	**1·0**
Fuel Required:	106	13·5
Margin:	30	3·5
Total Fuel:	136	17·0

Some Operators like to carry an extra safety margin of 10%, and their fuel calculations may appear thus:

Stage	min	USG
Destination:	28	3·3
Alternate:	33	3·9
Flight Fuel:	61	7·2
Reserve:	45	5·3
Total:	106	12·5
+10%:	**11**	**1·3**
Taxi:	–	1·0
Fuel Required:	117	14·8
Margin:	19	2·2
Total Fuel:	136	17·0

This is getting fairly complicated, although, if you use the one procedure all the time, you soon get used to it.

WEIGHT AND BALANCE, and PERFORMANCE.

Before inserting the final fuel figure, it is good airmanship to consider:
- Weight and Balance; and
- Take-off and Landing Performance.

The aeroplane must be loaded so that no weight limitation is exceeded, and so that the Centre of Gravity lies within approved limits. This is dealt with in Chapter 33 of Volume 4 of this series – The Air Pilot's Manual.

The performance charts should be consulted if necessary to confirm that the aeroplane is able to operate from the planned runways.

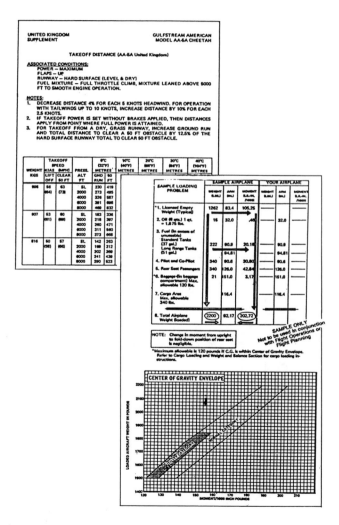

Fig.13-19. Consult the Relevant Performance Charts and Complete a Weight and Balance Calculation.

SOME TYPICAL FLIGHT LOGS.

Example 1: The Completed Flight Log for the Flight from **Elstree.**

FROM /TO	SAFETY ALT	ALT / TEMP	RAS	TAS	W/V	TR °T	DRIFT	HDG °T	VAR	HDG °M	G/S	DIST	TIME	ETA	HDG °C
ELSTREE		2400													
	1920	+10	98	102	270/30	069	-6	063	5W	068	130	60	28		068
IPSWICH		2400													
	1772	+10	98	102	270/30	286	-5	281	5W	286	73	40	33		287
CAMBRIDGE		2400													
	1920	+10	98	102	270/30	208	+15	223	5W	228	84	38	27		230
ELSTREE											TOTAL	138	88		

CONSUMPTION RATE 7 USG/hr		
Stage	mins	US Gal
Route	88	10·3
Reserve	45	5·3
Fuel Required	133	15·6
Margin	80	9.4
Total Carried	213	25·0

Fig.13-20.

Example 2: A Flight Log for a Flight from **Staverton.**

FROM /TO	SAFETY ALT	ALT / TEMP	RAS	TAS	W/V	TR °T	DRIFT	HDG °T	VAR	HDG °M	G/S	DIST	TIME	ETA	HDG °C
STAVERTON		3000													
	2770	+12	90	95	250/20	056	-3	053	6W	059	114	59	31		
DESBOROUGH		FL35													
	2070	+11	90	96	250/20	164	+12	176	5W	181	92	24	16		
CRANFIELD		FL40													
	2570	+10	90	96	260/25	231	+7	238	5W	243	73	27	22		
BECKLEY		FL45													
	2570	+10	90	97	260/25	299	-9	290	6W	296	76	6	5		
KIDLINGTON		FL45													
	2690	+10	90	97	260/25	276	-4	272	6W	278	72	31	26		
STAVERTON											TOTAL	147	100		

CONSUMPTION RATE 8·5 USG/hr		
Stage	mins	US Gal
Route	100	14·2
Reserve	60	8·5
Fuel Required	160	22·7
Margin	122	← 17·3
Total Carried	282	40·0

Fig.13-21.

Example 3: A Flight Log for a Flight from **Manchester**.

REGISTRATION		DATE	PILOT		CHOCKS OFF	CHOCKS ON		FLIGHT TIME
6-BGWY		4-9-86	E. PAPE					

RUNWAY	RH LH	QFE	QNH	QNH		W/V	VAR	DEV	TAS
24						280'25	6	-	90

STAGE	HEADING C	DEPT TIME	LEG TIME	ETA	RTA ATA	SAFE ALT	TRACK T	HDG T	HDG M	GS	DIST
MANCHESTER CREWE	223		13			1600	201	217	223	82	17
CREWE WARRINGTON	334		15			"	343	328	334	74	19
WARRINGTON WIGAN	334		08			"	343	328	334	74	10
WIGAN BARTON	126		06			"	116	120	126	114	12
BARTON MANCHESTER	168		05			"	149	162	168	104	8

EMERGENCY 121.5

CONSPICUITY	4321
EMERGENCY	7700
RADIO FAIL	7600

CLEARANCES

SAMPLE ONLY
Not to be used in conjunction
with Flight Operations or
Flight Planning

STATION FREQUENCY	CALLSIGN TYPE	POSITION HEADING	ALTITUDE QNH	FROM TO	ESTIMATE	REQUEST
MANCHESTER TOWER 118·70						
MANCHESTER APP. 119·40						
BARTON RADIO 122·70						

CONSUMPTION		5 IGPH
STAGE	TIME	FUEL
FLIGHT	47	4
DIVERSION	30	3
CONTINGENCY	0:45	4
TOTAL		11
+ 10%		1
+ TAXI & TAKE OF RUN		1
FUEL REQUIRED		13
TOTAL USABLE FUEL		25

Fig.13-22. Flight from Manchester and Return.

225

Example 4: A Flight Log for a Flight from LEEDS.

LEEDS – NEWCASTLE										
WINDS			RUNWAY							
2000	300/20		QNH		SAMPLE ONLY Not to be used in conjunction with Flight Operations or Flight Planning					
5000			QFE							
T.A.S.	90		WIND							
STAGE	MSA	TR (T)	HDG (T)	VAR	HDG (M)	DIST	GS	TIME	ETA	ATA
TAKE OFF								→		
SET COURSE								→		
HARROGATE	1500	034	021	6°w	027	9	90	6		
SCOTCH CORNER	1500	349	339	6°w	345	28	76	22		
NEWCASTLE ZONE BDY	2000	358	347	6°w	353	30	78	23		
NEWCASTLE	1500	358	347	6°w	353	6	78	5		
ALTERNATE TEESSIDE	(SEE	NEWCASTLE	– TEESSIDE	SHEET	TIME =	20				
LANDED								→		

LEEMING RADAR 132.4
TEESSIDE TWR 119.8
        APP 118.85
NEWCASTLE TWR 119.7
        APP 126.35

FUEL REQUIRED
Fuel on Board = 98 Ltr
Consumption = 24

	Time	Fuel
Route	56	23
Alternate	20	8
Reserve (45 min)	~	18
TOTAL		49

	TWR	APP	RAD	
LEEDS	120.30	123.75	121.05	DISTRESS 121.50

Fig.13-23. Flight Log from Leeds, and Return.

PLANNING THE CLIMB.

In the previous examples no allowance has been made for the increased fuel consumption during the climb. Whilst this is not significant for the low-level flights that have been covered, when you come to plan a long-range flight at a higher altitude, then, to improve the accuracy of your planning, it will be necessary to calculate fuel/time/distance on the climb and use these in your flight log.

As this is not a requirement for you as part of your basic-PPL training, we have included this as an Appendix entitled **'Planning The Climb'**, which we recommend you go through when you get a chance later on. It is APPENDIX 2, located at the back of the book.

☐ Now complete **Exercises 13 — The Flight Log.**

14

THE FLIGHT PLAN

The flight plan is an ATC message, compiled by or on behalf of the Pilot in Command (PIC) to a set CAA format and then transmitted by the appropriate ATC authority to organisations concerned with the flight. It is the basis on which ATC clearance is given for the flight to proceed.

Correct use of the flight plan form is most important, the more so in these days of automatic data processing. Incorrect completion may well result in a delay to processing and subsequently to the flight. Full instructions for the completion of Flight Plan form are contained in an Aeronautical Information Circular (AIC).

Note that a Pilot intending to make a flight must in any case contact ATC (or other authority where there is no ATC) at the aerodrome of departure. This is known as '**booking out**' and is a separate and additional requirement to that of filing a flight plan.

Private Pilots may, if they wish, file a flight plan for any flight. They are advised to file a flight plan if intending to fly **more than 10 nm from the coast or over sparsely populated or mountainous areas.** Flight Plans must be filed for flights:
- within controlled airspace *notified* as IFR only;
- within controlled airspace in Instrument Meteorological Conditions (IMC) or at night, excluding Special VFR (SVFR);
- within controlled airspace in Visual Meteorological Conditions (VMC) if the flight is to be conducted under the Instrument Flight Rules (IFR);
- within certain Special Rules Airspace irrespective of weather conditions;
- within Scottish and London Upper Flight Information Regions (UIRs – i.e. above FL245);
- where the destination is more than 40 km from departure and maximum total weight authorised exceeds 5700 kg;
- to or from the UK which will cross a UK Flight Information Region (FIR) boundary;
- during which it is intended to use the Air Traffic Advisory Service.

NOTE: The fact that **night flying** is conducted in accordance with IFR procedures does not, of itself, require that a flight plan be filed. Equally, IFR flight in 'open FIR', by day or night, does not of itself require a flight plan.

Flight plans should be filed at least 30 minutes before requesting taxi or start-up clearance (60 minutes in certain cases where the controlling authority is London, Manchester or Scottish Control).

If a Pilot who has filed a flight plan lands at an aerodrome other than the destination specified, the Air Traffic Service Unit (ATSU) at the specified destination must be told within **30 minutes** of the estimated time of arrival there.

FILLING IN THE FLIGHT PLAN FORM.

The Pilot should fill in the appropriate white spaces on the Flight Plan form using **BLOCK LETTERS**, or **numerals** for the time in UTC and the number of Persons on Board. A typical Flight Plan could be as follows:

Item 7: Insert the **aircraft registration,** say **G M E G S,** five letters with no hyphens.

Item 8: Insert **V** for **Visual Flight Rules**.
Insert **G** for a **General Aviation** type of flight.

Item 9: Insert, in this case, **PA28** for **type of aircraft** using four characters only, and **L** for **Light** aircraft-wake-turbulence category. The first box (2 spaces), labelled *number,* is left blank unless there is more than one aircraft in your group.

Item 10: Insert **V** to signify that you have **VHF** communications radio, and **C** for that category **Transponder** for Secondary Surveillance Radar (SSR). The Letter **S** is used to signify **S**tandard radio equipment, which is considered to be VHF, ADF, VOR and ILS.

Item 13: Insert **EGBB** for **Birmingham** (ICAO code for each aerodrome is listed in the UK AIP or in *Pooley's Flight Guide*), and the **estimated** *off-block* taxying time of 1210 UTC.

Items 15 Insert **N0105** to indicate the cruising **TAS** in **N**autical miles per
& 16: hour (kt) to the value of 0105 (i.e. TAS is 105 kt), and **A025** to indicate a **cruising Altitude** of 2500 ft AMSL, and **DCT** to indicate the **Direct** route with no turning points to the destination Northampton (EGBK), which is inserted in Item 16, and with the total **Estimated Elapsed Time** of 0026 (00 hours and 26 minutes). The **Alternate** aerodrome nominated for Northampton is **Leicester** (EGBG).

Item 18: Insert **0** to indicate no **other information**.

Supplementary Information —

Item 19: Insert **Endurance** of 0215 (02 hours 15 minutes), and 003 to indicate 3 **Persons on Board** (Pilot plus two passengers).

No **Emergency Radio** is carried, so each of these is struck out, as for the **Survival Equipment,** none of which is in this particular aeroplane.

The **Aircraft Colour and Markings** are a distinctive red and white, with a blue eagle on the rear fuselage, so insert these details.

No further **Remarks** concerning survival equipment or matters of importance in a Search and Rescue situation, so strike out the **N.**

Insert the Pilot-in-Command's **Name.**

There are rules to follow in filling in the Flight Plan correctly and you are directed into the AICs (Aeronautical Information Circulars) for more detailed instructions.

The size of the Flight Plan form is that of an *A4* sheet (about 12" x 8") and a reduced reproduction of the completed plan, as detailed in the text, appears on the next page. Having studied that, you should then be able to complete:

☐ **Exercises 14 — The Flight Plan.**

FLIGHT PLAN   ATS COPY

PRIORITY   ADDRESSEE(S)

<< ≡ FF →

<< ≡

FILING TIME   ORIGINATOR

→   << ≡

SPECIFIC IDENTIFICATION ADDRESSEE(S) AND/OR ORIGINATOR

| 3 MESSAGE TYPE | 7 AIRCRAFT IDENTIFICATION | 8 FLIGHT RULES | TYPE OF FLIGHT |

<< ≡ (FPL   – GMEGS   – V   G <<≡

9 NUMBER   TYPE OF AIRCRAFT   WAKE TURBULENCE CAT.   10 EQUIPMENT

–   PA28   / L   – V /C <<≡

13 DEPARTURE AERODROME   TIME

– EGBB   1210 <<≡

15 CRUISING SPEED   LEVEL   ROUTE

– N0105   A025 → DCT

<< ≡

TOTAL EET

16 DESTINATION AERODROME   HR MIN   ALTN AERODROME   2ND ALTN AERODROME

– EGBK   0026   → EGBG   →   <<≡

18 OTHER INFORMATION

–

) <<≡

SUPPLEMENTARY INFORMATION (NOT TO BE TRANSMITTED IN FPL MESSAGES)

19 ENDURANCE   EMERGENCY RADIO

HR MIN   PERSONS ON BOARD   UHF   VHF   ELBA

–E/ 0215   → P/ 003   → R/ ☒ ☒ ☒

SURVIVAL EQUIPMENT   POLAR   DESERT   MARITIME   JUNGLE   JACKETS   LIGHT   FLUORES   UHF   VHF

→ ☒ / ☒ ☒ ☒ ☒   → ☒ / ☒ ☒ ☒ ☒

DINGHIES

NUMBER   CAPACITY   COVER   COLOUR

→ ☒ / →   → ☒ →   <<≡

AIRCRAFT COLOUR AND MARKINGS

A/ RED/WHITE WITH BLUE EAGLE

REMARKS

→ ☒ /   <<≡

PILOT IN COMMAND

C/ KEMPFE   ) <<≡

FILED BY

SPACE RESERVED FOR ADDITIONAL REQUIREMENTS

Fig.14-1. Completed Flight Plan Form.

Intentionally Blank

3

EN ROUTE
NAVIGATION

15. En Route Navigation Techniques 232
16. Navigation in Remote Areas 276
17. Entry/Exit Lanes and
    Low Level Routes 281

15

EN ROUTE
NAVIGATION
TECHNIQUES

DEDUCED RECKONING is the primary means of visual cross-country navigation. It is commonly known as *Dead Reckoning* or **'DR'**. It is based on:

- starting at a known position (called a **Fix**);
- measuring the Track and Distance on a chart to the next point chosen along the desired track;
- applying the best estimate of Wind Velocity available to determine:
    - **Heading** to steer to achieve the desired track,
    - **Ground Speed** to find estimated time of arrival over that next point.

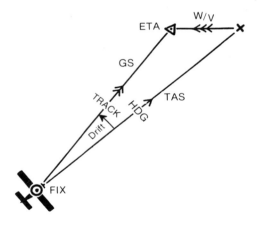

Fig.15-1. 'Dead Reckoning' is the Fundamental Method of Navigating Visually. The Angle between Heading and Track is the Aircraft's 'Drift'.

Dead Reckoning navigation, in which the Pilot flies the estimated Heading for the Estimated Time Interval (both calculated when flight planning), should bring the aeroplane over the next checkpoint at the appointed time.

Map Reading is used as a back-up to *DR Navigation*. This enables the Pilot to pin-point the aeroplane's position (i.e. obtain a **Fix**) over some ground feature en route and to evaluate the success of the DR navigation.

A **FIX** is the geographical position of an aircraft at a specific time, determined by visual reference to the surface of the Earth, or by radio navigational equipment.

A **PINPOINT** is the ground position of an aircraft at a specific time determined by direct observation of the ground – (i.e. not by radio nav equipment).

Fixing the aircraft's position is **not** a continuous process second by second throughout the flight, but rather a regular process repeated every 10 or 15 minutes. (This may need to be reduced to 5 mins or so in areas requiring very precise tracking like Entry/Exit Lanes – covered in Chapter 17.) If you try to identify ground features to obtain a Fix at shorter time intervals than this, then you may find yourself just flying from feature to feature without any time being available for the other important navigational tasks, such as planning ahead and monitoring the fuel situation.

For normal en route navigation a Pilot should:

- fly accurate headings (by reference to the Direction Indicator and to the ground); and
- periodically identify landmarks.

Unfortunately it is generally the case that the actual **Track Made Good** (TMG) is not precisely the Planned Track (or Desired Track). The difference between the Desired Track and the actual TMG is known as the **TRACK ERROR (TE).**

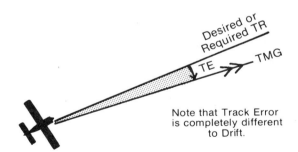

Fig.15-2. Track Error is the Angular Difference between Required-Track and Track-Made-Good.

ACCURATE TRACKING INVOLVES COMPENSATING FOR THE WIND EFFECT.

Most of the calculations in DR navigation are to compensate for wind effect, so if the wind differs in either speed or direction from the expected wind, then a Track Error will probably result.

If we assume that there is **no wind,** then the aeroplane will end up at what we call its **Air Position** (symbolised by a cross), i.e. its position relative to the air mass.

+
AIR POSITION

The **wind effect** will blow the aeroplane to its **Ground Position** (symbolised by a small circle), i.e. its position relative to the ground – and this is what we are really interested in. If we can actually *fix* or *pin-point* the ground position of the aircraft by reference to features on the Earth's surface, then we symbolise this on our chart with a small circle.

⊙
GROUND POSITION

If this is not possible, we can determine a **DR Position** by plotting the calculated track and distance flown since the last fix, and mark this point on our chart as a small triangle.

△
DR POSITION

Fig.15-3.

At the flight planning stage, a *forecast wind* was used to calculate a HDG for the aeroplane to make good a desired track. This wind will almost certainly not be precisely the same as the actual wind that is experienced in flight. This means that the actual drift in flight (the angle between HDG and Track Made Good) will most likely differ from that expected, to a greater or lesser extent.

Also, whether the Track Made Good (TMG) is left or right of the desired track will depend upon whether we have allowed **too little, or too much, DRIFT** to counteract the crosswind effect.

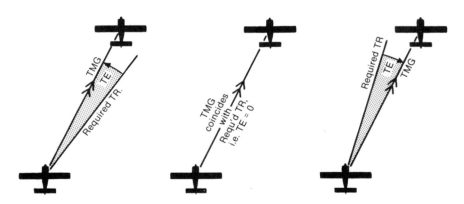

Fig.15-4. Track Error Results if We Allow Too Little or Too Much Drift.

En route **we can counteract a Track Error by modifying the Heading** to achieve more accurate DR navigation for the remainder of the flight.

It is also usual to find that the actual in-flight Ground Speed (GS) differs from that expected at the flight-planning stage, when all we had at hand was the forecast winds rather than the actual winds that we are experiencing in flight. This means that the original Estimated Time

Intervals (ETIs) to cover certain distances will be somewhat in error and will need to be modified once an accurate in-flight check of Ground Speed (GS) is obtained. The Estimated Time of Arrival at any point can then be revised.

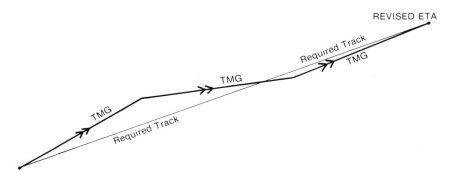

Fig.15-5. In-Flight Modification of HDGs and ETIs is Usual in DR Nav.

First and foremost, the most important way to keep in-flight navigation workload to a minimum is to **be thorough in your pre-flight preparation** (i.e. flight planning). For **in-flight navigation**, concentrate on:
• simple mental calculations; and
• simple computer opeartions.

This will allow you to modify the Headings and Estimated Time Intervals (ETIs) calculated at the flight-planning stage without too much *'head-down'* work, and the methods that we discuss here will be adequate for most situations.

NOTE: As mentioned earlier when discussing *'Track-Guides'* in the chapter on Chart Preparation, be very clear in your own mind that **Track Error and Drift are two different things** and should never be confused.

AIRMANSHIP FOR THE PILOT/NAVIGATOR.

Airmanship is **common sense.** Do not become over-engrossed in navigational activity; being also the Pilot of the aeroplane you are responsible for a safe flight path. Fly the aeroplane reasonably accurately at all times (HDG +/– 5°; altitude +/– 100 ft; Indicated Air Speed +/– 5 kt). Even though you are looking out of the cockpit most of the time to monitor the attitude and heading of the aircraft, and to check for other traffic, you should periodically check the Flight Instruments to achieve precise Heading, Air Speed and Altitude.

Setting the correct power and holding the attitude will result in the required performance in general terms but, to fly precisely, you will need to refer to the Flight Instruments and make suitable minor adjustments to the attitude and the power. This means a quick look at the relevant flight instruments every 10 seconds or so throughout the flight.

Scanning the essential instruments in flight quickly and often is an important skill to develop. A good Pilot has a fast **scan rate,** which is necessary for accurate flying.

Ensure that the aeroplane is in trim, and can fly itself accurately *'hands-off'*; not that you will actually fly it hands-off, but correct trimming will considerably lighten your task of maintaining height and heading. Check that the IAS used in your calculations is within 5 kt of that actually being flown, and that the altitude is within 100 ft; if not, do something about it by adjusting the power and the attitude.

Keep your paperwork in the cockpit neat and accessible – do not work *'head-down'* for more than a few seconds at a time, and:

KEEP A GOOD LOOKOUT!

Continually observe weather conditions, not only ahead of you, but also to either side and behind (just in case you have to beat a hasty retreat). You must assess any deterioration in weather and modify your flight accordingly. Ask the Flight Information Service (FIS) or Air Traffic Control (ATC) for an update on the weather en route and at your destination aerodrome if you desire this information. Their function is to provide a service to the Pilot.

Take appropriate action to avoid hazardous conditions. For instance, it is good airmanship to divert around thunderstorms instead of flying near or under them, and to avoid areas of fog and reduced visiblity, as well as dense smoke from fires because the visibility will be reduced and the air turbulent.

Obtain a Position Fix every 10 or 15 minutes if possible and update your Headings and ETAs; (more frequently in poor visibility and/or congested airspace, e.g. every 5 minutes).

Also, carry out **Regular En Route Checks** of the:
- Magnetic Compass and Direction Indicator alignment;
- engine instruments;
- electrical and other systems.

This En Route Check can be remembered by the mnemonic **'FREDA'**:

F – Fuel *ON* and sufficient;
Fuel tank usage monitored;
Mixture, leaned as required for the cruise;
Fuel pump (if fitted), as required.

R – Radio frequency correctly selected, volume and squelch satisfactory, any required calls made.

E – Engine: oil temperature and pressure within limits; carburettor heat if required; other systems checked, e.g. the electrical system, suction (if vacuum-driven gyroscopes are fitted);

D – Direction Indicator (Heading Indicator or Directional Gyro) aligned with the Magnetic Compass, and your position checked on the map.

A – Altitude checked and the correct subscale setting (usually Regional QNH).

Maintain a time awareness, particularly with respect to FUEL and LATEST TIME OF ARRIVAL.

THE FLIGHT SEQUENCE

DEPARTURE FROM AN AERODROME.

For a trainee Pilot, the simplest method of departure is to set heading from directly over the top of the field at cruise speed and at the cruising altitude. Since most VFR cross-country flights in the UK occur at 3000 ft AMSL or below, the appropriate altimeter setting for cruising is the Regional QNH.

The actual method of departing an aerodrome will depend upon the circuit direction, and the nature of the aerodrome and surrounding terrain. Information on the particular aerodrome may be found in the UK AIP or in *Pooley's Flight Guide.*

Many aerodromes have no restrictions placed upon them, but this is not always the case. For instance, a number of aerodromes lie within the control zones and under the control areas surrounding major airports, and have Access Lanes for VFR flight which must be adhered to. Obviously if you are navigating to or from one of these aerodromes, you must plan your departure or arrival via one of the points where the Access Lane leaves or joins the control area. These are indicated on aeronautical charts with a large 'E'. Other aerodromes may have local restrictions due to heavy traffic, high terrain or nearby built-up areas calling for special departure or arrival procedures.

If you depart via an Entry/Exit Access Lane, or by any means other than departing from over the top, then a simple calculation of Actual Time of Departure (ATD) needs to be made. Your en route Estimated Times of Arrival (ETAs) will be based on this (at least initially, until Ground Speed checks allow you to update them).

We will consider **Two Possible Methods** of departing on a track of, for example, 150M from an aerodrome where the appropriate runway to use is RWY 06 and the circuits are left-handed. Assume aerodrome elevation to be 1200 ft AMSL.

Since your compass will be experiencing acceleration and turning errors while setting course, ensure that the gyroscopic Direction Indicator is aligned with the magnetic compass prior to commencing your take-off roll, and ensure that both the compass and the DI agree at least approximately with the runway direction.

Method (1): Turning in the Direction of the Circuit.

After take-off, climb out to 500 ft AAL (i.e. 500 ft on QFE, or 1700 ft on QNH) and turn left in the direction of the circuit. Continue left turns in the circuit direction and set course overhead the field at a height of at least 1000 ft AAL and climbing clear of the circuit (i.e. 2200 ft on QNH in this case). Log the Actual Time of Departure (ATD) in the appropriate place on the flight log. The ATD will be your time of setting course overhead the aerodrome.

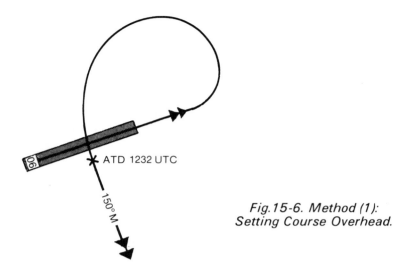

*Fig.15-6. Method (1):
Setting Course Overhead.*

Method (2): Climbing Straight Ahead until well clear of the circuit before turning to take up the desired Heading.

In this case you will not set course overhead the field, so once you have joined track you will need to estimate your Actual Time of Departure (ATD) as if you had set course from directly overhead. A GS of 120 kt is equivalent to 2 nm per minute, so if you set course at say 4 nm from the aerodrome at time 1234 UTC and your estimated GS is about 120 kt, the ATD would be 2 minutes prior to this at 1232 UTC.

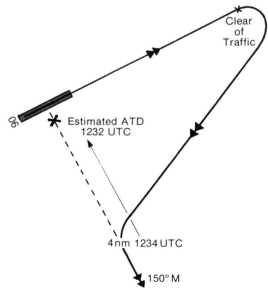

Fig.15-7. Method (2): Setting Course En Route and Calculating ATD.

If there is a laid down departure route via a specific point, then you can log your time of departure from the point. The main purpose is to have a starting point in time for your en route time calculations (although remember that fuel is being burned from the moment the engine starts).

This second method can be used whenever you intercept track rather than setting course from over the top.

Immediately after setting heading and becoming established on track, you would:

- log the Actual Time of Departure (ATD) and insert the *estimate* overhead the first checkpoint, based on the ATD and the flight-planned Estimated Time Interval);
- make a departure report by radio if required (frequencies are shown on the aeronautical charts).

NOTE: The terms *Estimate* and *Estimated Time of Arrival (ETA)* are used fairly loosely to mean the same thing, i.e. the *time of arrival overhead*, although in a strict sense ETA applies only to the aerodrome of intended landing.

Rough Check of Departure Track.

On departure you should have in mind some ground feature en route which is within 10 or 15 nm of the aerodrome, against which you can check that you are indeed departing in approximately the right direction.

Example 1: After take-off from a certain aerodrome and taking up the calculated heading to achieve our desired track of say 150°T, we should pass slightly left of a large lake at about 8 nm from the aerodrome. To confirm that it is the correct lake, our charts show a large hill and radio mast on its north-west side, so we should use these to confirm our identification of it.

Fig.15-8. Check Approximate Tracking Direction Soon After Departure.

You should ensure within the first few minutes that you are making good the correct track. If you are in any doubt, check the Direction Indicator against the Magnetic Compass. For accuracy, apply the deviation correction found on the card in the cockpit to amend °M to °C.

Set Heading on Departure Visually.

If you do not overfly the aerodrome to set heading, then prior to take-off it is not a bad idea to note some features directly on track from the aerodrome and within 5 or 10 nm of it, and then to make sure that you track over that feature. You can do this sometimes just prior to take-off by looking in the direction that you intend tracking, otherwise have in mind some feature or checkpoint selected off the chart as illustrated above.

Once clear of the circuit area, Aerodrome QFE is of little value, so QNH should be set so that the altimeter reads height above mean sea level and gives you guidance on terrain clearance.

CRUISE.

On reaching the cruise level you should ensure that Regional QNH is set. If you are cruising above the usual UK Transition Altitude of 3000 ft, it may be good airmanship to cruise at a Flight Level (based on 1013 mb rather than QNH), the same as all the IFR traffic will be doing.

Establish cruise speed and cruise power and trim the aeroplane. Scan all the vital instruments and systems for correct operation. Verify that the gyroscopic DI is aligned with the magnetic compass. It may be a good time to do a full *FREDA* En Route Check.

It is good airmanship to check straight away that you are achieving the desired True Air Speed (TAS) on the cruise. This may be done very quickly by:
- computer (by setting pressure altitude against temperature, and reading-off TAS on the outer scale against IAS on the inner); or
- approximation (at 5000 ft TAS is about 8% greater than IAS, and at 10,000 ft TAS is about 17% greater than IAS);
- setting the adjustable temp/TAS scale, if fitted on your ASI, so that, as well as reading IAS on one scale, the other scale indicates TAS. This is a feature found on some (but not all) Air Speed Indicators in general aviation aeroplanes. It is a scale similar to that on your *CRP-1* computer where, by setting pressure altitude against true outside temperature, TAS can be read-off against IAS, at least in the cruising range.

NOTE: These aspects were discussed in Chapter 2 on *Speed*.

If the achieved TAS is significantly different to that expected then you should check:
- correct power set;
- correct aircraft configuration – flaps up, landing gear up (if appropriate), position of cowl flaps.

As soon as possible on the Cruise obtain a Ground Speed check.

From two position fixes separated by about 20 to 30 nm, you should be able to **establish an accurate Ground Speed** and determine if your Heading is achieving the Desired Track or not. (Naturally, if you are about to fly over featureless terrain or water, where position fixing will be difficult, there is nothing to stop you using fixes obtained on the climb. Good Airmanship is common sense.)

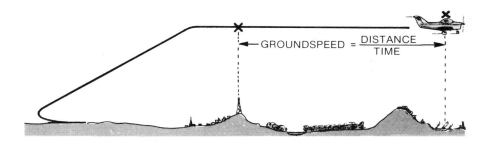

Fig.15-9. Obtain a Check on GS and Track Early in the Cruise.

If the actual GS is significantly different to that expected at the flight-planning stage, then you will have to revise your ETAs. If the Track Made Good (TMG) differs significantly from the desired track, then you will have to make a HDG change. Make use of the best available information to estimate a suitable heading.

Of course, to get good fixes you need to **select good check features** and make use of your *map reading* skills.

MAP READING IN FLIGHT.

The success of Map Reading depends upon four basic factors:
1. A knowledge of **Direction.**
2. A knowledge of **Distance.**
3. A knowledge of **Ground Speed.**
4. The selection and identification of **Landmarks** and **Check Features.**

Select Good Checkpoint Features. Landmarks and checkpoints that can be easily identified, and which will be within your range of visibility when you pass by them, are best. Just how conspicuous a particular feature may be from the air depends upon:
• the flight visibility;
• the dimensions of the feature;
• the relationship of your selected feature to other features;
• the angle of observation;
• the plan outline of the feature if you are flying high;
• the elevation and side appearance of the feature if you are flying low.

Preferably the feature should be unique in that vicinity so that it cannot be confused with another nearby similar feature. A feature that is long in one dimension and quite sharply defined in another is often useful, because:
• if a long feature (such as a railway line, canal or road) runs parallel to track, it can assist in maintaining an accurate track; and
• if a long feature crosses the track it can be used as a position line to aid in determining an updated Ground Speed (GS).

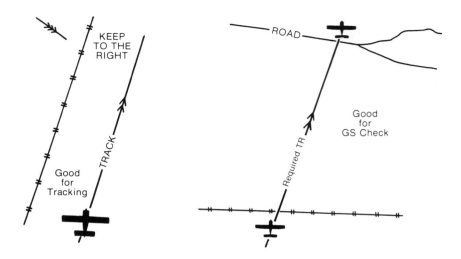

Fig.15-10. Long, Narrow Features are Particularly Useful.

NOTE: Remember, when tracking along line features, stay to the right (i.e. keep the line feature on your left where you can best see it out of the Captain's seat). Aircraft flying along the same line feature, but in the opposite direction, should be doing the same, thereby minimising collision risk.

The relationship between your selected feature and other nearby ground features is very important for a positive confirmation of your position. For example, there may be two small towns near each other, but you have chosen as a feature the one that has a single-track railway line to the West of the town and with a road that crosses a river on the North side of the town, whereas the other town has none of these features. This should make positive identification fairly easy.

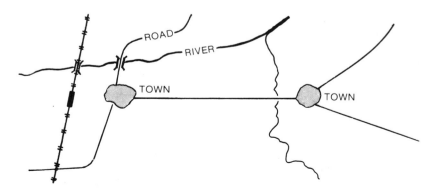

Fig.15-11. Confirm Identification of your Selected Feature by its Relationship with Other Features.

'Position Lines' Can Be Very Useful.

A **Position Fix** is obtained when you can positively identify the position of the aeroplane relative to the ground. A **Position Line** is not as specific as a *Fix* because you can only identify the position of the aeroplane as being somewhere along that line, and not actually *fixed* at a particular point.

A **Position Line** is an extended straight line joining two points, somewhere along which the aeroplane was located at a particular time.

You may see a Position Line referred to as a *PL* or a *line of position* or *LoP*. Position lines can be obtained:

- from long narrow features such as railway lines, roads, motorways, coastlines, etc;
- from two features that line up as the aeroplane passes them (known as *'transit bearings'*);
- from magnetic bearings to (and from) a feature – (this need not only be visual, it can also be a radio position line, i.e. a magnetic bearing from an NDB or VOR).

Fig.15-12. Each of these Aeroplanes is on the Same Position Line.

It is usual to show a Position Line on your map as a straight line with an arrow at either end, and with the time written in UTC at one end.

Fig.15-13. Marking a Position Line.

Of course, if you can obtain two Position Lines that cut at a reasonable angle, then you can obtain a **good position fix.** For the aeroplane to be on both Position Lines at the one time, it must be at the point of intersection.

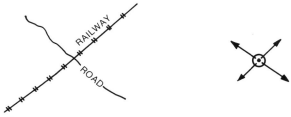

Fig.15-14. Two Position Lines with a Good Cut Can Give You a Fix.

Select Good Features 10 or 15 Minutes Apart.

Do not choose a multitude of landmarks and checkpoints. Just one good checkpoint every 10 or 15 minutes is sufficient. At a Ground Speed (GS) of 120 kt, this puts them 20 to 30 nm apart.

Knowing direction, distance and Ground Speed, a Pilot can think ahead, and **anticipate the appearance of a landmark.** This anticipation allows time for:

- flying the aeroplane (HDG, height, airspeed, engine, systems, checking DI against compass); and
- carrying out navigational functions such as performing simple calculations (estimating new headings, revising ETAs, checking fuel) and then keeping an eye out for the next checkpoint; and then
- looking ahead at the appropriate time for the checkpoint which should be coming into view.

Look for a definite feature at a definite time.

Choose a unique feature to avoid ambiguity.

Example 2: From his chart, a Pilot chooses a small hill with a radio mast as a suitable checkpoint about 4 nm right of the desired track and about 20 nm ahead. The GS is 120 kt, so the 20 nm over the ground should be covered in 10 minutes.

If the present time is 1529 UTC, the Estimated Time Interval (ETI) of 10 minutes gives an estimate at, or abeam, the checkpoint at 1539 UTC. He will, of course, be keeping an eye out for it for some minutes prior to this.

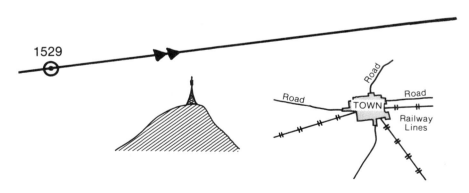

Fig.15-15. Look For a Definite Feature at a Definite Time.

If, instead of passing 4 nm abeam of the feature as expected, the aeroplane passes directly overhead, the Pilot recognises from this **fix** that he is off-track. It is appropriate to confirm that the feature is indeed the selected feature and not another nearby similar one. This can be done by checking the surrounding area for additional ground detail, say a small nearby town with a railway junction – i.e. relate to the whole picture.

244

Once he is certain that he has fixed the position of the aeroplane at a particular time, the Pilot can calculate very simply a new heading to achieve the desired track. Two easy ways to do this are by using *track-guides* (or *fan-lines*) already marked on the map by you at the flight planning stage, or by using the *'1 in 60 rule'* (to be discussed shortly).

Map reading is used to assist DR navigation, not as a replacement for it.

CHART ORIENTATION IN THE COCKPIT.

In flight, the Pilot must relate the land features and their relative bearing from the aircraft to their representations on the chart. To do this it is best to place the map (chart) so that your desired track is *'up the map'*.

If, according to the chart, a landmark is 30° off the track to the right from the present position of the aeroplane, then the Pilot should be able to spot it by directing his attention out of the aircraft window approximately 30° to the right of track. (Note: It may not be 30° to the right of the heading of the aeroplane because the heading may differ from the track, depending upon wind velocity.)

TRACK

*Fig.15-16.
Orientate the Chart
in the Cockpit.*

With the chart oriented correctly in the cockpit, the features shown to the right of the track drawn on the map will appear on the right of the aircraft's track as you fly along (hopefully). The only disadvantage is that it may be difficult to read what is printed on the chart, unless you happen to be flying North.

In normal medium level en route navigation:

READ FROM MAP TO GROUND.

This means, from the chart select a suitable feature some 10 minutes or so ahead of your present position, calculate an ETA at, or abeam, it and then at the appropriate time (some two or three minutes before the ETA) start looking for the actual feature on the ground. Your chosen landmark need not be in view at the time you choose it, but you should anticipate it coming into view at the appropriate time.

LOG KEEPING.

The purpose of keeping an in-flight log is to record sufficient data:
- to enable you to determine your position at any time by DR;
- to have readily at hand the information required for radio position reporting.

Logged data is invaluable if you
feel uncertain of your position at any time.

Keeping an in-flight log, however simple, helps in the methodical sequence of navigational activity of:
- calculation of HDG to achieve a desired TR;
- calculation of GS and ETI to determine ETA at the next checkpoint;
- anticipation and recognition of checkpoints;
- recalculation of HDG, GS and ETIs if necessary (and the cycle repeats).

An in-flight log need only be very basic. On a normal cross-country flight you should log:
- Take-off Time on the flight log;
- Actual Time of Departure (ATD) on the flight log;
- Fixes (position and time) on the chart;
- Track Made Good (TMG) on the chart;
- changes of HDG (and airspeed), and time of making them;
- calculated GS;
- ETIs and revised ETAs at checkpoints;
- altitudes.

This sounds like a lot, but it isn't. Indicating TMG and fixes on the chart simplifies things for you, as these cover the two fundamentals of your progress towards your destination.

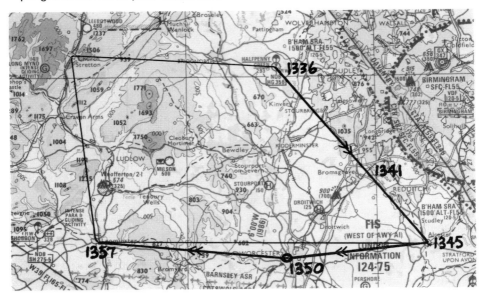

A.T.Dep. 1336

FROM/TO	SAFETY ALT	ALT / TEMP	RAS	TAS	W/V	TR °T	DRIFT	HDG °T	VAR	HDG °M	G/S	DIST	TIME	ETA	HDG °C
H'PENNY GREEN	2035	2500 / -5	105	106	L&V	141	–	141	6W	147	96	23	13	1349	
ALCESTER	1904	FL45 / -10	104	108	L&V	271	–	271	6W	277	97	32	18		
LEOMINSTER	2697	FL45 / -10	104	108	L&V	352	–	352	6W	358	97	19	10		
CHURCH STRETTON	2697	2800 / -5	105	106	L&V	093	–	093	6W	099	96	20	11		
H'PENNY GREEN											ToT	94	52		

Fig.15-17. Keeping A Log.

USING POSITION LINES FOR GROUND SPEED CHECKS.

You should continually update your Ground Speed (GS) as the opportunities arise. Time is of vital importance in navigation and your time of arrival anywhere will depend upon the GS that you achieve.

Position Lines that are approximately at right angles to your track can assist in updating your GS. Noting the amount of time it takes to cover the distance between the two position lines allows you to calculate the GS.

Example 3: 1351 UTC   Crossing a railway line perpendicular (at right angles) to track.

1359 UTC   Transit bearing of a radio mast and a bend in a river perpendicular to track 18 nm further on.

18 nm in 8 minutes = GS 135 kt.

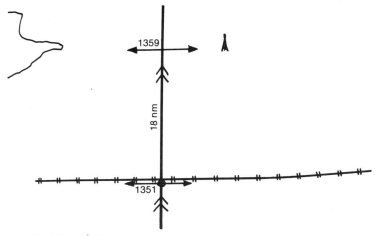

Fig.15-18. Ground Speed Check Using Position Lines Perpendicular to Track.

These position lines need not only be visual. You could also make use of radio position lines from an abeam NDB or VOR radio navigation station.

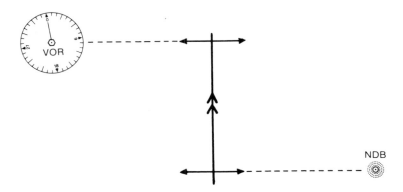

Fig.15-19. GS Check Using Radio Position Lines from Abeam Radio Nav Beacons (NDBs and VORs).

NOTE: Although the use of radio beacons for navigation is not part of the United Kingdom 'basic-PPL' syllabus, we have included some examples to illustrate that basic navigation techniques are the same no matter where our information comes from. Experienced Pilots always use a mix of information sources so as not to get caught out if one source suddenly ceases to be available during the flight. Radio Navigation is covered in Vol.5 of the Air Pilot's Manual – IMC Rating.

You can also carry out very simple GS checks using *Distance Measuring Equipment (DME)* radio navaid stations directly on track, either ahead or behind.

Example 4:   1325 UTC   DTY DME 67 nm and tracking directly towards DAVENTRY DME.

1331 UTC   DTY DME 60 and tracking directly towards DAVENTRY DME.

7 nm in 6 minutes
= GS 70

Fig.15-20. GS Check Using DME.

USING POSITION LINES FOR ESTIMATING DRIFT,
(Visual and Radio Position Lines).

If you have a position line roughly parallel to track you can use it to estimate the drift angle. Tracking directly overhead a long straight railway line makes a visual estimate of your drift angle quite easy, as does tracking along a radio position line to (or from) an NDB or VOR radio navaid station.

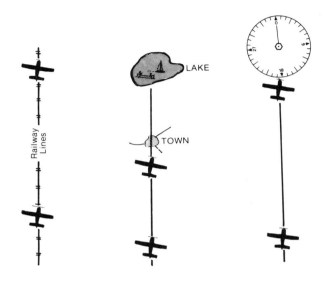

*Fig.15-21. Determining Drift Angle from
Position Lines Parallel to Track.*

☐ Now complete **Exercises 15 — En Route Nav Techniques-1**.

OFF-TRACK HDG CORRECTIONS.

It is usual to find that the actual Track Made Good (TMG) over the ground differs from the desired track that you plotted on the chart at the flight planning stage. If this is the case, then you will have to make some precise corrections to the HDG so that you can return to track at some point further on.

Since the in-flight workload for the Pilot-Navigator can be quite high, we will concentrate on quick methods of mentally calculating track corrections.

1. The Angle between the Track Made Good (TMG) and the Required Track is called **Track Error** (TE).

2. The Angle at which you want to close on your required track is known as the **Closing Angle** (CA). The size of the CA will depend upon how much further down the track you wish to rejoin it – obviously the sooner you want to rejoin the desired track the greater the CA will have to be.

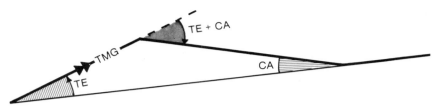

Fig.15-22. Track Error and Closing Angle.

It is obvious from our diagram that to rejoin the desired track at the chosen position will involve a *track change* equal to **TE** + **CA**. (This makes use of a Theorem of Geometry which you may remember from school and which says *'the external angle of a triangle equals the sum of the two interior opposite angles'.)*

It is at this point that we make an approximation that simplifies our in-flight calculations. We assume that a **Track Change** of, say, 15° can be achieved by a **Heading Change** of the same 15°. This is not perfectly accurate because the effect of the wind may cause a different drift angle after making a significant heading change, but within limits it is accurate enough for visual navigation.

For angles up to about 15°, we can assume that a **Track** change
can be achieved by an equal **Heading** change.

The big advantage for Pilot/Navigators in doing this is that it allows us to make track corrections without having to calculate the actual wind velocity.

METHODS OF ESTIMATING CORRECTION ANGLE.

(1) With 'Track-Guides' (or 'Fan-Lines') already drawn on the chart at the flight planning stage and emanating from certain checkpoints along the route, the estimation of Track Error (TE) and Closing Angle (CA) to regain track at that next checkpoint is made very easy. After obtaining a fix, you can estimate TE and CA, which, when added together, will give you the required track change (and the required heading change) to close track at the next checkpoint.

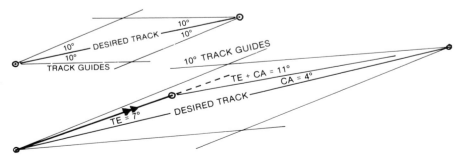

Fig.15-23. Track Correction Using 'Track-Guides' (or 'Fan-Lines').

An **advantage** is that you do not have to measure distance off-track, although this is in fact quite simple to do. A **disadvantage** is that you must have passed over the point from which the track guides emanate behind and you will rejoin track at the point ahead to which the track guides close. Sometimes this is not the situation and other methods need to be employed.

If 5° and 10° Track-Guides (just 10° adequate if short stage) are drawn either side of your desired track on your map, then estimation of track error in flight becomes very easy.

(2) The 1 IN 60 RULE can be used to estimate Correction Angle. This is the **most useful method of regaining track** for the VFR Pilot/Navigator. Time spent here really understanding this will make your en route navigation tasks much easier.

The 1 in 60 rule is based on the fact that:

---

1 nm subtends an angle of 1° at a distance of 60 nm.

This statement can be extended to say that:
5 nm subtends an angle of 5° at 60 nm,
10 nm subtends an angle of 10° at 60 nm;
15 nm subtends an angle of 15° at 60 nm.

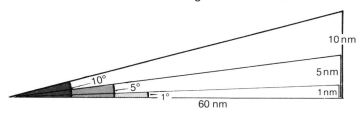

Fig.15-24a. The '1 in 60' Rule.

Now of course we cannot always wait until we have flown 60 nm to find our distance off-track, but that is of no concern because it is **ratios** that we are interested in.

Example 5: 4 nm off-track in 30 nm distance run is the same as:
8 nm off-track in 60 nm, i.e. a **Track Error** of 8°.

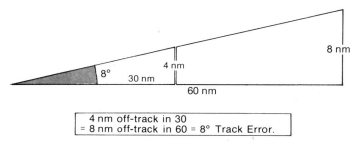

4 nm off-track in 30
= 8 nm off-track in 60 = 8° Track Error.

Fig.15-24b. Example 5.

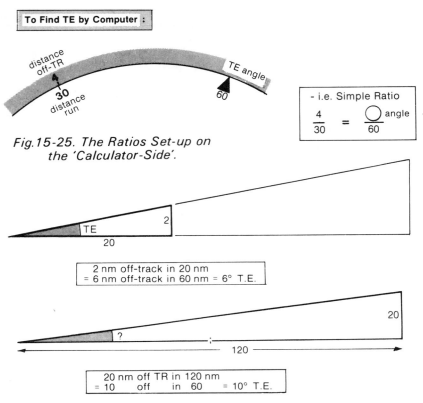

To Find TE by Computer :

distance off-TR

TE angle

30

distance run

60

- i.e. Simple Ratio

$$\frac{4}{30} = \frac{\bigcirc}{60} \text{angle}$$

Fig.15-25. The Ratios Set-up on the 'Calculator-Side'.

TE

2

20

2 nm off-track in 20 nm
= 6 nm off-track in 60 nm = 6° T.E.

20

?

120

20 nm off TR in 120 nm
= 10 off in 60 = 10° T.E.

Fig.15-26. Determining Track Error using the 1 in 60 Rule.

We can do this calculation mentally or by computer.

☐ Now complete **Exercises 15 — En Route Nav Techniques-2,** for practice in calculating Track Error using the 1 in 60 Rule, before we move on.

Knowing The TRACK ERROR, We Can Parallel Desired Track.

If we change our TR by the amount of the calculated Track Error, we will **parallel Track.** (We can do this approximately by changing our HDG by this number of degrees – accurate enough for angles up to 15°.)

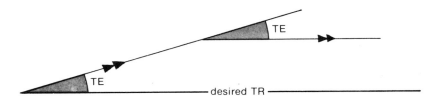

TE

TE

desired TR

Fig.15-27. Paralleling Track by Altering HDG by the Angle of TE.

The same 1 in 60 Rule can be applied to the Closing Angle (CA) once we have chosen the point at which we wish to rejoin track.

Fig.15-28. Calculating Closing Angle by the 1 in 60 Rule.

Now, knowing both Track Error (TE) and Closing Angle (CA) allows you to make a **Heading Change** (TE + CA) that should change your track by the same amount.

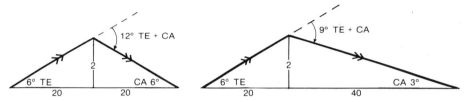

Fig.15-29. Changing HDG (and TR) by 'TE + CA' to Rejoin Desired Track.

Notice that to regain track at a distance ahead **equal** to the distance already travelled you can simply change heading by **double the Track Error** (because in this case the Closing Angle will equal the Track Error). If you had determined your Track Error at the halfway point, then this method would bring you back on-track at the next checkpoint.

This is also a convenient method of regaining track if you have to make a diversion, say around a thunderstorm en route. Turn a suitable angle off-track for so many minutes, and then turn back double that angle for the same number of minutes, and you should find yourself roughly back on track (depending upon wind effect).

This is an extremely important means of DR navigation for you to understand so we will do a few sample problems.

Example 6: After flying 25 nm on a HDG of 085°M, you find yourself 4 nm left of track. What should be your new heading to regain track 25 nm further on?

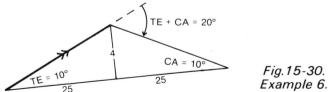

Fig.15-30. Example 6.

4 nm left of track in 25 nm = TE 10° left.
To close 4 nm in a further 25 nm = CA 10°.
Therefore we need to change heading 20° to the right, i.e. to 105°M.

Example 7: After 40 nm on HDG 320°M we find ourselves right of track by 4 nm. What heading should we steer to regain track in a further 20 nm?

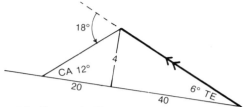

Fig.15-31. Example 7.

4 nm in 40 = 6 in 60 = 6° TE to the right.
4 nm in 20 = 12 in 60 = 12° CA.
Therefore change heading 18° to the left, i.e. to 302°M.

☐ Now do **Exercises 15 — En Route Nav Techniques-3.**

Example 8: We obtain a fix 6 nm right of track, and 30 nm further on find ourselves 10 nm right of track after flying a steady heading of 065°M. Find the heading to steer to regain track 40 nm further on.

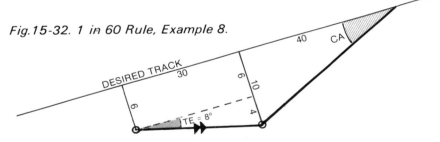

Fig.15-32. 1 in 60 Rule, Example 8.

We only have sufficient information to determine the TMG between the two fixes. To find the Track Error we will have to relate it, not to the desired track itself, but to a line parallel to the desired track.

TE = 4 nm in 30   = 8 in 60 = 8°.
CA = 10 nm in 40 nm = 15 in 60 = 15°.

Therefore to regain track 40 nm further on we need to change heading by 23° to the left, i.e. to 042°M.

Example 9: We obtain a fix 3 nm **left** of Flight Planned Track (FPT) and take up heading 080°M to rejoin FPT after 50 nm. 20 nm further on, we obtain a second fix 2 nm **right** of FPT and immediately change heading to rejoin FPT at the 50 nm point (which is now obviously only 30 nm further on). Calculate the new heading.

Since we have no information regarding the tracking of the aeroplane prior to the first fix, we can only be sure of the Track Made Good (TMG) between the two fixes. The track, and therefore the heading, will have to change by an amount equal to TE + CA.

NOTE: By definition, **Track Error (TE) is the difference between Desired Track and TMG,** i.e. the angle between FPT and the TMG between the two fixes.

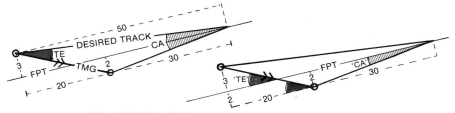

Figs.15-33a & b.
Example 9.

The CA shown on the left above is the usual closing angle – in this case between desired track from the first fix and desired track from the second fix. The *CA* shown on the right is a different angle – between original FPT and desired track from the second fix.

The *sum* of TE + CA from Fig.(a) is the same as the sum of *TE + CA* from Fig.(b). The latter method is used in this example (as illustrated on the right) because of its simplicity.

Working: TE = 5 nm in 20 = 15°.   CA = 2 nm in 30 = 4°.

Therefore to rejoin track at the desired point we need to alter heading by 19° to the left (to port), i.e. to 061°M.

☐ **Exercises 15 — En Route Nav Techniques-4.**

THE RATIO METHOD FOR ESTIMATING TRACK CORRECTIONS.

This method is an extension of the 1 in 60 rule that may assist you.

- If you wish to regain track in the same distance (or time) since you were last on-track, then change heading by double the Track Error (because the CA will be equal to the TE).

- If you wish to regain track in double the distance that it took you to get off-track, then the CA will be equal to only one-half the TE.

- If you wish to regain track in only half the distance that it took you to get off-track, then the CA will be double the TE.

The following four figures illustrate the **ratio method** of using the 1 in 60 Rule.

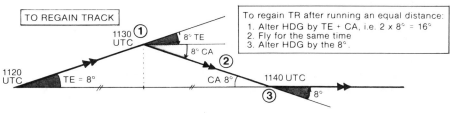

Fig.15-34a.

Now we can regain Track at any point we like. To do this we:
- alter HDG by the TE to approximately parallel the flight-planned TR;
- alter HDG further by the CA (Closing Angle) to close on the TR wherever we want;

and then:
- when TR is regained, alter HDG back by the CA.

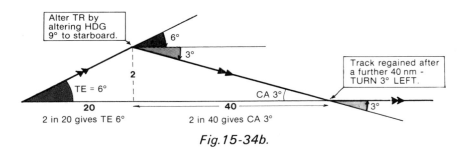

Fig.15-34b.

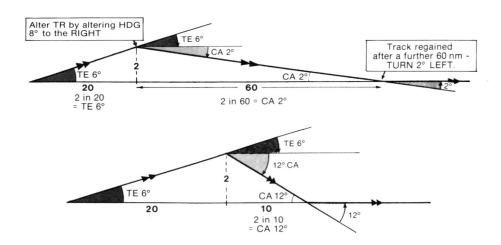

Figs.15-34c & d. The Ratio Method of Finding CA (Closing Angle).

Now, so far we have only discussed how to regain the desired track. Once we do this, if we do not alter the heading we used to regain track we will fly straight through the desired track.

MAINTAINING A DESIRED TRACK (Having Regained It).

From the preceding diagrams it is clear that to remain on track you will have to alter your latest TMG (i.e. the TMG flown as you returned to the desired track) by an amount equal to the chosen Closing Angle (CA).

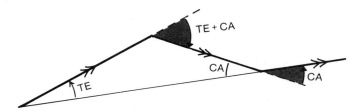

Fig.15-35. When Back On-Track, Change Heading by the chosen Closing Angle.

☐ Now complete **Exercises 15 — En Route Nav Techniques-5.**

THE INVERSE-RATIO METHOD.

In the United Kingdom, it is seldom possible to fly direct visual routes over long distances because of the presence of Controlled Airspace, Restricted Areas and Danger Areas. Normally we have to fly a series of shorter tracks with a number of turning points to avoid such areas. It is sound planning to select turning points that can be easily identified, say over a prominent landmark.

With short legs, the 1 in 60 rule can be simplified even further by concentrating on the Closing Angle (CA) to the next turning point and using what is known as the **'inverse-ratio'** method.

Using the Inverse Ratio Method at the Half-Way Point.

Previously we saw that, to close track in a distance equal to that already travelled since we were last on track, TE = CA. We would then alter heading by this amount which (since TE = CA) is equal to 2 x CA. This is the situation if we fix the position of the aeroplane at the half-way point along a straight track leg.

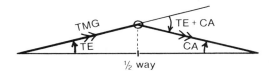

Fig.15-36. If 'Distance-to-go' = 'Distance-gone', then Alter Heading by '2 x CA'.

Using The Inverse-Ratio Method at Other Points En Route.

At any common fraction of the track gone then, to regain track, alter heading by *'CA x the inverse of the fraction of the distance gone'.*

- At the 1/2-way point, alter heading by 'CA x 2', as we have just seen.
- At the 1/3-way point, alter heading by 'CA x 3'.
- At the 1/4-way point, alter heading by 'CA x 4'.
- At the 1/5-way point, alter heading by 'CA x 5'.

Example 10: A track leg is 45 nm. After travelling 15 nm, you are 2 nm left of track. Aim to regain track at the next turning point.

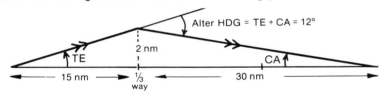

Fig.15-37. Example 10.

Previous Method:
> TE is 2 nm in 15 nm = 8 nm in 60 nm = 8° TE.
> CA is 2 nm in 30 nm = 4 nm in 60 nm = 4° CA.
> Alter Heading by TE + CA = 12°.

Inverse-Ratio Method:
> 1/3 of track gone.
> Alter Heading by CA x 3 = 4° x 3 = 12°.

'EYE-BALLING' AND THE INVERSE-RATIO METHOD.

Proper preparation of our chart can make in-flight track corrections easy.

1. Mark 5° and 10° track-guides either side of the desired track from the **end** of that track;

2. Divide the track into quarters and mark these points.

It is now easy to 'eye-ball' both Closing Angle and fraction of track gone for any fix that we obtain.

Example 11:

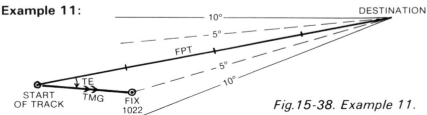

Fig.15-38. Example 11.

By 'eye-ball', CA = 5° and fraction gone is 1/4.

AH (Alter Heading) by 5° x 4 = 20° to the left.

NOTE: The same 'inverse-ratio' method can be used to revise the Estimated Time Interval (ETI).

Time gone from start to fix is 7 min,
therefore total time for leg = 7 x 4 = 28 min.

A limitation of the inverse-ratio method is that it only allows for one alteration of heading per stage, and it only regains track at the next turning point. For short legs this is not a significant disadvantage and the method is more than adequate. Its simplicity greatly reduces the workload in the cockpit for just a little extra effort at the flight planning stage.

☐ Repeat the **En Route Nav Techniques-5** exercises using the Inverse-Ratio Method.

A SLIGHTLY HARDER APPLICATION OF THE INVERSE-RATIO METHOD.

Some Pilots have trouble accurately estimating the fraction of the distance gone. 'Eye-balling' will not be perfect but, as long as your estimate is reasonable, a track correction sufficiently accurate in practical terms can be made.

Example 12: Calculating an *'alter Heading'* and a revised ETA.

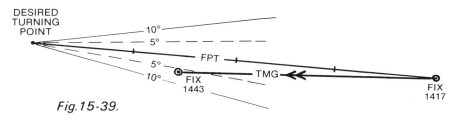

Fig.15-39.

By 'eye-ball': fraction gone 2/3.   CA = 6°.

Alter Heading by '6° x 3/2' (3/2 being the inverse ratio of 2/3) = 9° to the right.

> Time gone = 26 min.
> Revised total time = 26 x 3/2 = 39 min.
> Revised ETA = 1417 + 39 = 1456 UTC(GMT).

Answer: AH by 9° right. Revised ETA 1456 UTC (and no computer manipulations were necessary).

DIVERSIONS

EN ROUTE DIVERSIONS AROUND THUNDERSTORMS AND THE LIKE.

Occasionally, en route, you have the need to divert around a thunderstorm, a heavy rain shower, a town, etc. **If there are suitable landmarks** you can use these to assist you to divert around the 'obstacle' and then to return to track.

If there are no suitable landmarks, then it is a good idea to follow a simple procedure such as:
1. Divert 60° to the desired side of track for a suitable time (and note the HDG and time flown).
2. Parallel track for a suitable time (and note the time flown).
3. Return at 60° for the same time to return to track.
4. Take up a suitable HDG to maintain track.

NOTE: A 60° diversion is very convenient because an **Equilateral** (equal-sided) **Triangle's 3 Angles are each 60°.**

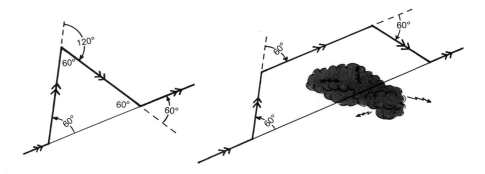

Fig.15-40. The Angles of an Equal-Sided Triangle are 60°.

With a 60° diversion followed immediately by a 60° return to track, the actual distance flown on the diversion is double the on-track distance. In nil-wind conditions this will take double the time.

If the initial 60° diversion HDG is flown for 2 minutes, and the 'return to track leg' is flown for 2 minutes, i.e. a total of 4 minutes, this will then exceed the direct on-track time interval by 2 minutes. Our ETA at the next checkpoint will therefore be 2 minutes later than previously estimated. If we had flown 5 minute diversion legs, then it would add 5 minutes to our ETA.

The length of the leg flown parallel to track will not affect the ETA.

NOTE: We have assumed nil-wind conditions in this discussion. If a significant wind is blowing, then you have to make appropriate allowances for it.

DIVERSION TO AN ALTERNATE AERODROME.

Occasionally it may be necessary to divert from our planned destination, for example, due to deteriorating weather at the destination, or the possibility of running out of daylight if you continue the flight to your original destination, or a suspected mechanical problem that suggests an early landing would be advisable, etc.

If the diversion only entails a small change in HDG (say up to 15°), then using the 1 in 60 rule is adequate.

Example 13: You are tracking 320°T to your destination aerodrome which is 135 nm further on when you receive a met report to say that a large thunderstorm is approaching it. Your HDG is 315°M and your GS 133 kt.

You decide to divert and land at a small aerodrome which, from your present position, is located 10 nm to the right of track and 42 nm distant. Calculate an approximate HDG to steer and an approximate ETI.

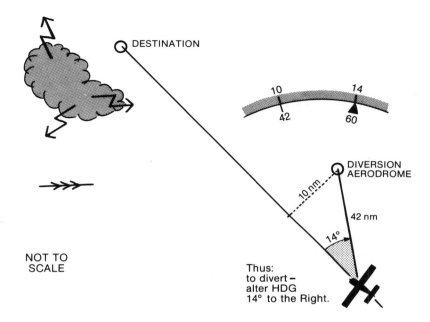

Fig.15-41. Example of a Diversion Slightly Off the Desired Track using the 1 in 60 Rule.

10 nm in 42 nm = 14 in 60 = 14° to the right of your present track.

Because the change in direction is only 14°, a track change of 14° will be achieved reasonably accurately by a HDG change of 14°. (This is because the wind effect will not differ greatly between the two tracks.) Similarly, we can assume the GS to be unaltered due to the similar wind effect on the two reasonably similar tracks.

Therefore: Steer a HDG of (315 + 14 =) 329°T to achieve a TR of (320 + 14 =) 334°M.

42 nm at a GS of 133 kt = ETI 19 mins.

If a diversion requires a **significant change of heading** (and this is usually the case), then the wind effect on the new track may differ significantly from that on the original track. The drift experienced may be quite different on the two different headings. In this case it will be necessary to use your computer to calculate the HDG and GS on the new TR using the latest and most accurate W/V that you have.

Example 14: En route from ALFA to BRAVO. Approaching CHARLIE, you decide to divert to DELTA.

The best technique to use is to maintain HDG and original TR to the next checkpoint (say CHARLIE) and carry out calculations to enable you to divert from that known position. (5 minutes should be more than enough to get yourself organised for an accurate diversion.)

Measure **Track and Distance** from your diversion point to the diversion aerodrome, and, using the known TAS and the most accurate wind velocity (W/V) to hand, calculate (on the wind-side of your flight computer) the Heading (HDG) to steer, and the expected Ground Speed (GS), from which you can find an Estimated Time Interval (ETI) and Estimated Time of Arrival (ETA) overhead the aerodrome.

Check your answers with quick mental approximations.

Calculations: CHARLIE to DELTA, TR 352°T, 27 nm, VAR 5°W.

TAS 105, W/V 240°T/30

By computer: Drift angle 15° right, Steer HDG 337°T, 342°M.
GS 112 kt, ETI (for 27 nm) 15 min.

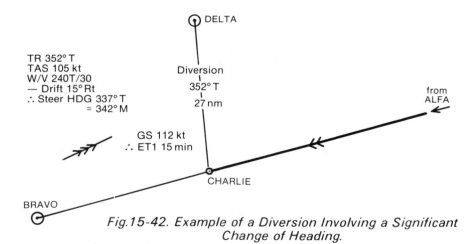

Fig.15-42. Example of a Diversion Involving a Significant Change of Heading.

SOME PRACTICAL HINTS ON DIVERSIONS.

Diversions sometimes become necessary at the most inopportune moments, possibly when you have other problems on your hands. It therefore pays to have a few tricks up your sleeve to allow you to make quick and practical diversions without having to get your computer out and go 'head-down' in the cockpit.

If you can estimate direction and distance by 'eye-balling', then your diversion will be made considerably easier. Direction is most important and, once you have taken up an approximate diversion heading and settled into the diversion track, you can calculate an accurate heading, distance to go, Ground Speed, ETI, etc, in a more relaxed atmosphere.

'Eye-balling' Track.

Estimation of track is surprisingly easy and, with a bit of practice, you can achieve a +/– 5° accuracy. In fact, you should **always** estimate track before measuring it with a protractor or plotter – this will avoid making 180° or 90° errors as has happened from time to time. Estimating before measuring will also develop faith in your ability to estimate to a practical degree of accuracy.

'Halving known angles' is the simplest means of estimating angles. Halving the angle between a quadrantal point and a cardinal point will give you an angle of 22·5°, say 22°, and halving this again will give you 11°. An accuracy of +/– 5° will be achieved with practice.

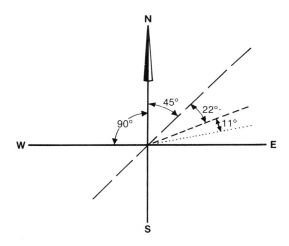

Fig.15-43. Halving Angles as a Means of Estimating Track.

Estimating Distance.

The average adult male *'top thumb-joint'* will cover about 10 nm on a 1:500 000 chart (and 5 nm on 1:250 000). Check yours! This makes it very easy to estimate short distances.

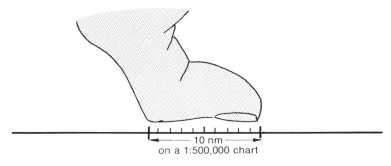

Fig.15-44. The Top Thumb-Joint Covers approx 10 nm at 1:500 000.

A full hand span might measure 60 nm on a 1:500 000 chart. Check yours!

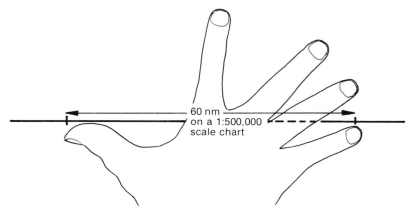

60 nm
on a 1:500,000
scale chart

Fig.15-45. A Full Hand Span is approx 60 nm on a 1:500 000 Chart.

If you have a 60 nm span and a 10 nm top thumb-joint, then you have an in-built 1:60 measuring device, ideally designed to measure 10°.

10 nm in 60 nm = 10°, by the 1 in 60 rule.

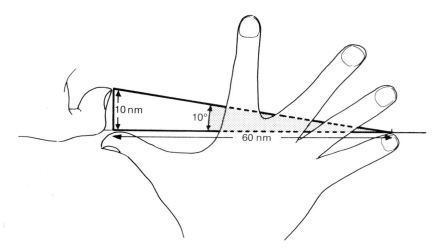

10 nm

10°

60 nm

Fig.15-46. The In-Built Personal 1 in 60 Measuring Device for 10°.

As part of your Navigation Competence flight-test you will be asked to carry-out a diversion. Should you elect to make use of Radio Navaids then these will also be examined. Radio Navaids (covered in Vol.5 – IMC Rating) need to be thoroughly understood before being used for navigation.

VISIBILITY

Cross-country flights by the holder of a basic-PPL (i.e. no IMC or Instrument rating) should only be carried out in good weather conditions which permit continual observations of the ground, according to the specific requirements laid down by the CAA for your licence level. This means that you should generally be able to spot each check feature at an appropriate time prior to actually reaching or passing abeam it.

Good Visibility decreases the Workload on the Pilot/Navigator.

POOR VISIBILITY.

Reduced visibility brings additional problems to the Pilot/Navigator. As you know from Aviation Law, it is permissible for a basic-PPL holder to fly, under certain circumstances, in visibility as low as 1·5 nm, which is really quite poor visibility.

As well as making the actual handling of the aeroplane more difficult (since the lack of a natural horizon makes holding an attitude more difficult), Poor Visibility also means that checkpoints may not come into view until you are almost upon them and, if the checkpoints are some distance off-track, you may not even see them.

Poor visibility may be due to smoke, haze, mist, rain, smog, etc. Sooner or later you will be faced with the problems that reduced visibility brings. Consideration should be given to turning back, or to diverting, if you feel that Visual Meteorological Conditions (VMC) cannot be maintained, or if the visibility (even if in excess of VFR minimum requirements) is still not adequate for your particular flight and your particular experience.

Consideration should also be given to slowing down and perhaps even extending some flap and adopting the 'precautionary' configuration. A slower speed gives a Pilot more time to see things, as well as reducing the radius of turn if manoeuvring is required.

If you are expecting poor visibility en route, it is advisable to select more en route checkpoints that are closer to your desired track. This reduces the time between fixes and reduces the anxiety if you do not spot one of the check features, but the next one comes up on time shortly thereafter. If several checkpoints fail to appear, you could have reason to feel 'uncertain of position'.

UNCERTAIN OF POSITION.

If you have flown for some time without obtaining a fix (say 20 or 30 minutes), you may feel a little uncertain of your precise position. You will be able to calculate a DR position (using expected TR and GS), but you may feel a little anxious that you cannot back this up with a positive fix over or abeam some ground feature. This situation is a normal one and is no reason for immediate anxiety. It is far from being 'lost'.

It is impossible to give a set of rules that covers all possible situations, but the following are general rules that may assist you.

If A Checkpoint Does Not Come Into View at the Expected Time:

1. Log HDG (Compass and Direction Indicator readings) and TIME.

2. (a) If the Direction Indicator is incorrectly set, then you have the information needed to make a fair estimate of your actual position, then reset the DI and calculate a HDG and ETI to regain the desired track; or
(b) If the DI is aligned correctly with the compass, then the non-appearance of a landmark, whilst it will perhaps cause you some concern, need not indicate that you are grossly off-track. You may not have seen the landmark for some perfectly legitimate reason, such as bright sunlight obscuring your vision, poor visibility, a change in the ground features not reflected on the chart (e.g. removal of a TV mast, the emptying of a reservoir, etc), or if you are navigating above even a small amount of cloud, the inconvenient positioning of some of this cloud may have obscured your check feature.

3. If you consider the situation warrants it, make an **Urgency Call** (PAN PAN PAN, etc) on 121·5 MHz. This should enable ATC to fix your position by 'auto-triangulation'.

4. If you obtain a fix, or if the next checkpoint comes up on time, the flight can continue and normal navigation procedures apply once again.

5. If still unable to fix your position, follow the procedure below.

PROCEDURE WHEN LOST

Becoming lost is usually the result of some human error. Being lost is totally different to being *temporarily uncertain of your position,* where you can determine a reasonably accurate DR position.

Once again, it is impossible to lay down a set of hard and fast rules on what to do, except to give you the advice that careful pre-flight planning and in-flight attention to the normal, simple en route navigational tasks will ensure that the situation of being lost will never arise.

There is one thing that is certain if you ever become lost.

You must Formulate a Plan of Action because:
it is futile to fly around aimlessly in the hope of finding a pinpoint.

If you change your thinking from one of being *'uncertain of position'* to one of being *'lost'*, then make use of the Radar Advisory Service, if available (see point (3) above). If still lost:

1. It is important initially to maintain HDG (if terrain, visibility and what you know of the proximity of controlled airspace permit) and carry out a **sequence of positive actions.**

2. If a vital checkpoint is not in view at ETA, then continue to fly for 10% of the time since your last positive fix, and

3. Deciding what your last positive fix was, **check the Headings flown since that Last Fix**, ensuring that:
   - the magnetic compass is not being affected by outside influences such as a camera, portable radio, or other magnetic material placed near it;
   - the gyroscopic Direction Indicator (DI) is aligned with the Magnetic Compass correctly;
   - magnetic variation and drift have been correctly applied to obtain your HDGs flown;
   - an estimate of track direction on the chart against that shown on the flight plan is correct;

4. **Read from Ground to Chart**, i.e. look for **significant ground features** or combinations of features and try to determine their position on the chart.

5. Establish a **'Most Probable Area'** in which you think you are. There are several ways in which this can be done, and we recommend you to consult your Flying Instructor for his or her preferred method.

Two Suggested Methods for Establishing a 'Most Probable Area'.

Method (1). Estimate the distance flown since the last fix and apply this distance, plus or minus 10%, to an arc 30° either side of what you estimate the probable Track Made Good (TMG) to be.

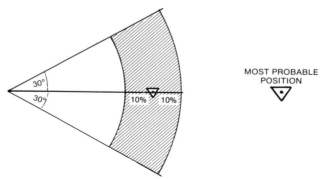

Fig.15-47. Estimating the 'Most Probable Area' that You are In.

Method (2). Estimate your 'most probable position' and draw a circle around it of radius equal to 10% the distance flown since the last fix.

Fig.15-48. Method (2) for Estimating 'Most Probable Position'.

- **Establish a safety altitude** at which to fly in order to ensure adequate clearance of all obstacles in what you consider the general area to be. Be especially careful in conditions of poor visibility or low cloud.
- **Check large features** within this area of the chart with what can be seen on the ground. Try and relate features seen on the ground with those shown on the chart, i.e. **read from ground to chart.** Confirm the identification of any feature by closely observing secondary details around the feature, e.g. a small irregular lake is confirmed by the position of a small town on a bend in the railway line as it turns from West to South. Double check any fix.

When you do positively establish a fix, re-check your Direction Indicator (DI) and recommence normal navigational activity. Calculate the HDG, GS and ETI for the next check feature and set course for it.

At all times continue to fly the aircraft safely, maintaining an awareness of time, especially with respect to the beginning of Official NIGHT (SS+30) and Fuel State.

If you are Still Unable to Fix Your Position, you should consider taking one of the following actions:
- Increase the 'most probable area' by 10, 15 or even 20% of the distance flown from the last fix.
- Climb to a higher altitude to increase your range of vision.
- Turn towards a known prominent line feature, such as a coastline, large river, railway line or road, and then follow along it to the next town where you should be able to obtain a fix. (Don't forget that it may also lead you into a control zone.)
- Steer a reciprocal heading and attempt to return to your last fix.

Note the following Important Points of Airmanship:
- If you want to cover as much ground as possible with the fuel available, you should fly the aeroplane for **best Range.**
- Keep a **Navigation Log** going.
- Remain positively **Aware of Time.** Keep your eye on the fuel and on the time remaining until the end of daylight. If darkness is approaching, remember that it will be darker at ground level than at altitude, and that it becomes dark very quickly in the tropics.
- If you decide to carry out a precautionary search and landing (i.e. a forced landing with the use of power), allow sufficient time and fuel to do this on the assumption that two or three inspections might have to be made before finding a suitable landing area.

WHY DID YOU BECOME LOST ?

If at any stage you became lost, you should systematically try to determine the reason (either in flight or post flight) so that you can learn from the experience.

Common reasons for becoming lost include:
- incorrectly calculated HDGs, GSs, and ETIs (hence the need for you always to make mental estimates of approximate answers to these items);

- incorrectly synchronised Direction Indicator (Heading Indicator) i.e. gyroscopic DI not aligned correctly with the Magnetic Compass – (this should be done every 10 or 15 minutes);
- a faulty Compass reading (due to transistor radios, cameras and other metal objects placed near the Compass);
- incorrectly applied Variation (Variation West, Magnetic Best; Variation East, Magnetic Least);
- incorrectly applied drift (compared to TR, the HDG should be pointing into wind, i.e. flying North with a westerly wind blowing would mean that the HDG should be to the left of track and into-wind);
- a wind velocity significantly different to that forecast, and not allowed for in flight by the Pilot;
- a deterioration in weather, reduced visibility, increased cockpit workload;
- an incorrect fix, i.e. mis-identification of a check feature;
- a poorly planned diversion from the original desired track;
- not paying attention to carrying out normal navigational tasks throughout the flight.

With regular checks of Direction Indicator alignment with the magnetic compass, reasonably accurate flying of HDG, and with position fixes every 10 or 15 minutes, none of these errors should put you far off-track. It is only when you are slack and let things go a bit too far that you become lost.

FURTHER POINTS
on En Route Navigation

RANGE AND ENDURANCE FLYING.

The performance of most aeroplanes is fairly flexible, and you as Pilot would operate your aeroplane in the best manner for your purposes according to your own judgement. Guidance is given in the various manuals associated with the aeroplane.

If your desire is to fly a given route using the minimum amount of fuel (or conversely, fly the maximum distance on a given amount of fuel) then you would fly for **Range**. **Range Flying** is concerned with **Distance** and **Fuel**.

If your desire is to stay in the air for the maximum time possible, with the distance covered not being a consideration, then you would fly for **Endurance**; for example, holding near an aerodrome waiting for some bad weather to pass, or holding due traffic before you make your approach. **Endurance Flying** is concerned with **Time** and **Fuel**.

Performance figures for Range or Endurance cruising will usually be found in the Pilot's Operating Handbook for your aircraft. The topic is discussed in more detail in Volume 4, Chapter 32.

THE AIR PLOT.

Pilots mainly use the *'track plot'*, which is path **over the ground** described by **'Track'** and **'Ground Speed'**. Occasionally the **air plot** is used, where passage relative to the air mass is plotted, i.e. wind effect is not taken into account. The symbol for an *'air position'* is shown.

Fig.15-49. Symbol For an 'Air Position'.   ✛

An air plot may be used for an aircraft who has requested navigational assistance because of being lost. By plotting HDGs and TASs flown since the last fix (i.e. the passage of the aeroplane relative to the air mass), it is possible to determine where the aeroplane would have been if there was nil-wind.

By applying an appropriate wind vector for this time to the final air position, **a DR ground position** for the aeroplane may be deduced. The wind blows the aeroplane from its air position to its ground position.

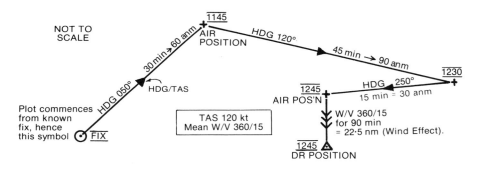

Fig.15-50. Example of an Air Plot.

NOTE: It is not usual for a Pilot navigating visually to use an air plot, although it may be of use when flying over featureless terrain or the sea, where obtaining fixes or tracking information is difficult. The principle, however, is fairly simple.

MENTAL DEAD-RECKONING.

If you develop the skills of mental 'dead-reckoning', then it becomes less likely that you will ever make a gross navigational error. Each time you are flying, not only on 'cross-countries' but also out in the local training area, practise estimating tracks, distances and heights.

Wind Components Applied to TAS and Planned or Desired Track.

When flight planning and also en route, it is a good idea to keep a mental check on all your heading and GS calculations. Some formulae based on Trigonometry can be memorised, but we feel this is a little too involved to include at Private Pilot level.

What you *can* do quite easily, however, is remember the following:
- a headwind component reduces Ground Speed to less than True Air Speed;
- a tail wind component increases Ground Speed to more than True Air Speed;
- to achieve the desired Track, the aeroplane must be headed somewhat into wind.

Example 15: If your desired track is West and the wind is from 220°. Having a headwind component, your GS should be less than TAS.

Your heading must be into-wind compared to desired track and so will be to the left of West, i.e. a bearing less than 270°. With this in mind, you check that your flight plan and en route calculations reflect this, i.e. GS less than TAS, and HDG less than the FPT/desired TR in this case.

Estimating Distances.

Also good to keep in mind is that a 'Sight Down' angle of 45° from the horizon gives a horizontal distance equal to your height AGL – either ahead or to the side.

Example 16:
(a) If you are 7000 ft above terrain which is 1000 ft AMSL, height AGL is 6000 ft (approx 1 nm), and so a sight down angle of 45° gives a horizontal distance of 1 nm.
(b) At 12 000 ft AGL, a sight down angle of 45° gives 2 nm.
(c) At 3000 ft AGL, a sight down angle of 45° gives 0·5 nm.

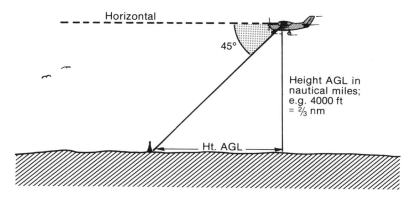

Fig.15-51. Estimating Distances Using
Sight Down Angle 45° Below the Horizon.

LOW LEVEL NAVIGATION.

Low Level Navigation means navigation at about 500 ft AGL. It is carried out in the same way as normal pilot navigation at higher altitudes, with a few special considerations.

At a low level you will have a limited field of vision. You will also have to keep a constant lookout due to your close proximity to terrain. This means that at the pre-flight stage you should study your charts very carefully and choose suitable check features, reasonably close to track and perhaps greater in number than for a similar flight at a higher altitude.

The elevation of nearby features above the general level of the surrounding terrain is more important for a low level flight, because they will be seen side-on rather than from above as in normal en route navigation at a higher level.

VIEW FROM ABOVE

VIEW FROM THE SIDE

Fig.15-52. The Side Elevation of Check Features is Important in Low Level Navigation.

Spot heights such as radio masts, factory chimneys, church steeples, etc, are very useful at low level, but may be almost invisible when flying at high altitudes. Railways lines at the bottom of cuttings may be very visible from altitude, but not visible from a low level unless you are directly over them.

The presence of unusually high and difficult-to-see obstructions and built-up areas must be anticipated and avoided.

The **Limited Field Of Vision** means that you need to **anticipate** the sighting of check features and recognise them quickly (hence the need for a very careful study of your charts before commencing the low level navigational exercise).

If a ground feature fails to appear at its ETA, there will be no time to be too concerned and search for it. Assume that it has been passed and concentrate on looking for the next check feature which should not be too far ahead. The number of check features required for low level navigation should in general be greater than for normal higher level navigation. Only if you fail to spot several consecutive check features should you become 'uncertain of your position'. Mental DR in such a situation is invaluable in determining the probable position.

Log Keeping on a low level exercise will necessarily have to be restricted because of the greater concentration required on things outside the cockpit. Due to aircraft handling considerations, and the need to keep a good lookout, it may at times be imposssible to make any but the briefest log entries or marks on your chart.

NOTE: Your attention is drawn to the **'Low Level Civil Aircraft Notification Procedure' (CANP)** which is a service aimed at improving the information available on low level civil aircraft to be disseminated to military operators to assist them in planned avoidance. It pertains mainly to such low-level localised operations as crop-spraying and banner-towing, however check with your flying instructor if he or she considers it affects your planned flight.

CANP is is described in AIP RAC and in Pooley's *Pilots Information Guide.*

DESCENTS FROM HIGHER LEVELS

Most visual (as distinct from Instrument) flights in the UK are carried out at 3000 ft and below, which makes an accurate descent calculation rather academic. Since it is so straightforward, however, we will consider a few simple cases for those times when you do cruise high.

Example 17: If your rate of descent is 500 feet per minute (abbreviated to either *ft/min* or *fpm*), how long will it take to descend from 8000 ft AMSL to 2500 ft AMSL?

Time to descend (8000 – 2500 =)
5500 ft at 500 ft/min = 11 mins.

Fig.15-53. Example 17.

Example 18: In the above case, if your estimated Ground Speed (GS) on descent is 162 kt, how far from the aerodrome should you commence descent to arrive overhead at 2500 ft AMSL?

(This would be a typical situation on arrival at an aerodrome of elevation 500 ft AMSL, where you wished to overfly at 2000 ft Above Aerodrome Level, i.e. 2500 ft AMSL, prior to joining the circuit for an approach and landing.)

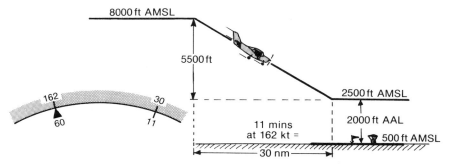

Fig.15-54. A Simple Descent Calculation.

Example 19: Your Estimated Time Interval (ETI) to a nearby diversion aerodrome (elevation 142 ft AMSL) is 8 minutes and you wish to begin descent immediately from 5000 ft AMSL to overfly at 2000 ft Above Aerodrome Level (AAL). What average **rate of descent** should you maintain?

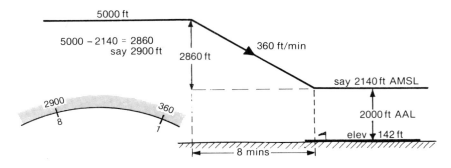

Fig.15-55. Another Simple Descent Calculation.

To descend (5000 – 2100 approx =) 2900 ft in 8 minutes = 360 ft/min.

Example 20: You are at FL75, 18 nm from an aerodrome (elev 21 ft AMSL, QNH 980 mb) and you wish to commence descent immediately to arrive overhead the aerodrome at 2000 ft AAL. If your True Air Speed on descent is 127 kt with a tail wind component of 25 kt, what rate of descent do you require?

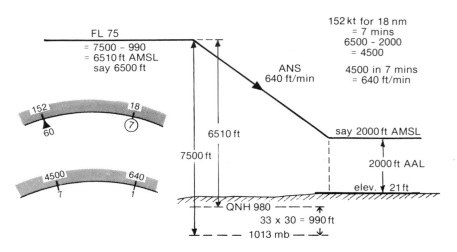

Fig.15-56. Example 20.

GS on descent = 127 + 25 = 152 kt.
Time to travel 18 nm at GS 152 kt = ETI 7 minutes.
Rate of Descent to descend (6500 – 2000 =) 4500 ft in 7 mins
= 4500/7 = 640 ft/min.

Example 21: You are to descend at 500 ft/min from 8500 ft with a GS of 157 kt, wishing to overfly an aerodrome, elevation 730 ft, at 2000 ft AAL. At what distance from the field should you commence your descent?

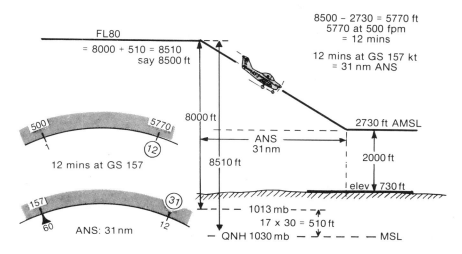

Fig.15-57. Example 21.

☐ Now, finally, complete the descent **Exercises 15 — En Route Nav Techniques-6.**

16

NAVIGATION IN REMOTE AREAS

One day, you will perhaps decide to make a journey into one of the world's remote and featureless areas, such as North Africa, the Middle East, India or even the Australian outback. The transition from cross-country flying in the more heavily populated areas of the UK to flying in the featureless areas however, should not be taken lightly. Navigation in remote areas is not necessarily more difficult, but **the lack of landmarks will require more disciplined flight planning and flying.**

A number of accidents have occurred in the past when inexperienced pilots encountered navigational difficulties in remote areas of the world. A common theme has been:

- lack of experience; coupled with
- inadequate flight preparation; and
- poor in-flight navigational technique.

Experience. Where does one gain 'experience'? Pilots are faced with 'lack of experience' many times in their flying careers; how do we gain experience, except by reading and studying and then finally 'doing'? First solo; first cross-country flight as a single Pilot/Navigator; we are extending ourselves to new limits all the time, and in the process building up experience.

Often we learn some lessons that have been learned many times before by other pilots. Listen to them! But make your own operational judgements. *Biggles* stories might have something in them for you. Read reports of trips where things did not go as planned (and learn from other Pilot's experiences rather than your own).

The term 'lack of experience' is used here in reference to navigational experience. We assume that, as a responsible pilot, you would only venture forth into a remote area in an aeroplane in which you had recent flying experience and whose systems (fuel system, electrical system, etc) you were fully conversant with.

Flight Preparation. There is no excuse for inadequate flight preparation, even for the most inexperienced Pilot. You must do your homework properly for a particular route, so that you can make reasonably correct in-flight decisions when the unexpected occurs. Of course, with proper pre-flight preparation, the *unexpected* seems to occur less often.

In-Flight Navigational Technique. Flying in remote and featureless areas requires some **good DR** flying. Following dirt tracks that meander through the desert (and then peter out) is **not** a good navigational technique for outback areas. This is not to say that following the only railway line up to Alice Springs or the one-and-only sealed road across to Perth in Australia shouldn't be done – this is an area for your own operational judgement – but we are referring here particularly to areas where such features are not available.

What can you, a Pilot-in-Command, do to avoid the pitfalls that can occur in remote area flying?

FLIGHT PLAN CAREFULLY.

The 'DAY BEFORE' Type of Pre-Flight Planning.

- Allow plenty of time to flight plan carefully without any pressure of time being placed upon you.

- Ensure that your charts are current and adequate for your intended route, plus or minus any reasonable planned or unplanned diversions.

- Examine your charts carefully for landmarks and distinguishing features along your proposed route, and to either side of track.

- Ensure that you are up to speed on your computer usage, especially in calculating HDGs, Ground Speeds and Times.

- Ensure that you carry the required radio and survival equipment and that it is in good condition and you know how to operate it.

- Make use of the local knowledge of other Pilots and Briefing Officers who know the area you intend flying over. Determine suitable fix points and obtain as much information as possible on suitable landing areas along the route. Ensure that this information is reliable and up-to-date, because it is not unknown for landing grounds in remote areas to be abandoned and possibly unuseable.

- If practicable, plan your route over suitable landing areas.

Obtain a Thorough MET BRIEFING.

- Ensure that you are briefed thoroughly on the route and for your destination and alternate aerodromes.

- Do not be embarrassed if you do not understand all aspects of the Area Forecasts or Aerodrome forecasts, or some of the abbreviations. Ask for clarification!

- Be wary of areas where visibility may be reduced in dust or haze.

- Do not plan on flying above a low layer of cloud for long periods where your visual navigation could be impeded.

- In hot, desert areas, try and determine an approximate altitude above which you will be out of the convective turbulence layer and its associated 'bumpy ride' for the time at which your flight will occur.

Obtain a Thorough OPERATIONAL BRIEFING.

- Flight Service and Air Traffic Control personnel are aviation professionals. They are trained to a very high standard and it is their job (and usually their pleasure) to assist you in any way possible. It is up to you as a Pilot to **request** their assistance.
- Pay particular attention to landing area and aerodrome serviceability along your proposed route, especially following rain.
- Determine availability of the correct fuel at appropriate landing points.
- Determine if any military activity is planned in the area. Military jet low level navigation exercises do occur at high speed in remote areas – some of these aircraft are camouflaged fighters which are hard to see, and some of them large bombers. It is nice to know if they are around.
- Verify the time of Last Light for your destination.

Submit a FLIGHT PLAN.

- Check tracks and distances mentally following your computer calculations to ensure there are no gross errors, e.g. tracks wrong by 90° or 180°. Apply Magnetic Variation correctly ('Variation East – Magnetic Least ...').
- Check that drift has been allowed for in the correct direction and that ETIs are approximately correct.
- Plan on flying as high as is practicable:
  - a better picture of the country can be obtained;
  - on hot days, the flight should be smoother;
  - VHF radio coverage is better.
- Allow adequate FUEL, plus reserves – not only for the planned flight, but for any possible alternative action, including what procedures you will follow in case selected fix-points are not located as expected.
- Allow sufficient TIME for the planned flight plus any possible alternative action, especially if flying in the latter part of the day when Last Light is a very real consideration. It is only an extremely (over-?) confident visual Pilot that would allow only 10 minutes or so buffer prior to Last Light for arrival over the destination.
- Early departure times in the desert areas generally produce better flights. Cooler air gives better take-off performance and a smoother ride. Visibility may be better and the pressure of impending Last Light removed. The benefit of the early start can be lost if you dawdle along, though, wasting time with inefficient flight planning, refuelling, etc.
- Allow for proper food and rest at appropriate intervals. It is not only the aeroplane that needs fuel.

IN-FLIGHT NAVIGATIONAL TECHNIQUE.

- Fly estimated HDGs accurately. Do not allow the aircraft to wander off-track simply through inattention. Have in your mind an awareness of approximate direction – and check that drift is applied in the correct direction for your desired track and the wind experienced. Check for drift soon after departure and adjust your HDG as necessary.

- Map read carefully as the flight progresses, but do not let this distract you from flying an accurate heading. Be aware that, following heavy rains in outback areas, large uncharted rivers and lakes may appear and disappear within a few days. Even if you cannot pinpoint yourself visually at all times due to the lack of landmarks, at least know your dead reckoning (DR) position at all times based on estimated TR and GS since your last fix.

- Maintain an in-flight log, recording all HDGs flown and the TIME of any significant changes. It takes a few seconds to do and may prove invaluable.

- Maintain a general sense of direction and ensure that the Directional Indicator is re-aligned with the Magnetic Compass at regular intervals (every 10 or 15 minutes).

- Do not deviate from your flight plan without any real justification. A flight plan should be adhered to unless a positive fix indicates that you are off-track, or unless you change your intentions in-flight and prepare a new flight plan. With a positive fix, you have data that enables you to make a reasoned correction to your HDG flown.

- Anticipate your fix points some minutes ahead of your estimate for them and commence a good lookout, not just ahead but also to each side of track. Do not just wait for planned fix points to show up – anticipate them. Continually study the surrounding countryside, but not to the extent that it disturbs your accurate heading keeping.

- Positively establish your position in relation to a selected fix point before continuing on to the next fix point.

- If you are unable to locate your selected fix point and you are uncertain of your position, commence your planned alternative action being aware of FUEL and TIME in particular. This alternative action could be to return to the last positive fix or to divert to some prominent landmark even if some distance away. In these circumstances you may have to abandon your original plan for proceeding to your original destination, in favour of a destination that is easier to locate and which is in a more accessible area. Maintain an accurate log in this procedure.

- If you depart from your original flight plan, notify your new intentions to the appropriate Flight Service or ATC unit, but do this after you have planned on your new course of action and flying the aeroplane is well in hand.

WHAT TO DO IF THINGS DO NOT WORK OUT AS PLANNED.

- Do not become flustered. With reasonable planning, you should have allowed fuel and time to sort out this sort of problem. Establish the fuel state and time remaining to Last Light.

- Do not assume that you are in a particular place because that is where you want to be. Keep an open mind and study the surrounding countryside carefully. Log all significant changes of HDG, and the times they are made.

- Follow the procedures suggested in the previous chapter on what to do if you are uncertain of your precise position or if you become lost.

- Advise the Air Traffic Service Unit the HDGs and times flown since your last positive fix; the SAR (Search And Rescue) organisation can plot your flight using the latest wind data and assist in establishing your position.
- If, despite your precautions, things go unexpectedly wrong and you are caught with insufficient fuel or daylight to reach your destination or a suitable alternate, be intelligent in the use of your resources.

Carry out a precautionary search and landing whilst you still have adequate fuel and daylight available. Stay with the aircraft and activate the Emergency Locator Beacon.

THE EMERGENCY LOCATOR BEACON (ELB).

In remote areas visual searches can be very difficult. The Emergency Locator Beacon (ELB), if properly used, can allow the search area to be reduced quickly so that the visual search can be concentrated in a small area.

ELB is a generic (family) term covering devices known as Crash Locator Beacons, Emergency Locator Transmitters, etc. They all operate on both 121·5 and 243 MegaHertz.

A few common sense points on the use of the ELB are:
- know how to use the ELB. Review the operating instructions for your particular beacon prior to flight;
- ensure that the battery is fully charged;
- ensure that the ELB is capable of operating properly (tests are restricted so seek the advice of the authorites before activating a test as it may result in the commencement of unnecessary SAR action, such as scrambling of aircraft, etc);
- if you are forced down, however, do not be reluctant to activate the ELB at an appropriate time.

☐ Proceed now to **Exercises 16 — Navigation In Remote Areas.**

17

ENTRY/EXIT LANES
AND
LOW LEVEL ROUTES

Special Entry/Exit Access Lanes and Low Level Routes are provided to allow Exit from and Entry to some aerodromes that lie within Control Zones (CTRs) or under Controlled Airspace. They are established to allow easier access for training aircraft, for example.

There may be other routes legitimately usable which do not infringe restricted areas or controlled airspace, but the **established access lanes** provide a readily identifiable channel through complex sections of airspace.

Entry/Exit Lanes and Low Level Routes are designed to simplify navigation and operational procedures for non IMC rated Pilots flying near busy control zones.

THE BASIC RULES FOR FLYING ALONG AN ACCESS LANE OR LOW LEVEL ROUTE.

You should refer to the UK AIP (RAC 3-4) (and/or to *Pooley's Flight Guide*) for instructions.

- Follow the published instructions.
- Adhere to the published tracks and entry/exit points (labelled 'E'),
- Conform with the general flight rules regarding terrain clearance, and flight over populous areas, danger areas, etc.
- Operate not higher than the altitude specified as the upper limit in the section being flown.
- Keep to the RIGHT; (traffic separation may not be provided by ATC).

Navigating through an Access Lane or a Low Level Route is based on the normal visual navigational procedure of flying accurate headings and backing up with frequent visual fixes.

Flight Plan Accurately.

Entry/Exit Lanes are very confined areas. Control Zones (CTRs) which you wish to avoid entering are adjacent. The traffic in the area may be concentrated in the Lane. For these (and other) reasons extra attention must be paid to keeping a good lookout outside the cockpit compared to normal cross-country flying, and to map-reading with more than the usual number of fixes.

The easiest way to achieve this is to **flight plan accurately and thoroughly.**

- Study the met forecasts and actual reports thoroughly. Note any significant weather, visibility, cloud ceiling and wind. Relate the weather conditions to the terrain or built-up areas that you will have to fly over, ensuring that adequate terrain clearance and clearance from cloud is available. Be aware that strong winds may give rise to turbulence in the low levels where you will be flying.

- Request an operational briefing from your Instructor, checking to see if any special considerations need to be made for your flight.

- Select the best route. Sometimes there are several Access Lanes to choose from, and sometimes you may choose to avoid one and fly a completely different route. Prevailing conditions may make a more circuitous route offering easier navigation, flatter terrain, better visibility, higher cloud base, more separation from controlled airspace, etc, more suitable than the published Access Lanes although, generally they are perfectly suitable.

- Study the chart carefully for suitable landmarks and specified points in or near the Lane. Read all relevant comments in the UK AIP (RAC 3-4) or *Pooley's Flight Guide.*

- Identify a landmark on the approach to the Lane over which you can accurately position the aeroplane to commence the transit of the Lane. This point is best chosen to be say 5 nm prior to the commencement of the Lane to allow you room for manoeuvre without penetrating controlled airspace.

- Check all computer work for accuracy, and do mental checks of HDGs, GSs and ETIs.

- Have an alternative plan of action ready in case poor weather or some other reason makes a transit of the Lane undesirable.

- Aim to reduce the in-flight workload to a minimum.

Navigate Accurately.

- You need to keep on-track in an Access Lane, because of the proximity of control zones in most cases, where large and small aeroplanes may be operating.

- Accurately position your aeroplane (over a landmark if possible) prior to entering the Lane. This is your starting point for accurate track-keeping through the Lane.

- Aim to have all other tasks (such as after take-off checks, a departure or position report, copying the landing information off the ATIS, alignment of the Heading Indicator with the magnetic compass) completed prior to entering the Lane.

- Check the weather ahead to see if it is clear enough for a safe transit of the Lane. If not, adopt your alternative course of action, which might be to return to the aerodrome of departure, or to try another track.

(continued)

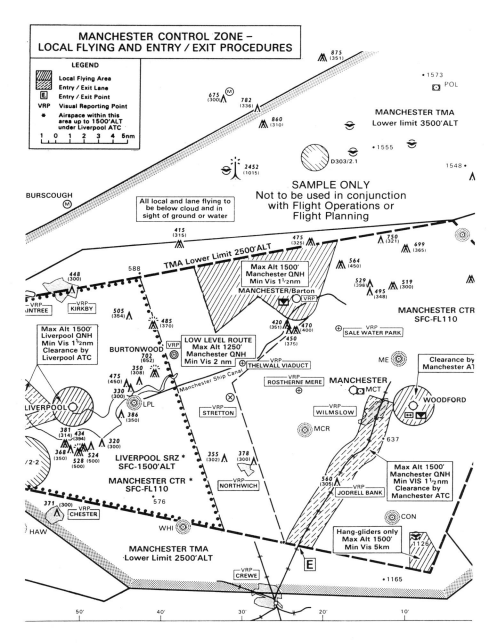

Fig.17-1. Manchester Low Level Routes, as shown in the UK AIP.

Wigan;
clear of the Route

Warrington; junction of
two arms of the Route

Northwich (VRP)

Approaching Crewe
(VRP)

Views when
Tracking Northbound

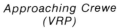

Fig.17-2. Navigating on a Manchester Low Level Route.

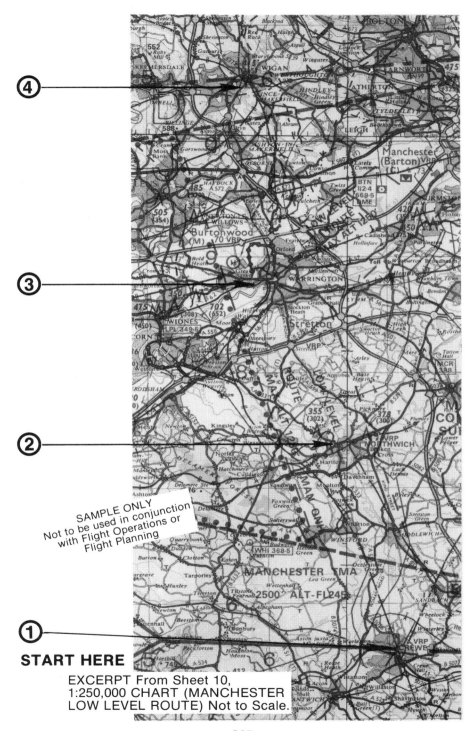

START HERE

EXCERPT From Sheet 10,
1:250,000 CHART (MANCHESTER
LOW LEVEL ROUTE) Not to Scale.

- Ensure that your Heading Indicator is aligned with the Magnetic Compass in straight and level unaccelerated flight.

- From your commencement point, steer your calculated or estimated HDG and continue with steady map-reading. Adjust your HDG to maintain the desired track and to avoid straying into controlled airspace.

- Be suspicious of any HDG that differs more than 10° from what you calculated was necessary at the flight planning stage. Many Pilots have tracked visually along wrong railway lines, when a quick HDG check would have alerted them to an incorrect track.

- Look ahead for navigation features. If you miss one, look ahead for the next one, flying your best estimate of HDG. This is very important if the visibility is reduced.

- You should aim to stay on-track and within the confines of the Lane by identifying the various features and either tracking over them or tracking abeam them on the correct side. Check that your HDG approximates the HDG that you calculated.

- Concentrate on navigation, but keep a very good lookout for other aircraft and for landmarks.

- Don't forget an occasional En Route Check of other items such as engine settings, fuel state, etc (i.e. *FREDA*).

- Listen on the radio for other traffic, and broadcast your own intentions if you consider it necessary.

- If you feel uncertain of your position, do not be reluctant to request assistance. You will often be in a radar environment, and in a situation where you are experiencing navigation difficulties due to, for instance, unexpected poor visibility, making visual fixes difficult. A request for a radar vector (HDG) to steer to remain in the Lane or Route may prevent an inadvertent penetration of the Control Zone.

These remarks have been directed at a Pilot who is not familiar with a particular Entry/Exit Lane. An experienced Pilot in good weather may feel quite happy tracking visually through a familiar Lane with very little planning, but if visibility decreases unexpectedly or some other unforeseen situation arises, these procedures give him something to fall back on. Local experience can count for a lot, but not always.

We all know very calm and proficient Pilots who always seem to be on top of the task at hand, no matter what situation arises. These Pilots are usually the ones that have done their homework and have done as much preparation on the ground as possible to minimise their in-flight workload. Having cards up your sleeve and alternative plans of action ready allow you to look calm.

Entry/Exit Lanes and Low Level Routes require extra vigilance and it is good to plan on a minimum in-flight workload so that your extra capacity is available to cope with any unforeseen distractions, which do occasionally occur.

☐ Now, finally, **Exercises 17 — Entry/Exit Lanes and Low Level Routes.**

APPENDIX 1

The Navigation Flight Test (NFT)

The Navigation Flight Test is undertaken after you have reached a satisfactory navigational standard during your training. It is completed prior to undertaking the qualifying cross-country flight.

The route of the NFT will be new to you, and will be advised 1–2 hours prior to the test. There will not be any intermediate landings and the route could penetrate regulated airspace, however no navigational assistance may be provided by radar controllers.

Pre-flight planning should enable you to carry out the flight comfortably. Your navigation plan and in-flight log are retained by the Examiner at the conclusion of the test, for forwarding to the CAA with the licence application, so train yourself to prepare **neat flight plans** and keep a **neat in-flight log**.

During the flight, **of prime importance** is to maintain the planned headings accurately and make sensible off-track heading corrections. Mental calculations or computer calculations of Heading changes should be backed-up by commonsense. For example, if you are **off-track to the left** it will be necessary to make a **correcting turn to the right** to regain track. During your early navigational dual training, your Flying Instructor will advise you on how to reach (and surpass) the required standard.

The Aim of the Navigation Flight Test is to check your ability to:

• apply simple visual navigation techniques;
• continue to navigate safely when forced by weather or other constraints to vary the planned flight profile, (e.g. descend early);
• carry-out an in-flight diversion; and
• liaise with ATC.

The following excerpt (on the NFT) is reprinted from CAP 53 — 'The Private Pilot's Licence and Associated Ratings'.

APPENDIX A   THE NAVIGATION FLIGHT TEST

1   The Navigation Flight Test (NFT) is intended to determine the applicant's ability to navigate safely by visual methods. It is a Pass/Fail Test and must, therefore, be completed in one flight and partial passes are not allowed.

2   TEST CONTENT

2.1 The test will consist of assessments of:

(a) Flight planning and self-briefing (including assessment of weather suitability) for a triangular route of approximately 1.5 hours airborne duration.

(b) In-flight recording of the progress of the flight.

(c) ATC liaison and compliance. Observance of Air Traffic Control Regulations and Rules of the Air.

(d) DR navigation (correction of track error, revision of ETAs, heading setting technique including synchronising the Directional Gyro with the Magnetic Compass in flight).

(e) Map reading.

(f) Maintenance of heading/height/airspeed at normal cruising levels and at lower levels (but not below 500 ft agl and without contravening Rule 5 of the Rules of the Air and Air Traffic Control Regulations) in conditions of simulated lowering cloud base.

(g) Re-establishment of position by visual methods following disruption of the original flight plan.

(h) Diversion following simulated adverse weather conditions en route.

2.2 Candidates will not be allowed to use either VHF radio or the radio navigation equipment fitted in the test aircraft to obtain position lines or ranges during the first two legs. However, should they wish to make use of radio navigation aids to assist in carrying out the diversion they may do so, and correct use of the radio navigation equipment and information will then be assessed.

2.3 A pictorial summary of the flight test is shown on the diagram at the end of this Appendix. The first leg will include setting heading and DR navigation to a destination about 30 minutes away. On the second leg, lowering cloud conditions will be simulated requiring the candidate to demonstrate an ability to navigate at a lower level for not more than 10 minutes. Subsequently, having climbed back to normal cruising altitude, a situation will be engineered requiring the candidate to deviate sufficiently from the planned track to check ability to establish position and to regain track or steer to destination from a point off track. At some stage during the remainder of the second leg, the candidate will be told that the weather is deteriorating and to carry out a practice diversion. The test will end when the candidate has demonstrated ability to track towards the diversion aerodrome for not less than 10 minutes, has told the Examiner the location of the aircraft, and has given an acceptable ETA.

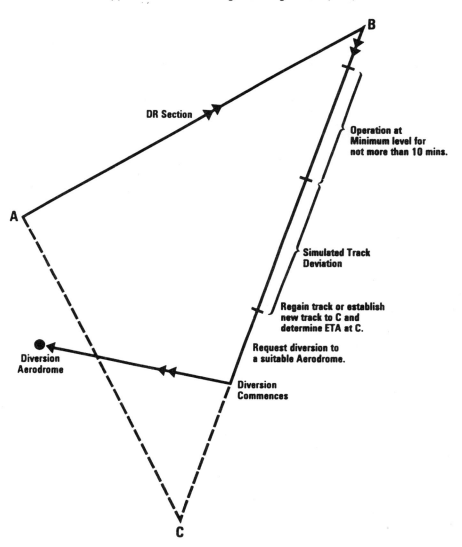

FLIGHT PLAN THE ROUTE A - B - C - A

Intentionally Blank

APPENDIX 2
Planning The Climb

In the CAA Examination on Air Navigation (and Meteorology) you will not be required to consider the climb, but will treat the whole flight as a cruise. On an actual flight, however, especially when you plan to cruise at a high altitude with a significant climb involved, you should allow time (and fuel) for the climb in your Flight Log calculations.

NOTE: No allowance need be made in a descent of a light aircraft – it is usual to plan as if the cruise continues to overhead the destination. The slight gain of the descent is offset by the fuel used in manoeuvring and approach.

CLIMBING TAS IS USUALLY LESS THAN CRUISING TAS.

It is usual to set climb power and climb at a particular climbing Indicated Air Speed (CLIAS). From Chapter 2 on Speed you will recall how, for the same Indicated Air Speed (IAS), the True Air Speed (TAS) will increase with an increase in density altitude, and how the profile of the climb is a gradual flattening out – especially as you near the performance ceiling of the aeroplane. On a climb at an approximately constant Indicated Air Speed (IAS):

- the True Air Speed gradually increases with altitude for the same Indicated Air Speed; and
- the rate of climb (RoC) gradually decreases.

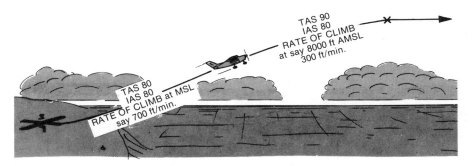

Fig.Appx.2-1. At a Constant Climb IAS, TAS Progressively Increases and the Climb Gradually Flattens Out.

A typical climbing IAS for a smaller aircraft is 80 kt.
Under ISA MSL conditions: 80 kt IAS = 80 kt TAS, RoC 700 ft/min.
At 5000 ft density altitude: 80 kt IAS = 86 kt TAS, RoC 470 ft/min.
At 10,000 ft density altitude: 80 kt IAS = 94 kt TAS, RoC 240 ft/min.

Because the rate of climb will reduce as you climb into the higher altitudes, it is usual to consider:
- the average climb TAS to be ⅔rd of the way to your cruise altitude;
- the average wind effect on the climb to be that of the wind at ⅔rd of the way to your cruising altitude. (To determine this wind, you could either extract it for the ⅔rd height approximately straight off the Area Forecast, or you could simply take ⅔rd of the wind strength at cruise level, which will usually be accurate enough.)

Once you have achieved your cruise altitude the normal procedure, having accelerated to the expected cruise Indicated Air Speed, is to set cruise power and let the speed settle. A typical cruising TAS for a smaller aircraft might be 110 kt TAS (and at cruise altitude, the IAS shown on the Air Speed Indicator would be less than this TAS of course).

PRESENTATION OF PERFORMANCE DATA.

Performance data may be presented in either **graphical** or **tabular** form. Either method is quite easy to extract data from. We show the *graphical* presentation for the PIPER WARRIOR and the *tabular* presentation of the CESSNA 172.

PIPER AIRCRAFT CORPORATION
PA-28-161, CHEROKEE WARRIOR II

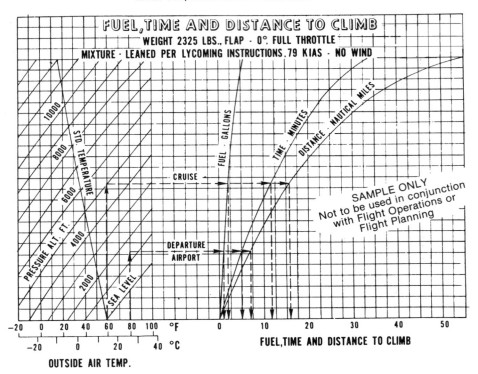

Fig.Appx.2-2. Fuel, Time & Distance to Climb – Piper Warrior II.

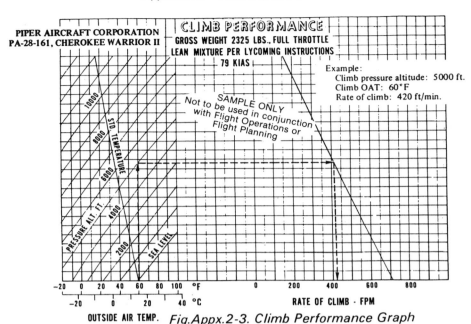

Fig.Appx.2-3. Climb Performance Graph

Fig.Appx.2-4. Best Power Cruise Performance – Piper Warrior II.

CESSNA
MODEL 172P

PERFORMANCE

TIME, FUEL, AND DISTANCE TO CLIMB

MAXIMUM RATE OF CLIMB

CONDITIONS:
Flaps Up
Full Throttle
Standard Temperature

SAMPLE ONLY
Not to be used in conjunction
with Flight Operations or
Flight Planning

NOTES:
1. Add 1.1 gallons of fuel for engine start, taxi and takeoff allowance.
2. Mixture leaned above 3000 feet for maximum RPM.
3. Increase time, fuel and distance by 10% for each 10°C above standard temperature.
4. Distances shown are based on zero wind.

WEIGHT LBS	PRESSURE ALTITUDE FT	TEMP °C	CLIMB SPEED KIAS	RATE OF CLIMB FPM	FROM SEA LEVEL		
					TIME MIN	FUEL USED GALLONS	DISTANCE NM
2400	S.L.	15	76	700	0	0.0	0
	1000	13	76	655	1	0.3	2
	2000	11	75	610	3	0.6	4
	3000	9	75	560	5	1.0	6
	4000	7	74	515	7	1.4	9
	5000	5	74	470	9	1.7	11
	6000	3	73	425	11	2.2	14
	7000	1	72	375	14	2.6	18
	8000	-1	72	330	17	3.1	22
	9000	-3	71	285	20	3.6	26
	10,000	-5	71	240	24	4.2	32
	11,000	-7	70	190	29	4.9	38
	12,000	-9	70	145	35	5.8	47

Fig.Appx.2-5. Tabular Climb Data format for the Cessna 172.

PERFORMANCE

CESSNA
MODEL 172P

CRUISE PERFORMANCE

CONDITIONS:
2400 Pounds
Recommended Lean Mixture

SAMPLE ONLY
Not to be used in conjunction
with Flight Operations or
Flight Planning

PRESSURE ALTITUDE FT	RPM	20°C BELOW STANDARD TEMP			STANDARD TEMPERATURE			20°C ABOVE STANDARD TEMP		
		% BHP	KTAS	GPH	% BHP	KTAS	GPH	% BHP	KTAS	GPH
2000	2500	- - -	- - -	- - -	76	114	8.5	72	114	8.1
	2400	72	110	8.1	69	109	7.7	65	108	7.3
	2300	65	104	7.3	62	103	6.9	59	102	6.6
	2200	58	99	6.6	55	97	6.3	53	96	6.1
	2100	52	92	6.0	50	91	5.8	48	89	5.7
4000	2550	- - -	- - -	- - -	76	117	8.5	72	116	8.1
	2500	77	115	8.6	73	114	8.1	69	113	7.7
	2400	69	109	7.8	65	108	7.3	62	107	7.0
	2300	62	104	7.0	59	102	6.6	57	101	6.4
	2200	56	98	6.3	54	96	6.1	51	94	5.9
	2100	51	91	5.8	48	89	5.7	47	88	5.5
6000	2600	- - -	- - -	- - -	77	119	8.6	72	118	8.1
	2500	73	114	8.2	69	113	7.8	66	112	7.4
	2400	66	108	7.4	63	107	7.0	60	106	6.7
	2300	60	103	6.7	57	101	6.4	55	99	6.2
	2200	54	96	6.1	52	95	5.9	50	92	5.8
	2100	49	90	5.7	47	88	5.5	46	86	5.5
8000	2650	- - -	- - -	- - -	77	121	8.6	73	120	8.1
	2600	77	119	8.7	73	118	8.2	69	117	7.8
	2500	70	113	7.8	66	112	7.4	63	111	7.1
	2400	63	108	7.1	60	106	6.7	58	104	6.5
	2300	57	101	6.4	55	100	6.2	53	97	6.0
	2200	52	95	6.0	50	93	5.8	49	91	5.7
10,000	2600	74	118	8.3	70	117	7.8	66	115	7.4
	2500	67	112	7.5	64	111	7.1	61	109	6.8
	2400	61	106	6.8	58	105	6.5	56	102	6.3
	2300	55	100	6.3	53	98	6.0	51	96	5.9
	2200	50	93	5.8	49	91	5.7	47	89	5.6
12,000	2550	67	114	7.5	64	112	7.1	61	111	6.9
	2500	64	111	7.2	61	109	6.8	59	107	6.6
	2400	59	105	6.6	56	103	6.3	54	100	6.1
	2300	53	98	6.1	51	96	5.9	50	94	5.8

Fig.Appx.2-6. Cruise Performance Data for the Cessna 172.

EXAMPLE:

Consider a climb from a Sea Level aerodrome to a cruising altitude of 7500 ft by a Piper Warrior under ISA conditions. (Assume the conditions such as weight, etc, are as specified on the climb performance graph above).

From the area forecast, the winds are light and variable at all altitudes. Our first checkpoint is say 45 nm from our departure aerodrome.

Climb from MSL to 7500: (from graph)

- 2·5 USG, 15 minutes, 21 nm, and since there is nil significant wind, this will mean 21 gnm (nm over the ground).

- There is no need to determine the average TAS on the climb, but if you do it is quite easy: 21 anm in 15 min = TAS 84 kt.

Fig.Appx.2-7. Computer Set-up.

Cruise (65% power) from Top of Climb (TOC) to First Checkpoint (at, say, 45 nm).

- Cruise TAS = 108 kt, nil wind, therefore Ground Speed 108 kt.
- Distance from TOC to first checkpoint = 45 – 21 = 24 nm.
  24 nm at GS 108 = ETI 13 min at 8·8 GPH = 1·9, say 2 US Gallons.

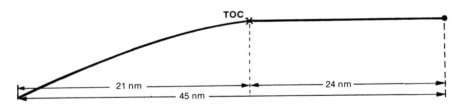

Fig.Appx.2-8. Profile of the First Leg.

- Time from departure
  to first checkpoint = 15 min climb + 13 min cruise
  = 28 min.
- Fuel burn from departure
  to first checkpoint = 2·5 USG + 2 USG
  = 4·5, say 5 USG.

What If We Had Not Considered The Climb?

If we had treated the whole of this first leg as a cruise, then:
- ETI is: 45 nm at GS 108 kt = 25 minutes ETI;
- Fuel burn is: 25 min at 8·8 GPH = 3·7 USG.

At the first checkpoint in this case, there is a 3 minute difference in ETI due to the consideration of the 7500 ft climb. Fuel burn as a result of climbing will exceed that of a pure cruise by (4·5 – 3·7 =) 0·8, say 1 USG.

What Do We Do About This?

Your Flying Instructor will give you advice on how to allow for the climb in your particular aeroplane. It may be that:
- for short climbs, no consideration of climb is required; and
- for longer climbs – a time and fuel allowance is made; or
  - a mean TAS is used for the leg; or
  - a full climb calculation is done.

A TYPICAL CLIMB AND CRUISE CALCULATION FOR A PIPER WARRIOR.

Departure Aerodrome: elev 1334 ft, QNH 1005, OAT +30°C
(so pressure altitude = 1574 ft).

Cruise Altitude: 7500 ft, Regional QNH 1009 (so pressure altitude is 7620 ft), OAT +10°C (use 65% Power).

Winds: from the Area Forecast: at 5000 ft: 10 kt headwind;
7000 ft: 20 kt headwind;
10,000 ft: 25 kt headwind.

Climb:
from MSL to 7620 ft PA (OAT +10C) = 3 USG / 18 min / 27 anm
from MSL to 1574 ft PA (OAT +30C) = 1 USG / 6 min / 8 anm;
so, from 1574 ft PA to 7620 ft PA   = **2 USG / 12 min / 19 anm.**

Note that both pressure altitude and temperature come into this calculation, i.e. we are really considering density altitude. (The performance of an aeroplane, both from the engine point of view and the flying ability or airframe point of view, depends upon air density.)

To obtain our actual climb figures from 1500 ft to 7500 ft AMSL we need to subtract one from the other (since the climb from MSL to 1500 ft does not actually occur – our take-off is at PA 1500 ft).

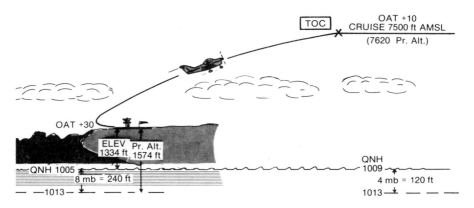

Fig.Appx.2-9. Climb Profile.

Now in this case we do not have nil-wind conditions. We will take the average wind for the climb to be that ⅔rd of the way up to cruising altitude.

The climb from 1500 to 7500 = 6000 ft, $\frac{2}{3}$rd of which = 4000 ft, so our average wind will be at 1500 + 4000 = 5500 ft. All of this is very approximate, so we will use the forecast 5000 ft wind of –10 kt (i.e. a headwind component of 10 kt).

- In 1 hour (60 minutes), the wind effect would be 10 nm;
- Since our climb lasts 12 minutes, the wind effect will be:
$$\frac{12}{60} \text{ of } 10 = \frac{1}{5}\text{th of } 10 = 2 \text{ nm};$$
- Since it is a headwind, the 19 air nautical miles on our climb will be reduced to 19 – 2 = 17 ground nautical miles.

To continue our flight plan to the first checkpoint, say 70 nautical miles from the departure aerodrome, the remaining cruise distance is 70 – 17 = 53 nm, and we proceed with the cruise calculations.

☐ Now complete **Exercises — Climb Planning.**

INDEX

acceleration errors, compass   41
access lanes   281-6
aerial tactics areas   176
aerodromes   199-201, 205
  alternate   260
aeronautical information   162
  Circular   227
agonic line   172
AIC *see* Aeronautical
  Information Circular
aircraft performance   204, 223
air
  Almanac   138
  density   18, 21
  nautical mile   6
  plot   270
  position   234
  pressure   102
  speed   15-27
  temperature   103
airmanship   235
AIRMET forecasts   195-7
airspace
  information   164
  restrictions   176, 202
  route considerations   204
Airtour CRP-1 computer   45, 79
altimeter   99
  cold effects   122
  subscale   108
altimetry procedures   113
altitude   98
  light effect   137
aneroid barometer   99
arc of longitude   129
Area of Intense Aerial Activity   172
  chart   176
atomic time   126

bearing measurement   185
bird sanctuary   170
British Summer Time   140

CAA Topographical Air Charts   157
CAS *see* Calibrated Air Speed
calculator-side of computer   79-97
calibrated air speed (CAS)   20
changing sea level pressure   111
charts   142, 150, 157-187
  folding   208-9
  orientation   245
  preparation   206
checkpoints   205, 241
circular slide rule   80
climb planning   226, 291-298
communications   202
compass
  acceleration errors   41
  checks   38
  deviation   33
  turning errors   40
contours   158
conversions   89-96
Co-ordinated Universal Time   126,
  131-2
crosswind   76
CRP-1 computer   45, 79
cruise   240-241
cruising levels   214-215
cultural features   161

date line   134
date/time figures   127
daylight   136
dead reckoning   232, 270
deduced reckoning *see* dead
  reckoning
density
  altitude   123
  error   21
departure   237-240
descent from higher level   273
deviation, magnetic   33-4
  card   35

direction
  indicator 43
  measurement 4, 5, 186-7
distance
  computer calculation 84
  conversions 149
  estimation 263, 271
  measurement 183-4
  units 5-6
diversion 259-264
  fuel 221
division by slide rule 82
drift 12, 234
  estimation 249
dynamic pressure 17-19

earth
  angles 150
  distance 148
  motion 125
  shape 142
emergency
  fuel reserve 220
  locator beacon 280
  procedures 279
endurance flying 269
entry/exit lanes 281-6
'eye-balling' 258, 263
estimated time interval 219
estimated time of arrival 246-7
ETA *see* Estimated Time of Arrival

fan-lines 208
fix 233
flight
  case 191
  fuel 219
  log 210-226
  plan 227-9, 277
  planning 19, 48, 69
  preparation 276
  sequence 237-259
foot-metre conversion 91
FREDA en route check 236
fuel
  consumption 86-7, 210
  planning 219-222
  weight 93

graticule 4, 171
Great Circle 5, 13, 143, 182
Greenwich Mean Time 126
ground
  position 234
  speed 8-9, 12, 15, 60, 64, 217
hachuring 160
hazard
  information 167-8, 176
  route determination 204

heading 6, 11
  accuracy 3
  calculation 217-218
headwind 76-8
hectoPascal 15
High Intensity Radio Transmission
  Area 172
hill shading 160
hypsometric tinting 159, 160

IAS *see* Indicated Air Speed
ICAO *see* International Civil
  Aviation Organisation
indicated
  air speed 16, 19
  altitude 99
International
  Civil Aviation Organisation charts
    152, 179
  Standard Atmosphere 15
instrument error 20
inverse ratio method 257-9
ISA *see* International
  Standard Atmosphere
isogonals 32, 172

kilometre-nautical mile conversion
  89
knot 13

lapse rates 100
latitude 4, 12, 144
  determination 180
  measurement 148
  scale 184
  time of sunrise 138
layer tints 159, 160
legend notes 166
local
  mean time 131
  time 130, 135
log keeping 246
longitude 4, 13, 145
  determination 181
  measurement 149
  time relationship 128
lost, procedure when 266-9
low level navigation 272
  routes 281-6

magnetic
  compass 30, 35-43
  deviation 33-4
  direction 29
  field 30-1
  North 30
  variation 30-1

map   142, 150
  reading   232, 241, 245
mean sea level   98
  pressure variations   105
mental dead reckoning   270
meridians of longitude   145
metre-foot conversion   91
military training area   170
minimum
  fuel required   220
  safe altitude   119, 215
multiplication by slide rule   81

nautical mile   6, 13
  statute mile conversion   89
navigation
  computer   23
  Flight Test   287-289
NFT *see* Navigation Flight Test
Nominated Air Traffic Service
  Unit   172
NOTAMS *see* Notices to Airmen
Notices to Airmen   158, 198

Official Night   141
off-track
  calculation   87
  corrections   249-250
ONC *see* Operational Navigation
  Chart
Operational
  briefing   278
  Navigation Chart   179
outside air temperature   25

parallel of latitude   144
performance capabilities   98, 204,
  223
personal navigation equipment   191
pinpoint   233
plotter, use of   186-7
Pooley's
  Flight Guide   177-8
  Planning Chart   205
position
  error   20
  information   171
  lines   243, 247-9
  plotting   181
pre-flight
  briefing   195-203
  preparation   190
pressure
  altitude   22, 24, 101
  measurement   15
Prohibited Area   169
protractor   185-6

QFE   110
QNH   107

radio facilities   170
range   169
RAS *see* Rectified Air Speed
Rectified Air Speed   20
reference direction   4
regional pressure setting   112
relative
  bearing   43-4
  density   93
relief, portrayal of   159, 160
representative fraction   154
Restricted Area   169
Rho   6, 21-3
Rhumb line   182
route
  segments   212
  selection   204

safety height   118, 214
scale of charts   154, 184
slide
  navigation computer   45
  rule   80
specific gravity values   97
speed   6
  computer calculations   84-5
spot elevations   160
static pressure   17
Standard Atmosphere   15, 100
Summer Time   140
sun, timing   125
sunrise   136
symbols   162-175

tailwind   76-8
TAS *see* True Air Speed
temperature
  conversion   100
  lapse rate   100
terrain clearance   98
time
  longitude relationship   128
  measurement   127
TMG *see* Track Made Good
topographical
  charts   152-3
  information   158
total pressure   19
track
  corrections   255-6
  error   11, 12, 233, 249, 252-4
  /GS   8-9
  -guides   208, 250
  made good   11, 12, 60, 64, 233
  measurement   185-7

traffic separation   98
transition altitude   116
triangle of velocities   10, 46
True
  Air Speed   6, 11, 14, 21-7, 216
  direction   28-9
turning errors, compass   40

UK flight procedures   199
UTC *see* Co-ordinated Universal Time

variation, magnetic   30-1
vector
  HDG/TAS   6-7
  plotting   47
  TR/GS   8-9
velocity   7
visibility   265-6
visual flight   191-3
volume-weight conversion   93

WAC *see* World Aeronautical Chart
weather forecasts   195-7
weight
  and balance   223
  conversions   93
wind
  components   76-8, 270
  correction angle   46
  down method   63-8
  effect   233-4
  -side of navigation computer
  45-78
  velocity   7-8, 12, 15, 57, 66
World Aeronautical Chart   180
W/V *see* wind velocity

Zone Time   133